Advance praise for *The Name Therapist*

"After forty years, *The Name Therapist* helped me finally figure out why I monogram everything: because growing up I could never find a keychain with my name on it! With her inventively fresh observations, impressive wit, humour, charm, and sometimes harsh real talk, Duana Taha has totally convinced me that we are more than just our names. But that names are, actually, everything. I love this book."

Elaine Lui, author of *Listen to the Squawking Chicken*

"If you've struggled with naming a baby, a character, a cat or a condition, this book is an essential companion and a total delight. Duana Taha's managed to write a smart, personal, trivia-stuffed (and kind of profound) treatise on why we pick the names we do, and how we're affected by the ones we're given. If there's a name for when a book takes you completely by surprise with its warm, dishy cleverness, so much so, you have to read it in one sitting, that's what happened to me."

Lisa Gabriele, author of *The Almost Archer Sisters*, and the *S.E.C.R.E.T.* trilogy under L. Marie Adeline, her nana's name

"So would a rose by any other name smell as sweet? Taha answers with a resounding "no"! *The Name Therapist* is both erudite and hilarious. It discusses the implications inherent in naming babies and the ways in which we discriminate against certain names. It answers questions you had as a child about all the Jennifers in the schoolyard and then asks, how do we really become who we are? It's a rollicking, fun read."

Heather O'Neill, author of *The Girl Who Was Saturday Night*

"I had no idea I needed therapy until I read this book. Wonderfully informative, utterly charming, and laugh out loud funny, I would prescribe *The Name Therapist* to literally anyone with a name. Which is everyone. That's how much I enjoyed it."

Dan Levy, co-creator of *Schitt's Creek*

"The magic of *The Name Therapist* lies in Duana's genuine curiosity and love for the psychology of naming. Her unique experience and background elevate the material from baby name encyclopedia to a deeply personal meditation on the phrase 'what's in a name?' Most impressive is her ability to romanticize even the most unlikely of monikers (Archibald, I'm looking at you!). There's no judgment or condescension, just an infectious sense of wonderment!"

Lauren (Felice) Collins, actor on *Degrassi: The Next Generation*, former sufferer of Middle-Name Pain

"I've been fascinated by the fine art of nomenclature since I was a wee girl. I love Duana Taha's unique, compelling take on why we choose certain names. It's so much fun and would be a great gift for anyone, but especially parents-to-be."

Sara Benincasa, comedian and author of *DC Trip*

"Marked at birth with a difficult-to-pronounce, gender-indeterminate, ethnically-confusing name, I've navigated the world of Jennifers and Michaels looking for someone who gets it. Well, Duana Taha does. She writes with charm, wit, and warmth about something so every-day but also so essential—names—those endlessly complex combinations of letters that help us make sense of who we are and where we come from. This book is basically the Magna Carta for people with weird names."　　　**Elan Mastai**, screenwriter of *The F Word*

"*The Name Therapist* makes it clear from the outset that this is a quali-tative study, yet the interviews and anecdotes, from Ronit and Shelica to Karen and many Jennifers, left this skeptic reevaluating her entire life as a Jessica, then a Jessie and finally a Jess; monikers all chosen for me by others, which have unconsciously helped shape my identity. I've seen the light. But the most illuminating story is that of Duana's. Her experiences, struggles and realizations regarding her own name are effortlessly weaved throughout forming a complete narrative that's both entertaining and heady. And they are beautiful, particularly one from Grade 4 where her path as a fine writer may have been determined, thanks to her unusual name."

Jessica Allen, digital correspondent for *The Social* and *Metro* columnist

THE
NAME
THERAPIST

HOW GROWING UP WITH MY ODD NAME TAUGHT ME
EVERYTHING YOU NEED TO KNOW ABOUT YOURS

DUANA TAHA

RANDOM HOUSE CANADA

PUBLISHED BY RANDOM HOUSE CANADA

Copyright © 2016 Duana Taha

www.penguinrandomhouse.ca

Random House Canada and colophon are registered trademarks.

Page 348 constitutes a continuation of the copyright page.
Images courtesy of the author.

Library and Archives Canada Cataloguing in Publication

Taha, Duana, author
The name therapist : how growing up with my odd
name taught me everything you need to know about yours / Duana Taha.

Includes bibliographical references and index.
Issued in print and electronic formats.

ISBN 978-0-345-81530-9
eBook ISBN 978-0-345-81532-3

1. Names, Personal. 2. Names, Personal—Psychological aspects.
3. Identity (Psychology). I. Title.

CS2367.T35 2016   929.4'4   C2015-905918-6

Cover design by Terri Nimmo with concept from Valerie Gow
Cover image © Peter Dazeley / Getty Images

Printed and bound in the United States of America

2 4 6 8 9 7 5 3 1

Penguin
Random House
RANDOM HOUSE CANADA

To my parents,
Who gave me this name and this outlook,
which gave me everything else

CONTENTS

INTRODUCTION

I love names. In fact, loving them has been one of my defining qualities as long as I can remember. I don't just have a few favourites, I love hundreds of them. How they sound, how they feel in your mouth, the impressions they give. I even love the names I hate—or at least, they fascinate me. Scores of names have firm-yet-evolving rankings in my mind, falling under subcategories like "fanciful" or "unambitious" or "bro you meet in university." So yes, I judge people by their covers—or by their handles, I guess.

I know it's kind of an odd preoccupation. People who don't love names like I do don't see the point in talking about them. "After all," they say to me, "we have no control over the names we were given at birth!" Yes, this is true—but I've always believed names are much more predictive than we give them credit for—they can make us who we are. Considering and analyzing this over my entire life has basically made me into a name junkie. I can't not notice them.

Sometimes, when I explain this, people say, "Why does it matter? It's just a name!" I'm not trying to criticize names just for sport, and if I don't love yours, it's not like I blame you for having it. But people who think it's unkind to judge names prove my point that names do matter. If they didn't, wouldn't we all just be called the same thing? Would people get so exercised about the idea that some names are good and some aren't? Our names come from our parents, but they're weighted and considered before they're bestowed. So why do we pretend that once they're given, they're all equal? It's not true.

Let me be clear: This is not a baby name book. In fact, there's no such thing as a baby name.

I know that's a preposterous statement. But think about it for a second. Names aren't only used for babies—in fact, they only really get useful once we've left infancy behind.

Sure, there are baby name books or websites that define names—but not really. They give Scottish or Slavic variations, and tell us a given name means "berry," or "warrior," but not whether or not the name will make the person honest or talkative or graceful. Most people look up their names in one of these books, read through them again when they're about to have a baby—and then never think about names again.

They may not, but I do. I always have. I've always known that people make decisions about who fills a job role or a friendship or an almost-impossible-to-get internship based on whether or not they can "see" a particular name in the role. Name bias is an under acknowledged "ism," but everybody knows the unwritten rules: Arthur is a much more likely CEO than Jace, Bella will get the choir solo long before Clovis, and if trying to be a ladies' man, Basil is fighting an uphill battle. Your opinion on the previous state-ment will depend on how much you like the individual names (or, in the case of Basil, *Fawlty Towers*), but I know you didn't feel neutral about them. You had a positive or negative reaction to each name, right? It's okay. Everybody does.

Are you getting that creepy feeling that I'm about to ask you to join my religion? I am, a little, because I think names are way more important than we give them credit for. A name isn't just a tool to distinguish you from the rest of the five-year-olds born the same year—it's the first key to becoming who you are going to be.

And I should know.

My name, Duana, is unusual at best. It looks like the feminization of "Duane" but is actually pronounced "Dew-ANN-ah." Sometimes. Depending who you ask.

In North America, where I grew up, it's on the furthest reaches of out-there. Nobody I know has ever had the same name; in fact, nobody's ever heard of it. It stuck out, a little odd and very unusual—kind of like I was. And so, early on, I had to explain and defend and try to understand it, because nobody else did. Those experiences made me who I am, and made me realize names are much more than just our distin-guishing labels. There's an old Latin phrase, "nomen est omen," which translates as "name is destiny," or implies that your name determines who you are. If it was true for me, why wouldn't it be true for everyone?

Relatively few people have my same name experience, but nobody's really neutral on names. Admit it, the name of your first love still sounds a little sweet, regardless of who that love was, and all the reasons why it shouldn't. The fourth-grade mean girl whose cutting remarks you still remember has ruined her name for you forever, right?

I went deeper. I'm a TV screenwriter, and I can't say I'm upset that obsessing over the real names of fake people is an important part of the job. The writers' room is a place that invites friendly debate, and I relish going several rounds over the most perfect nomenclature for the popular girl's sidekick. But even this professional name obsession turned out to be just the beginning.

My name nerdism evolved in tandem with my voracious pop-culture appetite, and I started writing a name advice column on a popular gossip website. People wrote to me mostly with questions about naming their expected babies, but sometimes it was friends of expectant parents, wondering how to tell them they were making a terrible mistake by choosing "Quinn." The questions were limitless. One writer wondered whether Aubrey was an androgynous name and whether that might negatively affect their child, while another asked whether a cousin who claimed to have reserved a certain baby name for life could be in the right, even if the claim happened when said cousin was twelve. And there were hundreds more.

I wasn't a parenting blogger nor even a parent, but I knew my stuff. I was thrilled to be an expert. In fact, I was something else. There are many name experts who know all about the origins of names and the people who have worn them through history, but I knew what names were today.

I became a Name Therapist.

This isn't to say I was the first person to have opinions on names, obviously. But not only do I have an unshakeable faith in the power of names, I have a secret weapon that money can't buy—my own ridiculously obscure name. So much of what people seem to worry about with names is what other people think—and my name was and is new to almost everyone I meet. Which means I have walked the walk. You wonder what kind of impact a strange name, or a name people mispronounce will have? I've been there. I will not sugarcoat it. I have opinions that a Steven or a Hannah just can't buy.

I've realized that while most people don't think their interest in names is particularly significant, everyone has a story about the name they were given, the one they should have been given, and the way their name has come to be synonymous with who they are. Unless, of course, it's not— which means a whole other relationship with the name and a whole other set of stories. Almost nobody feels neutral about their name, either. Everyone has an idea of how their name has either made them the person they are, or the ways it kept them from who they might have been. I want to tell them all.

So this book will explore how I came to think this way about names, and to interview people who have names of all types—common to uncommon, inherited to self-created. I'll explore the various ways a given name can affect your career, your personality, even your whole life. The key here is *given* name. Surnames, while they tell a story all their own, aren't chosen for each new generation by the parents and they don't fall in and out of fashion the way first names do.

What the book won't do is give an exhaustive rundown of the history of the name "Noah," or sixteen international variations on "Edward." Other books have those comprehensive listings, and they're invaluable. But I want to talk about what names mean once they're actually given to someone. In the age of Instagram and other, ever-more sophisticated means of personal branding, the idea that there are names that might make your child more unique, more unusual, more *special*—has become an obsession, one that often, but not always, ends in Madeleine.

We'll also explore a huge name factor—geography and culture. Names are of universal interest, but they're always seen through a culturally specific filter. Much, but not all, of this book's filter is North American, since the particular cultural rules and practices of Canada and the U.S. affect many of the people who supplied me with interviews and anecdotes, and because North American society is unique in borrowing many of its customs from Europe, Asia, and Africa, yet having a culture all its own.

Are you still unconvinced? Think of it this way. The only other thing you'll have for as long as your name is your body—and we know the relationship between people and their bodies is rich and complex. To me, names are just as fascinating, and I refuse to allow them to be seen as a "soft science" any more. In a fight to the death in the tournament of defining human traits, I am the champion of names, and why they matter today more than ever.

Is there such a thing as a universally unattractive name? Are there still rules for names, or people we should pity because they drew the worst straws? Is it better to have an unusual name people remember, or one that doesn't stand out? The answers may seem obvious, but it's a lot easier to make a sarcastic comment online if you call yourself Adam than if you call yourself Helmut, who's a lot easier to track down and identify—see what I mean?

Here's one thing I do know for sure—our interactions with people shape our opinions on names far more than their supposed meanings. The first time I met a real life (non-Muppet-dog) person named Rolf, he was a large and gregarious man with a thick German accent who talked enthusiastically about the fact that luxury sports cars are money pits: "So expensive, so many things break, these are for stupids." A beat, followed by a goofy, delighted grin, and then:

. . . "I am a stupid."

Come on! Isn't that everything you ever imagined about a Rolf? A guy who has serious interests, but can laugh at himself? Me too.

This is what makes an interest in names a constantly evolving game: Everyone brings their unique traits to enrich and colour their names. The human race makes up new people every day; ergo, we have new information about our impressions of "Kyla" or "Eleazer" every day. Your name is Esther? You're probably competent. Your name is Tyler? Everyone wanted to make sure you were popular, and I bet they got the job done. Your name is Ruprecht? Don't get up, I know exactly what derogatory name you were called on the playground. And maybe it made you into a bit of a comedian, so you could strike first before others used that very unattractive word for the male anatomy. It's human nature to categorize and assign meaning to everything, and names are no different—it's just that their associations and "off-label" meanings are far different than what can be found in a name dictionary, still bent on telling you that Leigh means "pasture, meadow." As if that tells you anything at all.

So, you still want to tell me you don't think that much about names? That's okay. I'm doing it for the both of us.

1

DEAR ABBY, WHO WAS REALLY PAULINE
Name Advice and Absolution

My dad went through a fifteen-year infatuation with self-help books. He's never really lost his respect for them, but his peak consumption of Tony Robbins and Mark Victor Hansen and Steven R. Covey, usually as books-on-tape, occurred while I was a teenager. Living in the suburbs requires your parents to drive you everywhere, so I was exposed to more than a few of these audio lectures in the car, and to Dad's enthusiastic repetition of key points. He knew, I guess, that repetition was the key to memorization, but would have gone as far as tattooing key phrases on my skin and my sister's if he thought it would help us to be more successful—which in his mind mostly meant "financially comfortable," but also "frequent public speaker."

One of the catchphrases Dad liked the most is admittedly kind of catchy. "Whatever the mind can conceive and believe it can . . .? It can . . .?" Because he never actually finished the phrase. He would wait, prompting us in an ever-louder voice, like a comedian trying to prime a punchline, until my sister or I caved and coughed up ". . . achieve."

It made an impact on us—I do think we both retain a lasting belief in the adage, but more importantly the phrase made it into each of our wedding speeches. Dad, you did it.

Still, if I had been told at fifteen that I was going to get to lecture people about names for money, I would have assumed it was a pity arrangement, where people tossed coins to the bag lady on the street while I talked about how Chris, Cathy, Carrie and Cory were, as a whole, an excellent collection of names for children in a trashy novel. It would never have occurred to me that all my time spent obsessing would have a real-life application and an audience. I'm *happy* about it—just a little surprised.

I am not the only one who feels this way. Recently I ran into a colleague who introduced me to the man he was speaking with, calling me a writer "and also a name expert." The stranger looked at me for a moment with a pleasant but confused look on his face, opened and closed his mouth without speaking, and then, finally, chose the phrase he wanted. ". . . For *commerce*?"

Yes, sir, for commerce, and also for joy.

The thing about names, and the way we talk about them, is that we don't. Disproportionately rarely, anyway. Still, there's much more discussion about them now than when I was young, wearing a name that belonged to only me. I assumed my interest in names was similarly rare—because I was a teenager Before The Internet.

My career as a name therapist came about because I couldn't keep my opinions to myself. More specifically, as a writer-slash-rabble-rouser on the website laineygossip.com, I would routinely groan at the unimaginative names I encountered as interest in celebrity baby names became more mainstream. When Jessica Simpson hinted in a 2012 interview that her first baby name would be somehow unusual, I scoffed online, at length. Mostly because at that point her *pregnancy* had been covered at great length and nothing about it had seemed all that newsworthy to begin with. You know I'm not wrong.

So I wrote an article on the blog about being a name snob, and about my expectations, such as they were, for Jessica Simpson's baby name, and the reader response— agreeing with me, disagreeing with me, confessing that they, too, were name snobs but thought they were all alone—was immediate and immense.

I have never believed people who say, "It all happened so fast," but in a very short time my name knowledge went from a nerdy pastime to a vocation it seemed I'd been in training for all my life. I got a request from a woman who wanted to know what I thought of the names she'd chosen for her babies, and I wrote an article responding to her in which my opinion was not favourable at all. The response to that garnered even more attention, and suddenly I was a baby name critic. Letters started pouring in much more quickly than I could answer them. I'd write an article online, hopefully before the baby in question was born, with an admonishment or praise and six to twelve alternative name suggestions—alternative, because the people who write in are almost never happy with the names on their shortlists. If they were, they wouldn't be writing to me.

There are few things that you can do so publicly while owning up to the fact that you have limited credentials. One of my early lines in the baby names column that I used a lot was "I'm nobody's parent yet." I wanted to be out in the open about that, in case my not having a child would influence the way someone chose a name, or listened to my advice. But it didn't seem to matter.

I was different because I wasn't being "nice." I was talking to people about names the same way I would talk to them about bad pants or bad boyfriends. I'd be straight up, explaining that the reason they were feeling bored with their choices was that the choices were, in fact, boring. Or because they were all variations on the same name. When you're limiting yourself to William, Henry and Harry, and Ben seems like too much of an outlier, yeah, you're going to be a little bored when it comes to babies two and three. This straightforward type of advice isn't uncommon, especially online, but there are stereotypes about fragile pregnant women that mean most conversations about names are filled with gentle praise and even gentler suggestions. Lucky for me, I was never that kind of advice-giver.

Instead, my advice is based on a few basic tenets. The first one, and the hardest for people to stick to is:

1. Don't be afraid.

Where names are concerned, people are pretty worried about allowing themselves to think outside the box. There are plenty of names that are popular because they're great, but the world doesn't need another Elizabeth. The philosophy of "if it ain't broke" works in a lot of circumstances, but it's a boring way to manufacture each new human, especially when we're telling these new humans that they're special snowflakes who are unlike any other. Sophie is a gorgeous name, but if seventeen girls in your child's school catchment area already have it, you have a slightly more uphill battle in explaining to your daughter that she's nothing like all the other Sophies and that nobody will ever make any comparisons between them.

The second tenet of my name therapy is one that, in theory, everyone seems to agree with, but in practice, is much less true:

2. A name should be yours alone (within reason).

I would get all these e-mails about name "stealing"—that your cousin took Angelica even though you swore you wanted it—and I'd think, Well, now it's used, so you don't want it. Pick another name, and don't be afraid. Also in this category are e-mails asking about whether this or that name will get your child teased. Kids tease about everything, not just names, so that's not a good enough reason to default to Jacob. I don't believe in being different just for the sake of it, or in "services" that will create an all-new name for your child—but I also don't think you should avoid Rowena just because it's never been done in your neck of the woods before. Different isn't bad, especially in 2016.

The idea that a name should be considered from all these angles, that less popular is better, and that it's unfortunate to run into someone who bears your same name is of course just my perspective, and clearly comes from my being the only one with my name. But I do think that whatever name you choose for your child—or hell, for yourself—should fall under the guidelines of tenet no. 3:

3. You should love it.

I don't care whether the name belonged to your favourite character or to the boy down the hall in boarding school, but it seems logical to choose a name that means something to you in particular, that sounds like music coming off your tongue, and that is special because it hasn't been given to the other sixteen babies born on the same hospital floor. You should love it, and be able to tell other people why it was the one, out of all the 10,000 in your baby book, that finally got the honour of being chosen.

I learned a few things, though, the longer I wrote the online column, now known as "Duana Names." First, that there are a lot more name nerds out there than I would have thought, most of whom are as eager to analyze every name as I am. They seem to understand that there are names that are usable for actual people, and then there are names that are just too "out there" for the average child—or adult—to wear in today's society, and should be confined to books. The disconnect comes from debating whether "Peregrine" fits into the first category or the second.

The more I wrote, the more I got letters saying "I never realized there were other name nerds" or "You're putting into words everything I have thought about my name, but didn't know why I felt that way." I feel proud to be helping and speaking to such a vast yet underserved community of name nerds.

Here's a fairly typical letter to receive:

We are expecting a boy next month and cannot agree on a name for the life of us. I love James Francis. James is a great, classic name that (I think) goes with our daughter Madeline and Francis was my grandfather's name as well as my brother and father's middle names. My husband is dead set on Lincoln Adler. Lincoln for his favorite president (history nerd) and Adler for the Adler Planetarium in Chicago (a place with special memories for us). I just don't think Lincoln Adler goes with Madeline Jean. I have tried to convince my husband that with James Francis our son will have the initials JFK (seriously) and that is presidential enough. We need help!

It's got all the essentials. Marital conflict, disparate influences from two parents, and a stalemate. When it comes to letter-writers, they are almost universally female. Given that they're often expecting mothers, that's not so surprising—but they are often also the ones more open to considering unusual names or names that weren't popular when they were growing up. Men—at least those whose partners are writing e-mails needing name help—seem to either want names that were popular when they were young, or just unassailably "normal" names. I don't want to misrepresent anyone though. Men have just as many opinions about names as women do, and just as often say things like "I didn't even know this bothered me until we were talking about it," but their solutions, where baby naming is concerned, seems to be to choose the tried-and-true, thoroughly run-of-the-mill alternatives. All the people pushing Hamish and Ichabod (well, other than me) seemed to be women who were pitted firmly against their male partners—but by comparison the gay couples I spoke to, both male and female, seemed more aligned with each other in their expectations for the types of names their children would have.

Another thing I learned was that people really are afraid to venture into uncharted territory because they're afraid their children's names will be made fun of on the playground. While I completely agree that kids can be the worst where finding other kids' weaknesses is concerned, I believe making fun of ethnic or unusual names is something we've outgrown as a multicultural society, particularly in the past twenty or so years in North America, because, think about it: What's the baseline "normal" name? I'm not naïve enough by a long shot to think that there aren't still names that are quietly snickered at, but now it's just the adults who are (maybe, privately) doing the snickering. Kids do not know the difference between Eleanor and Vishnu in terms of which name is "traditional"—which is a euphemism in itself—unless an adult tells them. Where there are names that rhyme with funny things or that sound lyrical in one language but comical in English, I think the new ethos of inclusiveness for everyone's differences trumps the base instinct to giggle at what rhymes with Dolores.

How to Name Someone Else's Baby

So my name advice focuses largely on "don't be boring," coupled with "don't be afraid," and a side of "actually try to pay attention to the names around you and account for them so that you don't replicate them." And then I proceed to have the most fun you can have naming children. I say this because unlike, say, my maternal grandmother, who had eleven children, I get to name child upon child upon child without having to raise them all, which really can't be overstated as a positive.

About 35 percent of the time I get an e-mail saying one of the names I suggested was the one the writers went with, which seems like a pretty spectacular batting average. I am elated when this happens, especially when I'm going out on a limb with a suggestion. Most recently I got a letter saying that my suggestion of Zeke had hit the jackpot, which is why you have to stretch the names you suggest! Sure, everyone agrees Emma sounds nice, but that's partly because everyone has heard Emma a million times before. I skew toward underused names for many reasons, one of which is that for every person who thinks Larkspur is a crazy name, there's another who thinks that's it! I've hit it! The bigger the gutsy name, the bigger the glory, right?

Then there's a smaller but still significant number of readers who write back saying despite the fifteen reasons they didn't want to go with Mason and the eleven alternatives I provided, they are going with Mason after all. These are the people who are interested in unusual names for other people, but happiest when their choice is unassailable. They can't face the prospect of lying awake six months in, thinking "I chose the wrong name"—something we'll get to later on. The rest of the time, the advice goes into the ether, at least for the parents who requested it. I assume this is because they are focused on the task of actually having and raising the baby in question.

Name advice, and its much more interesting corollary, name therapy, is easily the most fun job I've ever had, and at the risk of sounding egotistical, I'm good at it not just because I love names, but because I'm constantly trying to get better in a "field" where there aren't a lot of guideposts. So I ask myself the following questions to keep myself honest:

Am I suggesting enough varied names?

Sometimes I get into a real groove with a name that seems to suggest itself to every letter-writer and I have to curb myself. A while ago, it was Gregor. More recently I find myself pitching Helena and Enzo at every opportunity.

Am I wrong in ignoring what I thought of as "try-hard" names, like Indigo?

I tend to believe most people come up with these names on their own and don't need too much of my help. That is, if you're bound and determined to name your child Summer Raine, just like you thought up at sleep-away camp the year you were eleven, you're probably not looking to me for my help. And yeah, I guess we could expand that to say that I don't really think "Sunshine" is a name. I once went eleven paragraphs on a woman who was considering calling her son Kale. Still, if these kinds of names are your bag, I think it's because they live vividly in your imagination, and I love hearing about the names and what inspired them. Still, it might be that there's nothing I can suggest that will resonate with you if you hope to call your daughter Strawberry.

Am I giving enough examples for how they could be used in real life?

One of my go-to stipulations for a name suggestion is, "This is a name that can be used for both children and adults." But what if I am understating the case? Sometimes my posts are greeted with some pretty opinionated outrage, either by people offended that I have maligned their desired name, or by people offended I haven't suggested the name they chose when they were stuck in just such a dilemma. More recently I'm getting letters chiding me *for* recommending names—because parents who have chosen them want to keep them obscure and underused.

I have a ball writing the column—but that's not why it's a success. People like that I'm honest about names that are undeserving of acclaim, and because I have never once recommended a name due to its "meaning."

What Does It All Mean?

Do you like the name Sydney? Yes or no? It means "wide meadow." *Now* do you like the name Sydney? There's nothing wrong with the meaning "wide meadow," but what does it actually tell you about the person who wears the name?

I have never cared about the "meaning" of names—the origins of the words themselves, which are often words used as references to nature or faith in various languages where the names originate. Maybe it's my lack of a religious upbringing, but what makes a name meaning "God's gift" any different or better than "He who is like God"? My own name's meaning is "little dark one" and I'm dark but not little so . . . scoring 50 percent? Is that a good enough reason? Maybe I'm being too literal or simplistic, but with very few exceptions (Cecily, Deirdre, Claudia come to mind—and ironically, these names are fantastic), most traditional name meanings are positive. But to what end? Searching through

15,000 names on a database for your favourite girl's name that means "strong" isn't going to make your daughter any stronger. Apolline is a spectacular name, but choose it because you love the sound or the reference to Apollo, not because of the meaning "light and life," which sounds like a cliché from an online dating profile. After all, it's the proper noun— the name—that's walking around up front, not the meaning— and the more diverse our name culture gets, the less likely that meanings are universally acknowledged. It's fine that your name means "beauty" in Sanskrit if everyone knows Sanskrit. But when they don't, you wind up explaining a meaning more often than not. Similarly, it's fine if you chose Chandler because it derives from the French word for candle and you met in a candlestick factory—but most people don't know that, so if you don't explain it, you can't be offended if they assume you're a huge *Friends* fan.

What matters far more to me, where meanings are concerned, is the implicit meanings in names that we crowd-source and agree on mutually. BuzzFeed, the pop-news site, has had some of their biggest traffic days with articles like "What Guys'/Girls' First Names Say About Them: An Unscientific Discussion." The crowd-sourced opinions in the article are utterly unfounded and based purely in anecdote, but still totally resonant. An example: "Melanie's confidence is off the Richter. She's the one who gets you up to dance at weddings." Melanie and her friends and family can discuss whether this is true or false, but it has a lot more relevance for day-to-day life than the traditional meaning of Melanie—"dark," which my very smart editor pointed out comes from the same root as "melatonin." So I've never been much for traditional meanings.

There's one other question I am asked and the advice I give is apparently non-traditional, but I will defend it with my last breath.

Tell or Don't Tell?

The first time I was asked, in an interview, whether people who keep their baby names secret while still expecting weren't just being unnecessarily precious, I was stunned. Even more disturbing was that the interviewer clearly expected me to respond that yes, of course it was.

I could not disagree more.

This is a fairly modern trend, one that has evolved as most people learn the sex of their baby at roughly the half-way mark during a pregnancy. A generation ago or so, parents couldn't really commit to a name until they knew whether they were having a boy or a girl, but that problem is now obsolete in Western society. Once you know what you're having, current trends seem to say, you should be able to disclose *who* you're having not long afterward (in fact, choosing *not* to find out the sex is also considered in many circles to be ridiculously precious).

I am really shocked by this. Obviously pregnancy and impending parenthood are more than just opportunities to experiment with names, but my understanding has always been that the debate and weighing of names is part of what gets you through those long, swollen weeks. The weighing and choosing are a vital part of the process and it seems premature, if you'll pardon the term, to announce a name before it's been considered for the full forty weeks or more.

The journalist who spoke to me also wondered if it was indicative of greater secrecy—that if expecting parents didn't want announce the name up front, it was to guard against being "namejacked"—having their preferred name stolen by parents in the same circle who would take the opportunity to use it first. I used to think this was preposterous, but I've gotten the letters. This happens. There are people walking among us who are name-hoarders; who feel entitled to lay claim to dozens at once.

For these reasons I am always crystal clear: do not engage with people who want to know which names you're considering. Discuss them neither with your best friend nor your mother-in-law. You will either wind up sad, disappointed with yourself, or having promised to wrap in the name Eunice. Feign ignorance or, if you can't, think up some decoy names to talk about.

Who Cares about Names? Lessons from the Trenches

It became apparent very quickly that the names parents wrote in about, full of angst, weren't really about the children they were naming. Everyone knows, whether they articulate it or not, that the baby doesn't get a choice, and that choosing a name is really for the pleasure of the parents. If you want a Desdemona, you can make it so, and the kid will damn well like it, because how could your taste be anything other than excellent? Most parents worry more about the people around them, because judgment comes from your peers, not your kids or theirs.

In fact, the letters are barely *about* the kids. People who write in for name advice want to know what kind of people *they* will seem like if they choose this name or that; how they will be perceived if they betray their love for the Renaissance period or their secret truth that they always dreamed of surfing and will live vicariously through a son called Case. This follows both the parents and the kids everywhere. Recently I was watching a newsmagazine show that had parents debate whether or not their kids would lie in certain high-pressure situations while the parents watched on hidden camera. One father said that his son had better not, since his name, Tre, meant truth. No pressure.

I realized early on that the questions I was getting about baby names, involving parental approval and arguments with partners, and still-not-fixed junior high school wounds, was only a little bit about finding a name for a baby.

What it's really about is helping the soon-to-be parents become comfortable with their evolving taste in names, and maybe much more. That is, when your mother or best friend thinks your name choice is crazy or wild or boring, what they're really saying is "When did you stop being like me?" When you have the audacity to consider something someone else doesn't like, they wonder why you do and they don't. Since everyone considers their own taste unimpeachable, this either means they think you have bad taste in names—or they get defensive, because it means they think you suddenly don't like theirs.

Calling in the Professionals

As recently as the 1990s, the concept of baby name consultants for the public didn't really exist. There were countless baby name bibles, of course, and I knew them all because I would haunt the bookshelves they were on in the store or library. But I didn't buy them, because I knew some nosy checkout person would ask, "What does a ten-year-old girl need with baby name books?"

No, baby name dictionaries are meant to be bought by adults expecting a child, and similarly, the judging of baby names was left mainly to people in the privacy of their own homes after receiving printed baby announcements, or disbelievingly when driving away from nursery school meet-and-greets, or perhaps, for some judgment-free people, not at all.

But the Internet gives and gives, and so I've been able to find an entire community of name experts who study, opine and advise on names for love and commerce. The people I've assembled below are some of the heaviest hitters. Their styles differ and their opinions vary wildly, but their passion for names is incredibly familiar to me.

The Old School Sage

Dr. Albert Mehrabian, Professor Emeritus at UCLA, is the author of twenty books on various aspects of psychology—the impact of nonverbal messages, the idea that given personality traits can be predictive of success—and *The Name Game*, a guide for parents that details his research on the perception of names.

Dr. Mehrabian agrees that people will judge you by your name—the subtitle of the book is *The Decision That Lasts a Lifetime*. However, he attempted to quantify the value of names in six categories—Success, Morality(!), Warmth,

Health, and Masculinity or Femininity—with rankings based entirely on other people's perceptions of each name. That is, whether outsiders believe that Kirsten connotes health or that Alice ranks low on the success scale (it does, and so do Ignacio, Mordecai, Libby and Rose. Dr. Mehrabian never met Mordecai Richler).

I'm really torn here because on the one hand, judging names according to perception is exactly what all name critics or advice columnists advocate. But Dr. Mehrabian—who, in our brief e-mail correspondence, never invited me to call him "Albert"—has put together a sample survey of just . . . people. Regular people, participating in a scientific survey, who think Vanessa and Leonora connote a high degree of "femininity" and put Scott through the roof on a "warmth" meter? As for "morality," given that Dr. Mehrabian remarks that "A three-piece suit means one thing and a short skirt, quite another," and thinks any woman would choose to be called Elizabeth rather than Liz once she saw the numbers, I think we can assume that the "morality" test is just another way of saying "not a stripper name." (This concept will come up a lot—stay tuned for chapter 8.)

My name is, of course, too rare to be included in his book, but if I were called Jacqueline or Samantha I might have had more success, though I don't know when or how that "success" would be measured. Still, don't tell my dad. (A note on the success front—Jacqueline scores off the charts—a 103 on a scale of all six categories with 50 as a median. But the next most successful name, Katherine, scores only an 89—and the numbers fall from there.) Dr. Mehrabian's studies are very clearly aimed at anxious parents hoping they don't make a "tragic" decision about their child's name—no word on what to do if you're already named something low-ranking like Rufus.

The rankings seem . . . arbitrary. Which makes sense given that they were generated by polling participants in a survey. But, though I relish the judging of names, quantifying their success seems strange to me. I had trouble getting to this point, but I reluctantly came to the realization that I just don't agree with Dr. Mehrabian's research. I was delighted that so decorated a psychologist was taking on the study of names, but I ultimately think they're a qualitative subject, and that the impressions they give are malleable, not numerically scorable.

The New School Analyzer

There are still some numbers that matter, however. Most baby name sites now give a number ranking of how popular a name was, and that was originally the brainchild of Jennifer Moss, creator of BabyNames.com. Jennifer, a former computer programmer, explained to me that her name site was created when she was bored at work, and realized the algorithms she used in her job would be good at analyzing the popularity of names she heard on the playground at her daughter's school. She has also done private name consulting for parents, and agrees with me that people aren't as open to considering a range of names as they think they are. Generally something sticks with both parents early and doesn't let go. "After zeroing in on one name, like Allison, the more I would suggest other names, the more they would say 'Right, but how about Allison?' returning to the original name they had in mind," she laughs.

Of course. Because parents have definite ideas about the type of child they want to create, even if they can't fully articulate it. Enter Pamela Redmond Satran.

The Name Stylist

I've known of Pamela for a very long time, since the publication of *Beyond Jennifer and Jason: An Enlightened Guide to Naming Your Baby*. It is the first of her phenomenally successful baby name books, written with co-author Linda Rosencrantz, and it was published when I was just a teenage name nerd. Their books were formative for me because they included opinions about names, ones that Pamela and her partner, Linda, clearly espoused. They knew names were not merely a product or a numerical value, but a fashion statement and an indication of parents' personal style—and that meant there were names that were in style, and names that were hopelessly out. Best of all, the books didn't mince words. "Do not choose this for your child," it would say in so many words. The honesty is as refreshing as it is rare—there can be a lot of pressure to be "nice" about names, since all of them ostensibly already belong to someone.

But the straightforward approach worked, and spawned not only a series of very popular books, but begat the incredibly vast website Nameberry.com, which now bests all the other baby name databases by incorporating real-life opinions and perspectives on the names it profiles.

Pamela is so amenable to meeting and talking about the culture of naming and name books that I realize almost too late that I'm a little nervous about meeting her. I assume we are simpatico on the big name issues, but what if I'm actually a bit of a name rube?

A friend advises me, when in New York, to always meet in hotel bars, and it's a good idea—when she arrives at our meeting spot in a boutique SoHo hotel, I'm immediately struck by her glamour. I knew from my research that she worked in fashion magazine publishing for many years, and Pamela herself tells me those facts are related: "I think names are important because I'm a lifelong name nerd. So I don't understand people who say [names are] not important, but—" she takes a resigned sip of her drink, shrugging "—there are people who think clothes aren't important." Which, her expression implies, is their choice, but not the right choice.

Her name career began when *Beyond Jennifer and Jason* was published in 1988 and quickly became known as the first name book to truly express opinions on names. "I don't know exactly when babyGap was born, or *Parenting* magazine, but it was kind of like there were a lot of new products or ideas out there [at the time]." The consumerism of the Baby Boomers, she remembers, made all things related to parenthood—including names—a commodity in a whole new way.

Pamela's success, as she remembers it, was swift, partially tied to the fact that Prince Andrew and Sarah Ferguson named their daughter the then-unthinkable Beatrice. But *Beyond Jennifer and Jason* caught on for other reasons—mainly that it offered parents guidance they desperately wanted through a sea of names. No longer content to choose names based only on arbitrary meanings or family traditions, the book declared some names were terrible, not worth bestowing on a child—and that was revolutionary. "Nobody was saying any of this. Nobody had ever talked about it. When my friends were having babies, I had had my first baby, and we were sitting around talking, 'Oh, I like Nicholas but is it too trendy?' We were talking about 'Is it too weird?'"

This is the big, big elephant in the baby name room. It's the reason *Freakonomics* is still referenced ten years after publication and the reason baby names are still a hotbed of discussion. Names aren't just about style, they're just as often about class—and the fact that when parents choose names, they know they have the ability to determine their child's class, or at least others' perception of it.

It's a big deal, and not an easy topic. Pamela's book was the first to address the issue, and she understands why it was touchy. "[In 1988] there was a value to being like everybody else that I think was much stronger than it is today. In general, 'personal style'—that didn't really exist. It didn't." She explains that in the early 1980s, there was much less inclination to examine what constituted "stylish." You simply accepted what the experts said. She likens it to her work in fashion, when she realized that people didn't dress in head-to-toe Ralph Lauren or Calvin Klein as in the fashion magazines during the '80s, and proposing that they make a page "like us," mixing high fashion with low. Satran recognized that name culture could be similarly under-represented. Maybe there was a market for people who didn't want to name their children Katherine and Robert simply because those were the approved names up to that point.

Pamela and Linda wrote several editions and spinoffs of the first book, updating periodically as different styles of names became popular. The titles subtly cast aspersions on the most overused choices by parents of the day:

- *Beyond Jennifer and Jason* (1988)
- *Beyond Jennifer and Jason, Madison and Montana* (2004)
- *Beyond Shannon and Sean: An Enlightened Guide to Irish Baby-Naming* (1992)
- *Beyond Charles and Diana: An Anglophile's Guide to Baby-Naming* (1992)
- *Beyond Sarah and Sam: An Enlightened Guide to Jewish Baby-Naming* (1992)
- *Beyond Ava and Aiden* (2009)

It's right there in the titles—the frank valuations on the names that made these books different (and what made them incredibly successful—they are bestsellers many times over). Specifically, Pamela's and Linda's opinions were about the worthiness, the good-or-badness, of all kinds of names. Pamela knows that her opinions about what parents choose—and the fact that they're not as original as they think—is both a nod to and a step away from the cult of individuality. "I think the concept of being individual and distinct has been widely embraced, which of course was our message from the beginning. And yet I feel like at the same time people are still afraid to really step [away from the norm]. People are still looking for the name that feels different but that ultimately is really the same [as the one they are trying to avoid]. And so it is Ella, if it's not Isabella, it's Bella and then it's Ella and then it's Eleanor and then it's Nora."

Parents are reluctant to step too far outside the box, because the fear of giving the "wrong" name is very real, to the point where you sometimes hear stories of babies left unnamed after birth for a while, until the parents figure out something they, and their offspring, can live with forever.

Pamela and Linda's books allude to the idea that some names denote a higher level of economic or social class than others, but "allusion" is as strong as she's able to be in print. "We have not written about it as honestly as we might have, because it's such a touchy issue, because there are so many ways to define 'class.' In some ways I feel like [class, and the idea of passing it on, or trying to acquire it] is a really important question that's at the heart of what people really want from a name and they don't realize that that's what they're thinking *or* they're not willing to say it out loud."

I agree with Pamela. Because as soon as you broach the idea that a name has an inherent perceived value attached to it, people get defensive. Even if they asked for it, "advice" can quickly become "offence" if they don't like what you have to say. I know I'm a name therapist because of the way people unfold their name issues in front of me, but if challenged, I have no name-specific degree. In truth, all you have to do to be an expert online is to say you are. The reason people trust me is because they know they're not.

Most of my letter writers are trying to figure out how to subvert a partner (and maybe a set of parents or in-laws) whose opinions are much, much more conservative than their own. Or they're trying to find a way to reconcile their childhood dreams of what a baby should be called with the adult awareness of knowing that Aviana is ridiculous as a name and that Octavia might actually be the better option. People come to ask me my opinion not only because of my name expertise, but because I am not emotionally invested in the situation. Empirically I want what's best for your child but I don't actually have to answer for any of it. Plus, of course, there's the fact that the blog I write on is well-respected and very widely read. Being the expert there gives me cool cred that I savour, given that the search tag of the column includes the word "nerd."

I love giving advice on names. Writing the name column for the blog is easily the most fun part of my work week, and the rewards are most tangible—babies are being born all the time, and their parents write back regularly to let me know how the naming went.

Readers also write to tell me to stop suggesting Damian (which I appreciate, because everyone needs checks and balances), and they want to steer their siblings away from choosing names they think are trashy, and they are desperate to find ways to match their own Dutch heritage with their partner's Indian heritage and find a name that works for the grandparents— none of whom are English-speaking.

And I want to help them, and I scour things I've never read and look up the pronunciation of Martje (it's Matcha! Do you love it?) so that I can track down the solutions to their unique issues. But nobody chooses names in a vacuum. They're always reacting to their own name, their experiences growing up, and their expectations of themselves and of others.

But to understand that, I have to understand all the pitfalls of names and the experiences you can have walking around with one that doesn't quite fit. Luckily, I have some experience.

2

WHERE DO DUANAS COME FROM?
Personal Struggles with an Offbeat Name

So I'm a name nerd. Now you know. The question then becomes: Name nerd—made, or born? In my case, it was both.

My mother was born and raised in rural Tipperary, Ireland, while my father grew up in a downtrodden corner of Cairo, Egypt. They met in London, in 1970, and moved to Toronto a few years later. At the time, they didn't know when or if they'd ever be able to visit their home countries again. Even a simple transatlantic phone call was rare and prohibitively expensive—and travelling back home was out of the question. So when they had their first child in Canada, they agreed I should have a Gaelic first name to balance my Egyptian last name; it might be the only Irish and Egyptian culture I ever got. I don't think either of them knew that growing up amid Canadian multiculturalism in the 1980s would mean I had both too much and not enough of the places they came from—how could they have known?

So I was born Duana Elise Taha to Maureen and Gamal, who would have thought it was ridiculous that the fifty-fifty cultural mashup of a child they'd created was going to be so keenly *aware* of this name, all the time. I was in good company as a child of immigrants, but relatively rare as one who came from two cultures, yet belonged to neither. In Judy Blume's *Are You There God? It's Me, Margaret,* Margaret Simon says when you're part of two religions you're the thing that can't be. I remember thinking I understood the sentiment, but that I was also the thing that couldn't be without even broaching the topic of religion. I was a TV-deprived know-it-all with giant peach plastic glasses and boys' underwear, because my parents were never concerned with whether or not I was "on-trend" (and my grandfather sent the Egyptian cotton underwear so it had to be worn, boys' or not). I brought milk in my lunch thermos because my mother then thought it was "nature's most perfect food." All this not-fitting-in or not being typically "Canadian" had a lot to do with the cultures my parents came from, as it's extremely common for immigrants to focus on, you know, *survival* as opposed to aesthetics—but at the time I thought it was entirely a reflection on my name. I was sure it was the thing about me that actually made me different. In fact, I saw it as an active choice my parents made to *make* me different.

My name was different, I knew that much for sure. Growing up in the 1980s meant the same twelve names were heard over and over. My contemporaries were Michelle, Christopher, Stephanie, Andrew, Erin, and of course, over and over again, one name over all the others. *Love Story* didn't just produce the most pathetic excuse for being a horrendous person during arguments ("Love means never having to say you're sorry," which is not true, by the way— try it and see if I'm wrong), it also spawned the behemoth that was the name "Jennifer." Emblematic of the times, Jennifer was tinged with class, enough syllables to invite and celebrate excess, yet instantly familiar and aspirational. There were at least three of them on the street I grew up on, but there was nobody else named Duana. Not on my street or at swimming lessons or in the mall.

I used to think that I didn't notice the difference until I got to school, but the truth is that every time I told any adult my name they frowned in confusion. The lady at the bank who gave out the lollipops misheard me. "Diana?" she asked repeatedly. "No, DEW-anna," I replied, and still she didn't believe me. The dentist went with mockery, instead. "Your name is what? Doodoo? Ha ha, we have some doodoo here in the chair!" (You can imagine my feelings of vindication when my parents, for unrelated reasons, agreed that he was a jerk, and we found a new dentist.) My friends' parents, used to Carrie Ann and Jamie Lynn and Robert and Billy, somehow managed to make my name sound like a bit of a joke—"If Da-WAH-nnA wants to stay for dinner, set another place at the table."

I didn't have the words for it at the time, but I now understand that acquaintances' reaction to my name was a bit of stealthy xenophobia. I had long brown pigtails and freckles, and frankly, looked like a white girl. If you were judging me by my appearance, then there shouldn't have been any reason for the adults I encountered to struggle over my name. But when the name didn't compute with their eyes telling them *She looks like a Sarah*, it was a bit alarming for some of the adults I encountered and they weren't shy about letting me know.

So I was "other" very early on, and to me, it was all because of my name. It came to symbolize everything about my life that I disliked, and was a clear indicator of my parents' unwillingness to conform to North American culture. I was a typically myopic kid so I assumed that their immigrating to Canada meant they should have had total affection for and adoption of all the customs. Why couldn't they see that and leave their boring countries with terrible names that didn't fit in, behind? I was just a kid so I didn't vocalize any of this, of course, but I also didn't really believe that they'd *had* lives and families back home that they were sorry to have left. Going by other families I saw around me, I realized it was possible for grandparents and cousins to show up every few weeks for raucous meals or trips to the water park. Since I didn't have any of that, I assumed my family and I were basically from a pod. There didn't seem to be anything of note in Ireland or Egypt to cling to, so why was my *name* a throwback? Why wouldn't my parents just *conform*? To a kid in the status-obsessed 1980s, not conforming—on purpose—was basically the worst crime they could commit. I gave them a hard time about it, too.

No matter what lovely experience they gave me—whether a trip to the zoo or an amusement park or Niagara Falls—it was always punctuated by my dragging them over to the novelty "name" items in the souvenir shops. Despite the countless times I spun the racks of licence plates or mugs or hairbrushes, "Duana" never came up. The spaces near Denise and Donna never yielded anything good, and damned Diana was there mocking me every time, so close but so far.

The message was very clear. Here's a list of everyone who belongs, and you, Duana, aren't on it. All the things about me that were different—I could read before my fourth birthday, I skipped a grade at school, I wasn't allowed to watch television, I had this *hair*—could have happened to anyone, but combined, they became emblematic of what it meant to be a "Duana" and, by association, what it meant to be hopelessly out of touch. Which I assumed was an immutable position. As an adult I can see not all those qualities were negative, but as a kid I was only aware of them making me different. Making "Duana" different.

I quickly decided the best defence was being defensive. So I jumped in to say "I'm here," before a substitute teacher could mangle it while taking attendance. When I encountered slightly differently named classmates, I wondered what kinds of parents would think to name their kids Clemence or Nigel or Petula. Were these kids as obsessed with their names, or some other aspect of themselves that was just as maddeningly ever-present, as singular? They couldn't know, for example, how much significance I assigned to the day the teacher announced that we were going to have a new girl in the class called Savoury, and I thought "someone will finally understand me." When the poor girl showed up (and I had already transferred onto her all my eleven-year-old issues), her name was Alicia. The teacher had somehow gotten it very wrong, and my dreams of meeting someone who Truly Understood were crushed.

And then the tables turned.

By the time I got to high school, people were bending over backwards to be different. My name was still one of the many things that set me apart—but now it was suddenly, inexplicably, switched over to tally in the plus column. As we all donned Doc Martens, pierced everything we could get away with and tried desperately not to be ordinary (but still not too weird), I was suddenly way ahead of all the Katies. My name made me instantly identifiable, and, as my insecurity and my ego grew in equal measure (see above, re: I was a teenager)—it nursed a tiny, secretly held belief that maybe I had a leg up in being different than everyone else. That if names are destiny, maybe I had control of what my name could mean.

But I realized my interest in names, while not serial-killer-level strange, was not exactly shared by many of my peers. I tried to figure out exactly where I'd gotten the idea that my name, instead of my face or my family or my memorization of every lyric in the *Phantom of the Opera* libretto, was the thing that made me most unfortunately distinct from my peers. Like any right-thinking individual, I found the answers between two mildewy covers in the public library.

How 1980s Young Adult Fiction Created Name Nerds

For a certain type of outspoken, literary woman, Harriet M. Welsch is a touchstone figure. She is mouthy and candid and brutal in her pursuit of the truth. I mean, she has to be. She's a *spy*. For the uninitiated, I'm talking about *Harriet the Spy* by Louise Fitzhugh, and if you're reading this in a place that sells books, you should purchase that one to go along with this wonderful volume you're holding. I'm not saying an eleven-year-old Manhattan-based spy is my role model but, you know, listening to everyone talk about their names for years is a form of observation, and Harriet certainly taught me all about that—you see where I'm going here? She's not *not* my role model.

She's also not called Janie or Rachel or Beth or any of the names her classmates go by—she is Harriet. It's distinctive. It's not going to be mistaken for anyone else's name. She's always proud of it, and in fact, she even manufactures a middle initial. That's how proud she is of her name. The fact that she doesn't fit in with her peers is somehow kind of fitting. After all, she's *Harriet* and they're not.

The pattern repeats itself over and over with some of the most beloved books of the era. Beverly Cleary's "Ramona" series has Ramona Quimby as its heroine, another girl with an unusual moniker. And being unusual—in Ramona's case, outspoken and show-offy and jealous—and dealing with those traits, while not exactly loving them, is basically the theme of the series. It's noted that her sister, Beezus—a clumsy nickname for Beatrice—doesn't get off any easier. Beezus suffers from wearing hand-me-downs and sporting discount haircuts, and she sees herself as "other" as a result— but it's her name that announces her non-typicalness up front, before her old clothes even enter the equation.

Over and over again, novels written for young people in the 1970s and 1980s proposed that probably having an unusual name was going to be hard and make you an unusual person but, hey, at least you'd get books written about you. Anastasia Krupnik had a fear of moving to the suburbs and enjoyed talking to a plaster statue of Sigmund Freud. Judy Blume, whose canon figured largely in my understanding of being a kid, endorsed this theory in several books. In *Are You*

There God? It's Me, Margaret, Margaret and her friends take on "sensational" names to help themselves grow up and become sophisticated: Alexandra, Veronica, Kimberly, and Mavis. Deenie, the main character in the book of the same name, is supposed to be an actress or model, but we all know that's not going to happen because she thinks those things are kind of lame, but more importantly because the girl's name is Wilmadeene (no, really)! She's obviously destined for unusual adventures, ones the Janets and Alices on her cheerleading team couldn't ever conceive of. Boys don't fare any better—the titular character of *Superfudge* is called Fudge because his real first name is Farley. If you're going to be named Fudge—or Farley, for that matter—you're not going to remain one of the crowd. It's predestined. (Fascinatingly, especially considering all of the attention she gave to names, Judy Blume confessed to a friend of mine that, despite being the most beloved author of her time, none of her admiring fans had ever named a child Judy, after her. There's a way to show you're a truly devoted fan. . . .)

It was too late for the readers of these books, who, stats tell us, were overwhelmingly named Jennifer and Amanda and Nicole, to be original, name-wise. But these books created a generation of those obsessed with names, and as a result, were dissatisfied with their own (something that wouldn't manifest until almost a generation later)—who understood the power of a distinctive label for a distinctive person. It was too late, maybe, for their own names to be descriptive of how unusual they might be, but not too late at all for them to become fascinated by names so that they wouldn't inflict such ordinary labels on the next generation.

It's worth mentioning that the once-beloved Sweet Valley High series had Elizabeths and Jessicas and Lilas, but let me be the first to draw a line between the names in the books and their perceived relevance today. Who is more likely to be interesting to read about? Liz or Anastasia?

Big-Talk Backed Up

It was the rise of the Internet that did it, really. It's one thing to notice the coincidence of multiple Matthews in your statistics class or Shannons who live on the same floor of your dorm—but to realize it's a massively widespread phenomenon—that there are as many Shannons as there are aspiring actresses in Los Angeles—gives people an identity crisis. As soon as they enter a larger pool of people—a national swimming final or a freshman class at a university—it's abundantly clear that there are names that repeat over and over and over again, and usually there are similarities among the families that choose them.

But Duanas are still crushingly (or, depending how I'm feeling about the name, thrillingly) rare. I was an adult before I met another one, and it was all due to a guy named Mark. Zuckerberg, that is. He was the one who helped me find my people. For a fleeting time at the peak of social media's honeymoon phase, I was a member of a Facebook group called "My name is Duana—oh wait, so is yours!" I was unreasonably excited about this and so were my friends, since this was a time when people still paid attention to what other people did on Facebook. But the group disappeared, as did the associated Duanas. I'm not sure what algorithm to attribute that to, but I miss my friends I never actually met, knew, or spoke to.

Still, I had a jolt of joy when a few years later I searched on Twitter for the Duanas and found not one, but several! I had imagined that they were out there, waiting for me to find them again, but I didn't actually hope it could be true. No matter that our entire shared history was one Facebook joke. Twitter is where our kinship would begin again and be knitted. We would find so many things in common and realize that for the first time we would be understood! Ultimately, though I'm not sure I located the same Duanas I'd once bonded with, I found four Duanas—all of whom agreed to talk with me. Solidarity!

Er. Or, not. One Duana said that she pronounced the name "Dew-AHH-nah"—a pronunciation that I've run into but never been able to adopt authentically. She "doesn't really like the sound of it," though. She has a spectacular middle name, Saskia, that she uses instead and identifies with, so that may be part of her feelings on the name.

Duana Forrest is from Northern Ireland but currently lives in Virginia, and confessed: "You're the only other person I've found with the same name." She likes it, but offers up a third pronunciation. "I pronounce it as DUANE-AH. Like Duane (the boy's name) with an Ah at the end. I like the name because it's unique, but getting people to understand how to say it or spell it can be frustrating."

An aspiring journalist, Forrest says that having an Irish name wasn't of paramount importance to her parents when she was born, but that now—especially since she's studying in the U.S.—"The name definitely helps me to stand out, which I love. I'm still at college but it's helped me so far." I guess this is where I realize we're from different generations. She loves that her name helps her stand out! It's helped her so far! I kind of want to give her a hug and tell her to keep positive for all of us.

Okay! The breadth of Duanas begins to amaze me. We are united both in our differences and in our similarities! (Two of the four Duanas I spoke to were writers by profession. Coincidence?!) Different personalities, different pronunciations, but maybe a Duana is meant to be a writer? I turn to one more Duana for confirmation. Duana C. Welch, Ph.D, is the author of the book *Love Factually: 10 Proven Steps from I Wish to I Do*. Clearly she didn't agree with my childhood philosophy that all the trials in a Duana's life can be attributed to her name.

But there is another punch coming. Welch pronounces her name "DWAY-nah."

"I am friends with all the other Duanas in the world on Facebook and I met one other, once, when I was five. My parents named me after my father's middle name, Duane."

I can't avoid it any more. Am I walking around with the wrong pronunciation of my name? Did it take all the other Duanas to point it out? There are any number of online name databases that claim my pronunciation is the way it's supposed to be pronounced, or at least an accepted variant, but . . . have I had a false sense of my own name all this time? I try to seek out all of the Duanas that Welch mentions on Facebook, but I can find only one. Maybe privacy settings are very important to Duanas, and we set them quite high (and no, I'm not Facebook friends with Welch—she's never asked). This online caution isn't surprising to me actually—as I said before, it's a lot easier to have those questionable party pictures turn up in Internet searches if your name isn't Emily. From years of experience I know that my name only appears in a scant few name books—and believe me, I've checked every one I've ever seen. I would always look for those books in every bookstore—but with a few exceptions, like the *Beyond* . . . books, they never seemed to be on the shelves! However, I'll never forget when I did find my name—in a Satran/Rosencrantz book, no less! Their write-up (which now appears on their baby name database Nameberry) seems to acknowledge my pronunciation, but implies it's a choice. "Name your daughter Duana after a Duane relative if you like, but please pronounce it doo-ahn-a and not doo-wain-a."

So maybe I'm pronouncing my name wrong. You can't knock it if you haven't tried it, right? I decide the best way to decide whether I'm really entitled to my own pronunciation of my already unique name is if I walk around as Dway-nah. Or *Doo-wain-a* if you prefer. Some days this is not a problem, as my name is effortlessly mispronounced everywhere I go. So I try to recreate those situations. I go to a coffee shop and ask for an outlandish order just so they'll have a reason to write my name on my cup. But it turns out that spelling "Dway-nah" is virtually the same as spelling it Duana—I get "Duaneh" and barely noticed—a reaction I'll explore more later on.

When I enter another store and give "my" name, the attendant says, "Oh, wow. Is that like the feminine Duane?" I nod, and she smiles, satisfied. Maybe I need to stop swimming against the tide. But I can't get used to Dway-nah, and

I just feel like I don't know how to be her, whoever she is. I know it sounds preposterous, but there's a reason nobody's walking around calling themselves "Mireenda" or "Joecob."

Exhausted by Dway-nah, I am happy to return to being my version of Duana. And, my reward for my authenticity? At long last, corroboration! When I get home at the end of the experiment-day, I have another Facebook message. Duana Killalea lives in New Zealand, and her life looks so incredible I'm jealous—she surfs and takes exotic vacations and her phonetic description, over Facebook, of how to pronounce her name, is "do-arn-ah."

That sounds like my wacky pronunciation to me, as passed through a Kiwi filter. She says, "I hated it as a child, just wanted a normal name. Also if, there were ever any rumours or stories about Duana, there was only one option of who it could be! I always dreaded when teachers would call out my name on the roll, I'd always get a lot of interesting variations!"

DuaRna, my long-lost sister! Where have you been all my life? She goes on: "I like it now, I like having an original name . . . aside from the fact of constantly having to spell [it]. I get a lot of compliments on my name . . . I would definitely give a child a unique name." Duana's level of zen may just be because of her gorgeous lifestyle but I choose to believe she's embodying what "we" want for the name.

Bigger, Odder, Awesome: Unusual names as education and armour

I'm the only one I know walking around with this name, but walking around with an unusual name is not, in itself, unheard of. I'm always a bit cautious asking other people about their unusual (to me) names, because what if their unusual name is a dime a dozen in their reality? But curiosity always trumps politeness, so I always ask—and I feel automatic kinship whenever I hear someone in a coffee shop explain their name over and over or worse, give up trying to correct the pronunciation.

In fact, I remember interactions with unusually named people more vividly. In high school, I assumed I would be friends with the unusually named Ildiko. I still remember feeling crushing embarrassment when I misspelled the first name of our beautiful next-door neighbour, Cidalia (in my defence, the correct spelling makes me think of cicadas). But then, later, I met my people.

After high school, I was admitted to a small, intense program at Ryerson University. It was one of those places that like to tell their anxious pupils that one of the two people sitting on either side of you won't be back next year. I knew I belonged. Not just because television production was the thing I most wanted to do, nor because it was allegedly so hardcore that a third of us wouldn't last through the year, or the week, or something.

It was because of the names of my classmates. Ours was an unusually close group, and I have friends for life named things like Kelly and Dora and Matt and Ryan—but I have a special place in my heart for classmates like Cándida. Or Hilding. They know what it's like, man.

Cándida Lawrence admits her name had ups and downs. "Being an immigrant and attending ESL classes meant that I was surrounded with weirdly named people. For instance, my best friend in grade five was Zenith. Enough said. Then when I later clued in that Cándida was far from the norm, I took a bit of pride in the fact that it sounded pretty. . . . Melodic."

But of course, there's always a moment when your innocence about your name is shattered. Cándida remembers hers: "While working at my first real job at a fast food joint, a middle-aged gentleman was staring at my name tag and asked 'Is that really your name?' To which I answered yes. He then proceeded to ask, 'Do you know what it means?' To which I replied no. He concluded the exchange by informing me that my name, in medical terms, is a kind of yeast infection. OUCH."

I don't just feel Cándida's pain—I feel like I've been there. An unusual name is bad enough—one that people don't understand or hear often. But for someone to be shocked and disbelieving that your parents could choose the name at all is especially jarring. "What were your parents smoking?" is the kind of refrain "my people" hear over and over again.

If you asked Hilding Gnanapragasam, he'd say that was nothing. Hilding, a very old Scandinavian name, is a far cry from "normal," but Hilding said he had to learn to embrace it, and that meant developing a sense of humour. "I once heard that Leonardo DiCaprio's parents picked his name because the first time he kicked in utero, they were looking at a Leonardo da Vinci painting. I used to joke that the first time I kicked, the doorbell rang." He pauses for effect. "Hil-ding!"

After I stop laughing, I ask Hilding whether he was as bothered by not having items with his name on them as I was. "Yeah, that always sucked. And you know what, I always checked. Just in case. When we went to the Norwegian pavilion at Epcot Center, it was the one time I checked with actual hope and expectation. But no."

It's worth noting that Hilding's Sri Lankan last name, Gnanapragasam, isn't exactly easy either. But there are lots of surnames that are difficult no matter where you're from. (I went to school with someone whose last name was "Butt.") Hilding was born to a Norwegian mother and Sri Lankan father. Like me, he's an immigrant hybrid. But of course, surnames are inherited. Given names are given—apparently, out of love.

Hilding is cheerfully straightforward about the trials his name has given him. "I fully believe if my name is drawn as a contest winner, they would probably pick again because my name would be too difficult to say out loud," and, like me, he doesn't have much sympathy for unusual names that really aren't. He laughs telling me about the time his wife, Sylvia, implied that she had an unusual name. "This is going to sound insensitive, but I've always felt that other people with unusual names don't have anything as bad as Hilding. My name is a freaking verb. To *hild*."

But for all the trouble it's caused him, Hilding didn't choose to alter or hide or anglicize his name, as many do. I never heard him try to go by "Hil" or use a nickname. Ultimately, he says, he stuck with Hilding because the name belonged to his grandfather, who died before Hilding ever got the chance to meet him. There's a connection there, however theoretical, that he admits he doesn't want to lose. And he thinks there are other benefits, too. "Overall, I'd say my name is the origin for my sense of humour. It's always been a source of material for me. You don't grow up a chubby brown kid named Hilding without developing some defence mechanisms."

The trouble is in enduring the growing up, though. You can't reach out to that kid and tell them it's all going to be okay, and remind them that in the meantime they are gaining material for their eventual comedy routines or Ph.D level studies in human behaviour. To have an unusual name is to necessarily be alone in this particular way, and have to figure out how to navigate it all by themselves— and so they do. We do.

Everyone finds ways to cope with a label that screams "not like the others," and these days everyone seems to think they have one. Ultimately for me, it was about adopting an alter ego. I used to walk around calling myself Megan, because to my mind, Megan was the perfect North American kid—she was probably going to get the "Over the Rainbow" solo in the spring concert and be allowed to go to sleepovers and would never have weird foods in her lunchbox. Mostly Megan existed only in my head, but I will never forget the day a woman asked me my name, and I decided to tell her.

I was four or five years old at the most, and it was that forced social time waiting in the grocery line—I'm sure my mother was sniffing about the trashy tabloids, and I was probably hatching a scheme to beg for some Skittles. The nice woman behind us saw me, and asked me what my name was. Without missing a beat, I answered "Megan."

"No, it's not!" my mother, horrified, corrected me. The worst part was that her outrage trounced the poor woman, who had already begun saying "What a nice name . . . " My mother looked at me in disbelief. She didn't realize until then the degree to which I was longing to try on being someone else, and that I was already aware of how much my name announced that I was different. How casually I tossed aside the name she had chosen for me! This wouldn't have happened to Megan, whose name would never lead to such social awkwardnesses. As it was, all my mother knew was that I had lied about the name she worked so hard to find, and for what? For *Megan*?

This episode has stayed with me over the years, and I carry more than a little guilt about it. But maybe this is typical of people who have unusual names like this? I tried but didn't find anyone who would admit they'd tried to pass off a different name in front of their parents—at least, not without letting them know. Plenty have changed their names and lobbied their parents to accept this, but as far as I know, I'm the only one who tried to assume a new identity on the fly (at age five) and expected my mother to roll with it. What kind of a daughter was I anyway?

3

THAT MAN'S FATHER IS MY FATHER'S SON
Naming Tradition and Heritage

As a kid, I thought names were like a language. That their images and implications were something that everyone learned, expanded their vocabulary in, and thought about all the time. Once I figured out it wasn't true, I couldn't understand why everyone wasn't as interested as I was: evaluating each class list and bus schedule to see the names of the people who were about to be my friends and enemies. I would perk up at the appearance of Marcella or Adi and hoped every year there would be someone else outside the norm. This is not necessarily a normal preoccupation for a child, but I came to realize it wasn't solely my disease. It was genetic.

My mother's name is Maureen. When I was five or six, her brother Tony and his young family came to visit our family in Toronto. His Irish-by-way-of-London accent pronounced my mother's name more like "MAUR-ren"—like Lauren—and my father, tickled, proceeded to call her that for years afterward. But I soon learned that my mom wasn't actually Maureen, and Tony wasn't Tony.

They were not in a witness protection program. But they were two of eleven children from the large Clancy family in rural Tipperary, Ireland. As a kid, I spent my time learning my aunts' and uncles' names so I'd know them when I finally met them. I was taught that the eleven children in the family were Martin, Rita, Tommy, Pat, Michael, Josephine, Jimmy, Maureen (Mom), Larry, Tony, and Geraldine. Nobody I knew had names like these, which contributed to the foreignness factor. They seemed like the kinds of names only Irish people of a certain age would have—a fact that was corroborated when my Cabbage Patch Kid turned out to be named Coretta Rita. Everyone knew those Kids had old-fashioned awkward names like Elroy Ricardo and Clementine Juanita, and I assumed it was the gift of Xavier Roberts, the fictional "creator" of the Cabbage Patch Kids, who arranged for me to adopt a doll who bore a name shared with my aunt. "Xavier" is hyper-trendy now, but at the time was another name that was supposed to indicate how unusually named the kids from the Cabbage Patch actually were.

Regardless of their rarity, I repeated the names of my mother's siblings over and over, delighted that I had some family after all, even if I didn't get to have them come to my birthday parties. Unlike many immigrants, who take the plunge of moving to a new country with an existing brother or uncle or Aunt Elna already in place, my parents knew nobody in North America, and nobody came afterward to join them. So my copious family was kind of theoretical. My aunts and uncles and cousins existed in far-off Ireland, and the rhythm of those eleven names became a pleasant mantra that I boastfully rattled off whenever anyone idly asked if I had aunts and uncles—and then wished they hadn't.

Various Clancys at my sister's wedding.

But the flip side to having family is realizing that all families have secrets. In this case I learned that almost none of the adults who loved me—who provided stability and a sense of roots and culture, even from afar—was wearing their proper, given name. I was scandalized, and the more I researched, the more I realized the varying scope of the family transgressions. Herewith:

If the Clancy Birth Certificate Says:

Martin Francis: This is the man I know as my uncle Martin. No problems here, this is a clearly explained and understandable first and second name. Onward.

Margaret Mary: This is my aunt Rita. Pardon? Okay, so there's a world in which Rita is a derivative of Margaret, but why did my grandmother bother with a name that Rita has never used?

Thomas Joseph: Is Tom or Tommy. Another non-offensive and practical name that clearly derives from Thomas. Also, is Tom Clancy, but not *that* Tom Clancy.

Patrick Francis: Pat. Normal name, but let's notice that three boys in, my grandparents had already started repeating middle names. Steady on.

Michael Francis: Michael. (I'm not joking with the Francis.)

Johanna Mary: Josephine. Again, if you want to call Johanna "Jo," who am I to argue with you? But who nicknames their kid a longer and more formal name than the one they started out with? Also, how many girls, and how many Marys?

James Paul: Jimmy, and a name that seems in line with a less frilly, less fanciful family than the Clancys.

Mary Veronica★: My mother. Who was never, ever called Mary, or Veronica. She was called Maureen. We'll get to that asterisk. . . .

Lawrence Joseph: There we go again with the Joseph. He was called Larry.

John Anthony: Tony. What? Not Johnny? Not Jack? Of course not, why would you call someone by his first name? And finally, mercifully:

Geraldine Ann: called Geraldine. You thought I was going to fake you out there, didn't you? Nope. Maybe Granny was feeling like she had enough children to wear all the names she loved by then, and she no longer needed to triple up between given names and nicknames.

Of course, there's a very simple explanation for all this, as anyone who has a passing acquaintance with the grand old tradition of Catholic guilt (which seems to cross all kinds of ethnic, cultural and even religious barriers) will immediately recognize: that the need for a child to wear a saint's name trumps everything else, including what you might actually want to call your child—and if one saint's name is good, aren't two better? It has to be the right saint, though. That little asterisk on the opposite page is a reminder that the legend of my mom's name has many chapters.

My mother wasn't originally Mary Veronica, called Maureen. Initially, she was Mary Philomena, called Maureen. I can kind of understand Maureen a bit better knowing this, given that there are at least similar sounds in Philomena. Philo*men*a, Mau*reen*. Maybe?

But in 1961, when Mom was about ten, the Catholic church booted Philomena out of the club. No longer a saint—or at least, her "authorization of liturgical veneration" was withdrawn. I'm not sure what she did to get cut, but in my ten-year-old head it had something to do with back-talking Jesus, although I wasn't raised with the religious fervour and liturgical literalism of my mother's generation, and may be missing some of the complexity of the situation. Some parents might have shrugged, but for my grandparents, anything less than complete piety and adherence to the church's decisions was unthinkable.

So Philomena was out, and Mom—perhaps arbitrarily—became Mary Veronica. The trauma of changing names when she was already ten years into a personality was, on its own, a hard pill to swallow. Sure, it was a middle name, but it was part of Mom's identity. But it so happened that the nastiest, evillest, cruellest nun in the convent—because of course she went to convent school—was called Sister Veronica. So she was made to take on a name she hated. One that represented everything stifling and unfair about being a girl in the 1960s in a repressive Catholic school, and worn by a nun who hated her. Sister Veronica used to like Mom, I'm told, but went off her when Mom's long blond hair was cut very short, something the doctor thought would be more hygienic. The way my mother tells it, her parents really didn't get a say once the doctor said his piece. Alas, according to Sister Veronica, Mom no longer looked like the Blessed Virgin, and things went downhill from there.

And now Mom wears that nun's name. "I had no say in the matter, I was just told," she informs me. This was always one of my favourite stories of her growing up, and I worry that I've romanticized it too much.

I wanted to make sure I was getting the story right.

"Someone chose Veronica, I'm not sure who it was. I was told 'the records would be changed.'"

"But why not just leave it as it was? Like was it that big a deal?"

"Oh, well, you wouldn't, back then, you wouldn't. It just was what it was."

"Didn't you tell anyone that you didn't like Sister Veronica, and would have liked a better name, or a different name?"

Mom thinks about this, her head starts shaking in that little way that means she's thinking and sort of half-annoyed at the memory. "Oh well, at the time, I thought, 'Who cares?'

I would have liked to have had the choice, but you didn't back then. These things were never discussed or anything. The more outrageous thing to me, at the time, was that I was left-handed and the nuns—Sister Veronica in particular, I believe—told everyone I was from the devil."

"So you couldn't have anything else, like a dishonoured saint's name, dragging you down further?"

"I suppose, since you put it that way."

Still, she goes by Maureen.

Mom got the last laugh where names and nuns are concerned, in a story I'll come back to. Meanwhile, her siblings grew up, had children of their own, and netted me twenty-five first cousins on her side. Some of them are named obscure Gaelic things like Darragh and Grainne and Aisling—and some are called Paul and Richard and Michelle. I've always loved that in Ireland, these Gaelic and English names live together in harmony.

But mine was the only Gaelic name most people had ever come across. While that might have been my parents' goal, they definitely didn't expect the unending barrage of complaints I unleashed about it. To mitigate my whining, they ordered a custom-made Strawberry Shortcake nameplate for my door, and told me there were lots of Duanas back "home," in Ireland.

My father, for his part, might not have known he was telling a lie. As far as he knew, Duana was a rare, but beloved, Irish name. His English, though always excellent, wasn't finely tuned enough to pick up the specifics of the names of kids around us—all he knew was that he didn't want me to be another Sarah-Melanie-Jamie-Karen. I was going to have an original name and then live up to its rarity by being incredibly unusual in the best way possible. No pressure.

I realize now that part of Dad's impetus to have the name mean so much and be so unusual was based in his own name's origin. Though he goes by Gamal, his first name is Mohammed. Like millions of other Arabic men before him, Mohammed (or Mohammad, or Muhammed, or any number of other minute variations) was bestowed as a gift. To be named after the prophet is seen as an honour, and it's also the number one given name in the world, when you take into account all the spelling variations. It figures that for him—and for my mother, who was, officially at least named Mary—their child's name should have been borne by as few people as possible. This was a revelation. My parents bear, I realize, the two most common given names in the entire world, Muhammed and Mary. No wonder I never got a name hairbrush or keychain. They didn't want that for their daughter. I would resemble no religious icon or celebrity. Nobody.

But since "Duana" was fairly hard to bear alone at a time when even names like Daniella and Julian were "unusual" and "exotic," I couldn't wait to get to Ireland to meet all the Duanas.

We travelled back to Tipperary, where my mom is from, a few times before I was old enough to be indignant about my name. On those trips, as far as I know, the name passed without comment. But when we went to Ireland when I was nine, we stayed for most of the summer, visiting each aunt and uncle in various cities and tiny villages. Everywhere we went, waitresses and shopkeepers named Bridie and Katie smiled at me and said "Your name is *what*?" Then, when I clarified, something clicked: "Ohhh," they nodded, "You're Maureen *Clancy's* girl!" as though that explained it. I think in retrospect that my mother's "buck the trend" reputation was pretty established in her village, but I wouldn't understand the scope until a little later.

When I told my mother recently that I had a platform to expose her deception, she couldn't stop giggling. It seems she "thought" she'd heard Duana around Ireland when she was growing up. When I press the issue, she laughs: Okay, no, she didn't hear it growing up—but she found it in a baby book with Gaelic beside it, and it was Dubhaina, which told her that the correct pronunciation was Duana.

I ask her why her parents and siblings never gave her the side-eye about this name, given that, as previously mentioned, some of my cousins are called things like Deborah and Patricia and Joseph. She starts to giggle again. "Well, no, they couldn't say anything, because I told them all by telegram, so what could they say?"

This woman knew the name she was giving me was a cipher, at very least! That it was maybe an unpopular pronunciation, at worst. (Where my "Andrea-pronounced-like-Ohndrea's" at?) She chose it specifically because it was obscure!

Family Ties (You Down?)

I love all these stories—even the ones where it turns out my mother wasn't quite truthful about the Irish "Duana" population—but they're just *stories*. A lot of welcome insight into who my mom was as a kid, and the reasons she is the way she is today.

But, perhaps because my name isn't rooted in someone else's, there's nothing about these stories that makes me think "family names" are that important. Maybe because, as I detailed above, my family's names aren't actually their names. Or because they were chosen out of a sense of obligation, that saints' names were the only appropriate choices (In fact, many countries have lists of "legal" names that can be given, and you can choose only from this list). I'm not sure. All I know is that the concept of "family names"—of inheriting something that your parents wore, and your grandparents before them, doesn't resonate with me. I know why it should—being handed something as significant as a name that belonged to a significant person is, or should be, a spectacular gift. But I feel nothing, or worse, uncomfortable. To me it's like being asked to wear someone else's still-warm shoes. I feel as though this is one of the biggest struggles I have as a name therapist. I may not embrace the concept of an inherited first name to go with your inherited last name, but I at least have to understand it.

Family names used to just be "names." The concept of naming William Robert after his father and grandfather was a given, and what names lacked in originality, they made up for in the appropriate honours reflected back upon parents and grandparents who expected them. There is even apparently an algorithmic table that was used to help large families (in those days just called "families") to figure out what name should be passed to whom. God bless the Internet:

First-born son: named after the father's father
Second-born son: named after the mother's father

Third-born son: named after the father
Fourth-born son: named after the father's eldest brother
Fifth-born son: named after the father's second oldest
brother or mother's oldest brother

First-born daughter: named after the mother's mother
Second-born daughter: named after the father's mother
Third-born daughter: named after the mother
Fourth-born daughter: named after the mother's eldest
sister

I suspect that in addition to being too arduous to maintain—after all, who has five boys and four girls, exactly?—
this system resulted in boredom, which led to changing the
rules, which led to more hurt feelings. You know that the
first daughter-in-law to reject calling her first-born son after
the father's father was gossiped about for years.

My research has led me to any number of men who
are called Robert or David or Andrew because their grandfathers were, and who are in good company as their peers
are also wearing their grandfather's name. Like Hilding,
they understand the significance of carrying a name that's
been passed down from important man to important man
through the generations. But I had trouble finding any who
were delighted with their own names, who really said,
"Yeah, this name suits *me*."

Whether the honoured names are stuffed in the
middle or out front (but not used—these "stealth" first names
are a concept I'll explore at length later), a passed-down
Anne or John these days seems like a placeholder that just

never got fixed. Somehow, using names that belong to older family members used to matter more than it does today. Maybe because we're reluctant to predetermine a person's life based on an ancestor's personality? Maybe we take more risks. Most probably our impression of all the different things a person can be is much wider than it was in previous generations, and so thankfully, finally, we can expand into newer names.

But I hear myself. To say that a name as a piece of heritage is either unimportant or unattractive is completely subjective. Still, in my experience, it just doesn't seem as though a passed-down name has the kind of impact that matches the longevity of the tradition.

One problem with recycling family choices is that names fall in and out of fashion in roughly seventy-five-year cycles—so your daughter is embarrassed, not proud, to wear your mother's middle name Enid (and let's be honest, your mother didn't love it that much either). Baby name websites are filled with posts from readers saying things like "*Edgar and Ralph (Family names)—talk me into them, or help me talk him out of them!*" If the family name is inherited for the bearer, stressful for the namer, and elicits a wan smile from the honouree, who exactly is it for?

And then there are the nicknames applied to the wound to obscure the fact that it's the same name in the first place. If Dad is Robert, and uses that, how much does that wind up mattering to young Bobby? Doesn't the real meaning of "Bobby" become "We're trying not to confuse me with my dad, Robert," instead of whatever all the baby name books say?

My grandfather was Michael, called Mick (see above, re. they were Irish)—so it wasn't as if his son Michael (called Michael) felt an extra-special connection when they were called the same name—because essentially, they weren't. In fact, there's an entire subset of names that aren't really names in their own right, but that are issued to men whose names are the same as their fathers. They might actually be Alexander or Matthew— but since they're "the second," they're called Chip (as in off the old block) or, if they're the third, Tripp or Trey. This is also where the name "Trace" originated. Incidentally, Bill Gates is actually William Henry Gates III, and is "Trey" to his family. Of course not all families do this—but some "old" ones do, which is why you often find yourself associating "Trey" with "filthy rich." Maybe we do need an updated name dictionary.

So is the concept hopelessly out of date? Should we ditch it altogether? I asked an expert, whom we met in chapter 1— Jennifer Moss, founder and CEO of BabyNames.com, the biggest name database online and one of the original baby name resources on the web.

She told me that the act of using a family name is still in play, but the deployment is different. "A lot of families are choosing for first names surnames from the family tree, including the mother's maiden name. When you're trying to do so many things with a name, including having a name that crosses cultures, naming a son after the father [as a first name] is falling farther and farther out of vogue." As she points out, this tradition is still prevalent in many cultures, but as far as I'm concerned, names that have been used for several generations can feel boring—because not only is everyone using the same names, they're being repeated three families over.

There, I said it. Come and get me. Inheriting names from your ancestors feels like a relic from a time when we didn't have so many cultural mixes and other blended elements in our families.

The outlandishness of a name is usually attributed to how old it is, too. After all, isn't this what every amateur name enthusiast screams at the least provocation? "Albert?! You can't name a baby *Albert!*" Why can't you, except that it reminds that person of her grandfather? Until we start calling little boys Albie again, and then the whole cycle can repeat itself.

Some of the research from Dr. Mehrabian, whom we met in chapter 1, corroborates this—that the repetition of names based on our perception of their "strength" can ultimately limit our choices. In his book *The Name Game*, he surveyed two thousand participants, then graded five hundred names based a number of traits. Charles, Thomas and Alexander were high up on the successful list, as were Katherine, Margaret and Alexandra. Low on that same list? Elmo, Rufus, Bertha and Sadie. Later, we'll get into the fact that the women's names were actually ranked lower because of their perceived masculinity. But Mehrabian's research was designed to reflect the opinions of "average" people. So because of perceptions of success, we pass down the same names over and over again—creating a vicious cycle of names that aren't that fresh or varied. Scott and Eric were seen as popular in Mehrabian's experiment, where Muriel and Edwina weren't. So we aren't likely to hear them again. Instead, we stick to Charles—safe, but boring—and history repeats itself. There are two problems here. One, our ideas of success have changed. There are many more ways to be successful, and there are people with names like Kanye and Beyoncé and Mekhi to prove it. And two, inheriting a name doesn't automatically mean you're inheriting the first bearer's characteristics, or will follow in their footsteps. But if you can't guarantee you're passing down *some* traits, what's the point of passing down the name?

Dave Mueses tends to agree with me. Though he goes by Dave to his friends, his actual first name is Marco—after his father. "[Sharing my name with my dad], I actually felt like it wasn't *me*, and believe it or not, whenever anyone called me 'Marco' I hated it and it made me feel older than I actually was—and still does." I hadn't thought about this part—that not only would you be compared to the person who has your name, but that you might feel old before your time, or out of step from your peers, based on the fact that the name is somewhat "old." It's true that it's hard to think of a "young" Marco—the one that comes most readily to mind is "Polo," which unfortunately supports Dave's argument. It also answers why you might feel like a perfectly lovely name was unattractive—why I love Marco, but Dave can't. "Even though my passport, licence, and any form of identity says Marco, I managed to hide the fact that my first name wasn't actually David from many of my friends for many years, and most still don't know to this day."

What's most fascinating to me is that there's a level of willful dissociation from "Marco" here—ironic considering giving Dave that name was supposed to make him feel—or be—closer to the original Marco. In fact, my first instinct was to wonder whether Dave and his dad have larger issues, some reason why he doesn't want to be so closely associated with his father's name.

He swears they don't, and admits the name has actually benefited him in lots of ways. Still, he didn't pass the tradition or name on to his son. "I believe naming children should reflect an emotion or conjure up memory or some sort of significance or inspiration instead of just trying to be original or unique. That is probably more important to me than keeping family names. When I had my son, Marco was actually a name in contention only for the sake that it would be awesome to continue the tradition. But in the end we settled for Johnny-Phoenix London." I debated printing the name Dave chose here, because it seems over the top—but maybe that's the point. I think it explains the ricochet effect you can have when you name someone as a facsimile of someone you know very well.

Miklos Perlus didn't necessarily feel that way originally. As the son of Hungarian immigrants brought up in Montreal, he was told he had his grandfather's name, and according to family legend, one of his first phrases was a quick way to explain it to those who didn't recognize it, "Miklos. It's Nicholas with an M." He points out that it's "very Hungarian," and explains that "s," in Hungarian, is actually an "sh" sound, so the purest form of the name is pronounced "Miklosh." But the "Nicholas with an M" pronunciation worked very well for him, and allowed him to freely use the nickname Mik. "It just saves so much time!"

He shares some of my misgivings about growing up

with an unusual name, "There were no other Mikloses, and at the time, I didn't see that as a good thing." He notes that while the *Romper Room* teacher who looked through her mirror and "saw" everyone watching never said his name (a point that will come up over and over with the people I interview), Mick Jagger and Mick Dundee were great touchstones that gave his name attractive connotations.

But when he was around twenty, he was cast in a role on a teen sitcom, *Student Bodies*. Though he'd been acting for years, this was the first time he remembers being *asked* what he wanted to be called in the credits. "I don't think they were trying to dissuade me from using Miklos, I think they would have absolutely been fine with it, but when I asked them, 'Why are you even asking me?' they said, 'Well, some people would want to have a more relatable name, a cooler name, a name that the kids and the audience at home can connect with." I never thought about not using it until that moment, but I said, 'Oh. Well, that's okay, I'll just be Mik.' Because they all knew me as Mik anyway. So I went with Mik [in the credits] and really didn't think much about it until the show aired.

"And my father called, and was like 'What's with Mik?'"

Mik's father was upset, because he had given his son the name Miklos, his father's name. But Mik remembers thinking that it was his name too. That he had the right to distinguish it from his grandfather's name, and that shortening it was his prerogative: "I identify as a Mik." His eventual solution is that while he introduces himself as "Mik," he writes it "Miklos"—including in credits on other TV shows. The compromise works for him and his father, though he admits online genealogy sites sometimes mistake him for his deceased grandfather.

There's no doubt that wearing someone else's name can be fraught. This is where I buy into the Ashkenazi Jewish tradition, where parents use just the first initial of a beloved, deceased relative as inspiration for naming their children. Which means that only the initial represents the beloved relative, not the whole name. It's like tipping your hat to that person, instead of trying to lift them up and carry them around (just to murder a metaphor). I think it might make a lot more sense.

I ask my friend Tracy about this tradition—she and her husband, Ian, used her grandfather Maxwell's initial as the inspiration for both her son, who is also Max, and daughter Maggie Bea—though many families use only the first initial, thinking that using the full name of the deceased is too close. I ask whether this made the naming process easier—whether there was any debate between her and her husband over which relative to honour (it also occurs to me that this tradition is predicated on actually having lost someone whose initial means something to you).

She says they'd worked everything out beforehand—or so she thought. "The disagreements wound up happening with Max's Hebrew name," she confesses. "I wanted my grandfather's Hebrew name, Ian wanted his grandfather's. So Max is Max Edward (both my grandfathers), but his Hebrew name, David, [used] for synagogue, is Ian's grandfather's."

Another friend has a middle name that starts with F—Florence—because her grandmother's middle name started with F—Frieda. There's a link, but it's a private one, known only among her and her family. In fact, since she never met grandmother Freida, there's more freedom to feel honoured by carrying on a little part of her spirit rather than being overwhelmed by the obligation.

Maybe it's really all about the honouree, though. Perhaps having your name passed on and on and on is the real prize. I don't think Barack Obama spends all that much time counting the number of babies named after him, since he's busy—and he's lately been on a bit of a naming downslide in the U.S., after a high of baby Baracks in 2009—but it's a phenomenon that we can assume would not have happened had he remained "just" a senator. Still, maybe it means more to those with more localized accomplishments.

"My brother Mustafa named his son after me," my father tells me "and so my brother Hussein named his son Mustafa, and so forth"—all the brothers named their sons after their immediately-older brother. This is news to me, as I've never heard of a cousin named Gamal. Well no, it turns out he named his son Mohammed, after my dad's cast-off first name, and in fact, actually used one of the myriad variants. My cousin's name is Hamada—nothing you'd immediately associate with his uncle Gamal.

"Did it make you feel good?" I ask my dad.

"No, this is like you are trying to immortalize yourself. Where is the individual here?"

The appreciation is not exactly overflowing.

Turns out, family names are better received when the tradition is immediate and specific. It used to be that a family name lived as a middle name, particularly when the middle was a prime space for a woman's maiden name to live—a lively alternative to Anne or John—but given that many women keep their names (a study of the Harvard Medical School class of 2017 says 65 percent have kept or will keep their names), the mother's name is either used as a child's first name or remains as mom's last. Yet that middle-name tradition seems to be waning, according to a study by *New York* magazine. At least for now, the family tradition is in flux. How do you keep a common thread when nobody's playing by the same rules any more? Is the gravity of putting Aldous in the middle position, where it's been for four generations in your family, maintained if nobody knows it's there? If a family has all girls and lets the tradition die, how traditional was it in the first place?

In fact, fewer women seem to have inherited family names, but, perhaps because it's more rare, their stories have that much more significance.

Lesley Brett Saliwonchyk is one such woman who carries a family tradition in her name, albeit in a non-traditional way. I met Lesley, a talkative, effervescent presence, in our first year of university, and I remember thinking that she was the first person I knew whose bubbly personality made me think twice about the name "Lesley," which I'd dismissed as hopelessly sensible and grown up. I don't remember precisely when she explained where her name came from, but I remember that the story stayed with me for years.

When we meet up to discuss it many years later, she's as candid as she was back then. "I was adopted through

Children's Aid. I was one of the first adoptions through Children's Aid where my biological mother chose from profiles of three sets of parents, which means that my parents had some knowledge of who she was, including what her first name was, and she was Leslie." Lesley explains that, the way she remembers the story, her parents had three names in mind for a baby girl, Sarah, Alexandra, or Lesley—and when they learned the name of her birth mother, the choice to name her Lesley became obvious. (She also points out that her father thought "Alexandra Saliwonchyk" was too many letters. He might not have been wrong.)

Lesley's middle name, Brett, is actually the last name of the Children's Aid social worker, Jean Brett, who facilitated her adoption, and Lesley recalls fondly being close with Jean through her childhood. Lesley remembers thinking that "Brett" sounded cool, like it had a little "punch," something she appreciated when growing up as a tomboy. But the name Lesley wasn't as easy to identify with—something Lesley admits is partly because she knew something was "missing."

"I remember thinking it was a beautiful name for her, but not for me. Maybe because on some level I didn't know her and wasn't connected to her, and we were supposed to be sharing something, like an identity. I felt a bit cheated because I didn't know her. People were like, 'Oh no, you're connected, you have her name—but you can't meet her, or know anything about her life or where she lives,' because of the restrictions on adoptions at that time. I was wanting the connection [with Leslie], but I didn't have it."

Leslie and Lesley did ultimately connect when Lesley was a young adult, and their relationship continues to be one of the most important in her life. Obviously meeting her birth mother has allowed her to see the many ways they're similar genetically or in personality, but the experience has given her some blanket opinions about women named Leslie or Lesley—including the ones she's not related to. "I think Leslies are good communicators, both written and verbal. Because Lesley—" she emphasizes the hard "s"—"is such a crisp word. Articulate, for sure." I counter with "talkative," and Lesley laughs with rueful recognition.

Sure, those are anecdotal, but Lesley believes that meeting Leslie helped her grow into her name—as well as so much more. "Knowing Leslie has superseded everything. She's phenomenal."

Although we talk about men's names being the ones most often handed down, phenomenal women often have an outsized effect on the names we carry, matched only by their intentions for what the name will impart. Rachel Letofsky's mother knew from the time she was a teenager that she wanted to name a future daughter Rachel Lisa, after the Old Testament story where Rachel and Leah, Jacob's daughters, were both beautiful and smart. When the time came, her daughter arrived as something of a surprise: Rachel's hopeful parents found out that a baby was eligible for adoption on December 21, and brought her home a few short days later.

Rachel grew up knowing the story of her adoption, "I think I was around 18, and I applied to the adoption registry to find out more information about my real family, and they sent my original birth certificate. And on it, the name

THAT MAN'S FATHER IS MY FATHER'S SON   73

was 'Ehrin Burke.' Obviously I'd always wondered at my
heritage and my birth family, and I wondered if that spelling had to do with the old word for Ireland [Eireann]."
Rachel, who is Jewish, imagined Irish ancestry and an
entirely different life, culturally. Who would she have been
as an Ehrin?

"But when I met my birth mother, Theresa, she told
me she would have changed my name from Ehrin to
Memphis. And I mean . . . that's not a name that flies under
the radar. It's not like a nice, normal name that everyone's
heard of, like Rachel." Rachel thinks Theresa, who was *also*
adopted (and whose name was changed by her adoptive
parents), was trying to give her daughter a unique name
that would be memorable above all. And while she doesn't
feel any particularly affinity for the name Memphis—in
fact, she giggles every time she says it—Rachel thinks often
about the different life she might have led as Memphis.
"When I tell people about it, they say 'Oh, so you would
have been either a stripper or a country singer,'" she laughs.
But, though she definitely feels like her name fits her,
Rachel sees some ways that growing up as a Memphis
might have benefited her. "It's so hard to say, but [Memphis]
might have made me a bit more ferocious," Rachel, who's
often told she's 'too nice,' reflects. "Maybe, if I had been
Memphis, it kind of seems like a no-nonsense, take-no-
prisoners name, and maybe I would have pushed that side
of my personality more." And about that country singer
thing, "I always liked acting and singing and violin and
piano as a kid, but I was so painfully shy—the kind of kid
who would hide behind her mother's legs. It may have been

my natural inclination, regardless, but maybe if I had had the name Memphis, I would have had to get rid of that shyness." This is a theme that comes up over and over again. A unique name demands more of its wearer—either as a way to earn the name, or to defend it. It just hadn't occurred to me that even defending one's name is a privilege not everyone gets.

I found out there's another family tradition in my heritage, one I found somewhat alarming. I called my father frantically after watching one of those viral videos that was a lot more resonant to me than I expected. In it, a series of young Egyptian men are asked what their mother's name is. They squirm. They don't want to answer. Finally it's revealed that men don't mention their mothers' names in public, and that people don't use their mother's names—and in some cases forget their names altogether.

"Dad, is this real?"

My dad is usually pretty fast to condemn anything that he thinks I'm making up or exaggerating about. Let's just say we both have a lot of experience in this regard—it's a tendency I inherited from him. But he hesitates—I can almost hear his modern feminist sensibilities wrestling with the ingrained tradition.

After a long pause, he ventures: "In Egypt you insult someone by insulting their mother." I note that this tracks with the little bit of Arabic I know. Other than a few numbers and the word for "thank you," the only thing I can say with skill is a very colourful profanity. "So you don't say the woman's name, you call her by the name of her husband or later by the name of the oldest son."

"But her name doesn't just disappear!" I get very indignant very quickly. "Her friends don't suddenly greet her as 'Hello, Gamal's mother!'"

"There is no reason to say your mother's name. Not when you register at school or when you need a passport. You write your father's name."

"So what about on a birth certificate?"

A pause. My dad thinks about this one for a long time. You'd think it would be an obvious question. "Yes, I think so." Later he finds his birth certificate and confirms this.

But then where is a woman's name not used? My dad explains that the video I saw is referring to the tradition of never using a woman's name in public, among strangers. Among family, or at school or work, of course her name would be used. But on the street, you'd call her by her child's name if you needed to get her attention.

"It's seen as a matter of respect, or privacy."

It's hard for me to understand. How could not saying a woman's name be a mark of respect, when it's erasing her identity? Dad sighs, heavy with the weight of the cultural disconnect. "I know. It's very different. It's very difficult."

I pore over Arabic women's names—Aziza, Karimah, and my grandmother's name, Saniyah (which I'm pretty sure I spelled "Sonja" on a sixth-grade family tree assignment). What's the point in choosing such gorgeous names if they're going to be erased? I am irrationally upset that I don't carry an Arabic first name to buck the tradition. I'm half-contemplating adding one to my name, but I note the futility of this exercise, since I'd never have the chance to use it. As I struggle with this revelation—given the right context, I might care about family names after all, if they're about to be extinct—I realize I'd be the only one who would know the name was there anyway.

But then, that never stopped 1.2 billion Roman Catholics.

I wasn't raised in a religious household. My parents both felt there was more to criticize than to love in Catholicism and Islam, respectively, and didn't practise any religion. So I was pretty ignorant about the traditions from them, and was around ten or twelve when I discovered that in the Catholic faith, when adolescents are confirmed as "adult" members of the church, they get to choose a saint's name to add to their own. A name you get to choose yourself based on whatever you want! What a huge and awesome responsibility at the age of twelve! Sure, it has to be a saint's name (no Philomena here), but it's still a wide world of names left open for the taking. I was fascinated—and wildly jealous. The boy next door earned my scorn (and my realization that he would never be *that* kind of a boy next door) when, after my inter-rogation, he told me that he chose the saint's name "Peter." Except his name was *already Peter.* Who would waste such an opportunity? A chance to choose your own name—to define yourself as an emerging teenager—and he chose to be the same person he already was!

I've never ceased asking about confirmation names once I find out about someone's Catholic upbringing, even though in most cases there's a pause while they strain to remember. My father-in-law chose Alexander, various friends chose Valeria and Maria and Catherine, even as I hinted, retrospectively, that they could have made more ambitious, creative choices while still staying within the confines of Canon Law.

Veronica was popular, either as an *Archie* comics reference or, as one friend-of-a-friend pointed out, "because that's what Madonna chose."

By the time it was my mother's turn to be confirmed, she'd grown somewhat weary of the nuns, and of all the things she wasn't doing right. The priests and Christian Brothers spent most of their time concerning themselves with the transgressions of the boys, but made sure to turn up when it was time for the class's confirmation.

From my understanding of this story—I've begged my mother to tell it so many times I may have coerced her into remembering it the way I think she told it first—the girls had to tell the attending nun what saint's name they were choosing before going before the priest, who would then announce it to the congregation. Poetically, it was good old Sister Veronica who was ushering the confirmation class through the line as they waited to head to the altar.

"Well?" Sister Veronica demanding to know the confirmation name from my mother, who arrived behind classmates who chose Bernadette and Brigid and Marguerite.

Mom smiled at Sister Veronica. "St. Anthony of Padua."

I have to believe that she smirked.

Now this was Ireland, 1963. It was still six years before Johnny Cash's hit "A Boy Named Sue." Anything gender-bendy was unheard of at the best of times, let alone in the parish church of a Catholic village with a population of 900, including surrounding farmlands. Taking a male saint's name—Mom says it was on a dare—was unheard of and, as far as I know, unreplicated since. Remember what I said about bucking trends in her village? I assume my mother's rebellion was well gossiped about in the combination pub-grocery store in the centre of Drangan.

Apparently, Sister Veronica looked at my mother with nothing less than a sneer of scorn.

"You would," she snarled.

Mom did. Proving my thesis that this name thing is bigger than just me. But it's not the gift you're given that's important—it's what you do with it. So armed, I'm aiming to help other people figure out that names are as important as I know they are.

4

JASWINDER, CALLED JAY
Global Culture as Name Therapist's Minefield

Here's the reality. If I meet a guy named Archibald, there's a story about how his parents came to choose that name and chances are I'll hear it. If I meet a guy named Arjun, there's a story about how his parents chose that name, and chances are I won't. Because it's assumed that the inspiration for Archibald can come from anywhere—an affection for "old" names, a beloved grandfather, a secret affinity for Archie Bunker—but Arjun is obviously Indian, and so that's seen as enough of a story, right there—at least in North America. This has always struck me as kind of odd. Why is one name seen as that much more universal than the other?

Even though I'm a child of immigrants, I know my experience hasn't been as harsh or isolating as it could have been. This is because, as previously mentioned, I present as Caucasian. I once asked my friend Vera what the hardest part was about being a child of immigrants, and she rolled her eyes at my naïveté. No matter how much you assimilate to Canadian culture, she pointed out, "You can't hide being brown."

The party line is, of course, why should you have to? But immigration and assimilation into an Anglo community are fraught, and names get hopelessly tangled up in it. You'll rarely hear an expectant mother at a prenatal class say she's deciding between the names Kyra and Kaavya or between Chris and Chakradev. Those unusual names, not of European extraction, are well represented in our North American culture, but not in "name culture." Which is ironic, because the ways that uncommon names are problematic are common to all uncommon names.

What Are You?

Everyone with any kind of offbeat name relates to the story about the *Romper Room* lady who would never say your name, remembers spinning the rack of keychains or novelty licence plates thinking "maybe this time," and those same kindred spirits in naming know that being easily Googleable is both a blessing and a curse.

But it might only be Canadians of indeterminate ethnic origin who are squinted at and asked, in an almost aggressively straightforward tone, "So what are you?"

What are you? Can you think of a more reductive question that pretends to be innocuous? It tells you that there's something about you—either your name or the way you look or both, that deserves to be questioned or investigated, that is elusive. Something that doesn't quickly and easily quantify itself. Something about the way you present to the world isn't adding up to something easy to categorize, and, in general, people dislike the feeling of not being able to categorize someone. Of course, in Canada, there is a prevailing sentiment that says being not immediately classifiable is okay, because we acknowledge (most of the time, when we remember) that this is a country formed almost entirely by immigrants. Many Canadian family trees are comprised of some European/Caribbean/South American/Asian pick'n'mix, and particularly heavy eyebrows combined with blue eyes might cause people to ask about where Greek met Swedish, or where the "sultry" mouth come from in a family of thin- (stiff-upper-?) lipped Brits.

A face can elicit a question, a nod to a particularly interesting genetic combination, but a name doesn't always garner the same reaction. This is for two reasons. If someone's name is Allan, we don't think, "Well where did *that* come from?" There's no need to ask the question, as it "came from" everywhere and nowhere. But if someone is named Vilayanur, then the question is implicit (or explicit, depending where you are). What kind of name *is* that? What *are* you?

The truth is that the vast majority of "cultural" names, or "ethnic" names, are still conspicuously absent from the Baby Name Industrial Complex, which is absurd because most of us hear about them every day. Where "name trends" are concerned, they are unacknowledged and underappreciated.

Depending who you are, and what your fly-under-the-radar goals are, anglicization can be seen as a good thing. Aresh becomes Arthur, Samir becomes Sam. It's possible to know someone with an unusual name and never actually know it if you don't get a good look at their driver's licence.

I have very dark, coarse, curly-unless-beaten-into-submission hair. This is the most significant physical sign of my Egyptian side—though there are many others. Though it's a complete myth that all Irish are redheaded, and my blonde mother is one of the few in her family, it's still clear that somewhere along the way my looks tipped inexorably into "swarthy." That's the Egyptian in me.

But when I was young, it was easier to identify with being Irish. Sure, my first name was Irish and my last name was Egyptian, but additionally, we went to Ireland with some regularity. We knew people there. I could report about the family farm with authenticity. I wasn't able to draw the same references with my Egyptian side for a number of reasons. The language and cultural barriers meant that even if I knew things about my dad's family, I couldn't explain them easily in context. My grandmother didn't make me soup, and my dad couldn't tell me what kinds of schools my cousins went to. The divide was too big.

As I grew closer to adulthood, though, I learned I was more like my father, physically and in temperament, and that some of those similarities were about being Egyptian. I think. Were they?

It's debatable. Arguably Egyptian characteristics I possess include being hotheaded (this might also be an Irish trait, although we have to factor in my lack of red hair), hungry all the time, narcissistic. Everything I've just listed is part of a cultural stereotype—but it's one that might be charming if I were talking about jolly Italians. "Oh, man, you don't know eating until you've eaten with Italians!" Who hasn't heard something like that? It's the implication that I'm talking about an often unattractively depicted culture that makes it taboo. And if you don't believe me, shove the word "Americans" where I have "Egyptian." Now see why people might get mad?

Of course, these days Egypt is synonymous with "the troubled Middle East," but that wasn't always the case, it's relatively recent. Sure, "Walk Like an Egyptian," released in 1987, was full of stereotypes, but hey, it was still a feel-good tune! My dad loved it. Still, those stereotypes were all I really knew about Egypt in a concrete way until our first trip there in 1999. My sister and I went with my father to finally meet his relatives in Cairo. He'd been waiting to take us on this trip for years, because he thought the degree of poverty and ungracious city living we saw would be a shock to us (he didn't realize years of television would desensitize us). Finally, when we were in our mid/late teens, we went, Dad very anxious to show us the Pyramids of Giza and the Sphinx.

Much more memorable than seeing the Sphinx, though, was meeting my father's family for the first time. Three brothers, two sisters, all their respective spouses, and a passel of cousins. This was a highly momentous occasion, and my dad couldn't hide his giddiness. He had been insistent that we stay in one of the glamorous hotels he had gazed at dreamily when he was growing up in a downtrodden part of Cairo, and so, just an hour or so after we checked in, his family descended en masse to the Semiramis Hotel, on the bank of the Nile River. My sister and I were jet-lagged and had fallen asleep in the hotel room, but my father's pride and exuberance at a dream finally fulfilled superseded his own jet lag, rendering it irrelevant as he excitedly woke us and hurried us downstairs.

We entered the lobby and discovered fourteen beaming family members waiting to be identified. My sister and I huddled together on one of the lobby couches and allowed ourselves to be scrutinized, which, in this as in many cultures, is synonymous with being loved. We knew, from growing up with my dad, that sizing you up to your face was considered a totally appropriate and even affectionate way to interact, but it's still unnerving when it happens. I was nineteen and trying hard to be confident, Sheena was fourteen and saw absolutely no reason to pretend. The spectre of trying to be what they expected—whatever that was—was intimidating, to say the least.

One young cousin, Noha, spoke English pretty well, so my eyes darted between her and Dad, as I hoped to glean bits of conversation coming from the other dozen or so relatives in between. My sister and I were doing appreciably well understanding the conversations, and my dad, knowing how utterly lost we would be in the sea of Arabic, tried to help out—but he hadn't seen his siblings in a long while, everyone wanted his attention, and so it was hard to translate for us as much as he might have liked to.

One aunt talked rapidly to my dad as she gestured to Sheena and me, illustrating at length with her hands. I was pretty sure I understood what they were saying, and then Dad, beaming with the pride of showing off his children to his siblings, turned to us to confirm. "She says, 'Duana is Egyptian, but Sheena—no.'"

We smiled, because yeah, we'd joked for years that Sheena appeared to have gotten 100 percent of my mother's Irish genes, and I had 100 percent of the Egyptian ones. The mathematical impossibility of this aside, we'd known from the time we were very young that I take after my dad. Among my most resonant memories from my childhood were many trips to the beach, where my father would enthusiastically slather on some not-at-all protective "suntan lotion," with a maximum of SPF 2, then encourage me to "Put some oil, Du!" before looking pityingly at my sister's SPF 50.

Back at the Semiramis, my aunt kept speaking in Arabic. More gestures, more rapid speech. Sheena asked our cousin for a translation. Noha looked uncertain—it was obvious she knew what was going on, but maybe it was difficult to put into English words.

So Sheena spoke up again. "What's she saying, Dad?"

We both looked at him. He laughed, a nervous laugh we've known for years, usually when he's been caught in a traffic violation. Looking at me, he said, "Oh, she just says you're pretty."

Sheena and I traded looks. Our parents raised no fools. That was *not* what was being said, and there were enough nonverbal cues to make that clear, even if neither of us was ever going to learn a word more of Arabic than we knew in that moment.

In fact, it was very clear to me what was actually being said.

"She's saying I'm fat," I announced back. It's probably now that I should mention my aunt is—*almost* literally—five feet square. Where she lives, that's not uncommon. There are thin Egyptians, obviously, but women and men alike are generally short and squat, and carry most of the weight in their chests and stomachs. I could tell from her gestures that my body, more than my colouring, was what was leading her to assert my Egyptian inheritance. She wasn't insulting me.

There was a moment of shocked silence, and then my father burst out laughing. So did Sheena. So did I. And my aunt.

It's a good story on its own, right? Cultural acceptance and all that?

What if I tell you my aunt's name is *Fat*ima?

Yeah. In Arabic, the name is beautiful. In English, though, all you hear is that first damning syllable up front. I've only ever heard the "Fa-TI-ma" pronunciation in North America. In Arabic-speaking countries it's still FAT-ima or FAT-ma. Some would say this makes the name untenable as a given name in North America (and parts of Europe), though it's often heard, in the context of "Our Lady of Fatima," as the name of Catholic schools and churches. But there are others who'd say it's a beautiful name and it shouldn't matter. It really depends how each Fatima herself feels about it—but if she happens to be heavy (or thinks she is) she's going to assume her parents played a cruel cosmic joke on her, choosing that name.

In fact, the number of names that mean some version of "beautiful" in various cultures but that don't see the light of day in ours is astounding. Here's a partial list:

Beaufort (French)

Namaka (Hawaiian)

Yaffa (Hebrew)

Amara (Greek/Igbo)

Hermosa (Spanish)

My Dad (seated at left) introduces us to his family at the Semiramis Hotel.

Vashti (Persian)

Venus (Latin)

Shayna (Hebrew)

Anahi (Persian)

. . . right? Not all of these sound like what North American culture thinks of as beautiful names. None of them sound like "Bella."

But I am increasingly bothered by the idea that, even as we grow more and more culturally diverse in North America, the swath of names that are "acceptable" in the general populace is very narrow. No matter how much we trumpet the idea of cultural diversity, what constitutes a "normal" name doesn't expand. "Sure," we say to a guy called Dinesh, "Come to this country, set down roots, bring your traditions and help yourself to some of ours." But this has yet to translate to the "Canadianization" of the name Dinesh—instead, it's much more likely he'll name his son "David," so David fits into the landscape of his adopted homeland.

Names that are considered universally acceptable are either European or "North American," and that's about it. Sure, there's a widening circle of acceptance for, say, the French variation of Stephen, but imagine what would happen if I tried in my advice column to propose Jahmil to a couple of parents named Andy and Sarah? What about Leilani, a traditional Hawaiian name? Is that okay to offer up for grabs? Often girls with "exotic" names receive less scrutiny than boys—so what about Sachiko or Apeksha? Are these names acceptable, as in, common enough in North America not to turn heads of surprise at how "unusual" they are? If not—and I would say the answer is still decidedly not—how come?

Broadway actress and author Ipsita Paul has plenty of experience "testing" her unusual name. Adopted as an infant by East Indian parents in Toronto, she was given a traditional Indian name, 'Ipsita,' which in Sanskrit means "the most desired one." Her struggles with an unusual name were not unlike my own, but there was an added level of difficulty.

Physically, Ipsita presents as multiracial—a casual passerby might assume she was black. Her Indian name and notably non-Indian appearance were an especially complicated combination. "When I was growing up . . . I wanted my parents to change my name to Charlene," she confesses now. In fact, her parents called her bluff: "We were going to go to the courthouse to change my name— except we weren't *really* going to," she explains, with the hindsight of an adult who's now a parent herself. "I was making a big fuss about it, and when they were like 'okay, let's go' I thought 'Oh, no . . . I don't really want to be Charlene forever.'"

I'm amazed by this indulgence of her parents, especially since they had experienced similar name struggles. "[My dad] would introduce himself like this: 'My name is Mrinal. Sounds like urinal.' Charming!" Ipsita's mother, Shymali, on the other hand, resisted offers to anglicize her name. "A lot of people often asked if they could call her by a different name and she would just say no, because that wasn't her name. She believed [people should make the effort to learn her name]." So is it any wonder Ipsita didn't wind up defaulting to Charlene?

Still, her name didn't automatically become easy. "People are scared to say it," she explains. But she admits it was a career asset, in the sense that once she became an actress on Broadway, nobody ever forgot her name—particularly casting directors. Instead, she became another casualty of the "what are you" question, especially outside of her native Canada. "People would always ask, like "Oh, Ipsita, is that Spanish?" and when I said 'Nope!,' they were like 'Oh, did your parents make it up?'" At which point, Ipsita says, she'd say, "If you want to know the story, just ask me!" I joke to Ipsita that they were crossing their fingers she would say she was Cuban, and she laughs in recognition. "Or something! 'We want to know where to put you.' They don't always accept that, they want to be able to put you in a box." She notes the scrutiny of her unmatched name and face was stronger in the U.S. than in Canada—but understands that people will continue to try to find a "quick" place to slot her according to her name and appearance.

"I identify as mixed or multiracial, first. I am proud to be Canadian but that's definitely secondary." Ultimately, then, the name Ipsita is more of a gift than she realized initially. While it may raise the what-are-you question, it definitely doesn't answer it—which is just as Ipsita likes it.

The Elephant's Name Is Probably Elmer

We default to common, repeated names far more than we realize, I think. Yes, every elephant in a kid's book is called Elmer, and hell, Elmer's a cute name and it's not getting a lot of play outside of the preschool set, so why not? But it's emblematic, I think, of defaults that we don't realize we're relying on.

People talk all the time about wanting names that are "neutral." For their children, or for their creative endeavours, or for their company bios. But what about the names that are definitively someone or something, or a group of someones?

The concept of "Chinese names" is significant here, or rather its reverse—the understanding that a person of Chinese heritage in an English-speaking society will have a name for the North American public life, as well as a Chinese one that is for Chinese life and community, usually tucked away and rarely used in their English day to day. But Chinese culture is a superstitious one, resulting in Anglo names being chosen based on their sound relative to other lucky English words. In *The Joy Luck Club*, a character points out that her brother is named Vincent because it sounds like "Win Cent"—winning money. The fact that "Vincent" was out of common use (even in the context of the story) is not relevant. What matters is how lucky it sounds, not whether the name is current. But luck is not the root of everyone's naming philosophy.

For example, Philip Guo, an assistant professor of computer science at the University of Rochester, wrote an incredibly popular article on his blog (www.pgbovine.net) entitled "How to Choose an English Name." Guo, who says his blog is a mix of "the life of an academic," as well as observations from growing up "as sort of a nerdy kid . . . in an immigrant household," was born in China but immigrated as a young child, first to Switzerland and then to the U.S. He has vivid memories of his Chinese name and his English name being constantly confused on school records until his American citizenship and passport were finalized, and still cringes at the embarrassment.

Consequently, Guo's guide is aimed at new immigrant students—usually young adults—who are choosing names for themselves, and he maintains a strict policy that he puts right up front: "WARNING: DO NOT BE CREATIVE," based partly, but not only, on the e-mail he received from a student who chose Mortal Kombat (as in the video game *Mortal Kombat*), as part of his name and suggests they run squarely to the list of most popular names from the year they were born and choose only from that list. He also wanted to help course-correct some of his family members, who would often change their English names several times. He has further tenets of name-choosing he believes are paramount:

• Do not try to pick a fun or cute-sounding name from a
  movie, television, or video-game character.
• Do not pick a name that you think sounds cool or trendy,
  because Americans will think it sounds stupid.
• Do not pick a name because your friends think it sounds
  cute, because your friends are not the Americans you
  have to interact with in the future.
• Do not translate some positive-sounding word in your
  language into English and make that into your name.

Guo explains that having a well-known English name,
as opposed to one that's fallen out of fashion, helps mitigate
the realities of being a foreigner, and he strongly cautions
against choosing a nickname (rather than a full, fleshed-
out version) or a name that has a strong meaning—since
in North American culture, as I've mentioned, we don't
often know the "traditional" meanings of the names other
people wear. I wondered whether Guo always thought an
English name was a better choice than the name in the
language of origin, and he says it depends entirely on
context. His mother's name, Min, was easy to understand
and so she kept it, but his father's name, Nan, sounded
odd or possibly feminine, so for "purely career-based reasons," Guo explained, he changed it to Sam. "If a name is
easy to spell and pronounce, and doesn't have any sort
of ambiguous connotation, I would encourage [students]
to keep it. I definitely don't think you need to have a
Western name, but I do think that if it's long and hard
to spell, people might trip over it and feel awkward talking to you."

I can't disagree with him, and yet I'm frustrated that the choruses of "oh, your 'exotic' name is so beautiful" only extends to names that are easy for Western ears. As a dry, sarcastic friend once commented: "Let me know when hipsters start naming their babies 'Gurinder.'"

It bothers me as a name enthusiast that so many names from other cultures are left out of the running. Some are difficult to pronounce if you don't know the language they originate from, like Nguyen (Nu-wen) or Truc (Trook). Some have sounds, or vowel and consonant combinations, we don't hear in Anglo names, like Jaspreet. The sounds of the separate syllables are not unusual, but it's not the kind of name we choose for North American girls, whose names often begin and end with vowels, like Anna or Emma or with soft consonants, like Elizabeth or Margot. Then from Jaspreet it's just a short trip down a road of snickering elementary schoolers to the Hawai'ian name Puanani. (If you don't know, I'm not going to tell you.)

Basically, only Judeo-Christian names are considered mainstream in name books, products, and in general pop culture. Anything else is "other," and those names are, as a result, deemed less attractive. And they're lumped together in an unattractive "other" category, too. If I tell someone about two black men I know named DeShawn and Kofi, it's usually understood that they are both "black" names. The fact that one name originates from the American South and the other from Africa may get utterly lost in translation.

Meanwhile, friends who would never consider naming a child Yasir or Arjun happily tell me that Bodhi, their recent choice for their baby, means "enlightenment" in Sanskrit. Is choosing a name for its meaning—for that meaning in particular—gorgeous, or irritating? And why is it a more likely or appropriate choice than Daikaku, another name meaning "Enlightenment"? Why does the borrowing only become legitimate if the name from another culture is given to a young white baby with "enlightened" parents?

What I know is that the names I'm surrounded by don't reflect the cultures I'm surrounded by. Maybe this is not true everywhere. So I decided to go halfway around the world, in order to keep it in the family.

Putting the Irish in Delft

My cousin Paul is nine years older than I am. I met him once before—I was ten. You can imagine how much we had in common (if you're keeping score from chapter 2, Paul is my uncle Tom's son. *Tom Clancy*, yes!). Of my grandparents' twenty-five grandchildren, he is number three (I'm a middle-of-the-pack number fifteen). Still, Twitter is a magical forum that brings far-flung disparate people together, and why not follow your amusing cousin who has the same taste as you in television and coffee? Genetics are stronger than we think.

Paul moved to Delft, Holland, in 1999. He intended to stay a year, and—you know how these things happen—he met Inger. So they settled in Delft, and eventually, had their first daughter, Róisín. For the uninitiated, that's RoSHEEN, it's Gaelic, and the whole time I was talking with Paul I was surreptitiously trying to find the accents—called "fadas"—that go on top of each "i."

I ask how he decided to name their daughter an Irish name, but Paul says it was his wife, Inger, born and raised in Delft, who wanted their children to have Irish names. She thought they'd sound better with the (definitely Irish) last name Clancy.

This was how my conversation with Paul went:

PC: Also, and this is my theory, [with Irish names you'd] partially avoid the associations Dutch people have with Dutch names. You sidestep some of that with a "foreign" name.

DT: You mean that if she'd been called Elke or something that there would be Dutch stereotypes?

PC: Right.

(Paul and I digress a little bit, into our mutual understanding of the stereotypes people have of names. First he offers up a little something about Dutch names.)

PC: Jan-Willem.

Jan-Willem plays hockey, his dad works for the bank and drives an Audi.

DT: That guy wears turtleneck shirts, obviously.

PC: And is a WANKER.

(See? It must be genetics! Paul and I are simpatico. He then moves on to talk about his eldest daughter's name.)

PC: Róisín, as you probably know, is "little rose." In Dutch, that's "roosje." So a lot of the time she goes by "Roosje" or "Roos," which is an elegant solution.

DT: Rosie?

PC: Not ROSIE. Rosie milks cows. With her hands.

DT: HAHAHA. The indignity!

PC: "Roos" rhymes (almost) with "hose."

Paul and Inger have three more children: Twins Tomas and Niamh, and Grainne. Paul says if the kids were born in Ireland they might not have such Irish names, but the caveat there is that they consider themselves quite Dutch (though he says they might find it in their hearts to be Irish if the Irish ever make it to the World Cup finals). In this way, they're in both worlds equally—and seemingly quite happy about it.

My friend Heather has adopted this same philosophy. Heather is actually Melanie Heather (a concept I'll explore further later), and as resolutely Canadian as they come. She skis, and her parents, Rick and Ida, allowed any number of teenaged and post-teenaged girls to crash in her house, and everything about her upbringing just seemed thoroughly wholesome and Canadian. I mean, her name was Heather, for heaven's sake.

We became roommates at university and one day she met this guy, Gabriele. Heather calls him Gabe, but the full name is Gab-ri-*el*-eh, not quite like the girl's name, but not far. Gabe is from Rome. He and Heather were an excellent match right away, and not just because they're the tallest couple any of us has ever known. Heather taught him about skiing as a positive slant to the brutal Canadian winter, and in exchange she developed the cutest Italian accent when she pronounced certain words. You should hear how authentically she says "*amore mio*" and addresses their dog, Cesare.

But when Heather and Gabe had children, the kids were less Canadian. Well, actually, they weren't—they were Canadian through and through, and so their names were resolutely less Canadian. Heather explains: "For some reason we didn't consider the idea of having an English-sounding name combined with a super-duper Italian last name. We just felt that Benjamin Guiducci was too much of a stretch."

Heather and Gabe's children are named Davide and Olimpia. Olimpia is pronounced the way you'd think, but Davide is—well, it's pronounced the way you might if you were trying to fake that you knew Italian and met a guy named David. DAH-vee-day.

I thought they were gorgeous, but I did wonder about the Canadian factor. Specifically, it's one thing if you fall in love with a Roman guy who in turn falls in love with you and with poutine. Day-to-day, Gabe is as thoroughly Canadian as Heather is. Their life is in Canada. But this is not the same thing as naming your kid Gord. (Is there anyone outside of Canada whose name is Gord? Have we asked Gordon on *Sesame Street* whether he's Canadian?)

Heather acknowledges this: "My parents expressed concern about how they would pronounce Davide. They had questions. They said, 'What are we going to tell our family, like my relatively rural Canadian family?' And I said, 'Calm down.' My parents [ended up being] pretty great and my family was great. However, my brother actually gave us a hard time about the pronunciation of it."

Unlike Paul, Heather thinks her kids probably do think they're Italian (though they're still very young so such a question may be academic). I wonder how much of that is pride in heritage and how much is a byproduct of being Canadian, where "What are you?" is still a common question.

Say My Name?

Names are, of course, evolving. They're fluid. They fall in and out of fashion, some into utter obscurity and some just into prescribed periods of latency and hibernation. I'm quite sure that someday, my kid or someone else's is going to turn to me and with wide, shining eyes, say, "We're naming her Carol." It's inevitable.

I know that trends will come around, just like I know the next boy-names to make a big splash are going to be Stanley and Kendrick. But imagine my delight when I discovered a trend I could never have predicted: "Utah names."

The concept was introduced to me through a viral video, which is one of about ten thousand reasons why I will never believe it is inappropriate to waste time on the Internet. In the video on YouTube, a young woman looks earnestly into the camera and tells us her name is Honesty. And then, as you're processing that, she proceeds to spell it. "A–U–N–I–S–T–E–E. Aunistee."

The video continues with black text:

UTAHNS

HAVE NEVER LACKED

FOR CREATIVITY

IN NAMING THEIR CHILDREN

And then a parade of names, each one more phonetically mortifying and amazing than the last, delivered with effervescence and delight by two giddy actresses. A partial list: Kynslee. Emersyn. Nachelle. Skylei. Zerra. Taylee. Brinleigh, Brielle. Scotlyn is a particular favourite. Nakkole. Bexley. BREYANNIN.

I am on about my sixteenth gleeful replay of the video when I see they've also got a boys' version—and have actual squirming infants representing names like Tungsten. Creedance. Macrae. Kayze. Chancen. COIL. Draze. BRENR. Please trust me when I say all spellings are, ahem, original!

I am addicted to "Utah names." I need to hear more, like sweet bedtime stories. Luckily, the actresses behind the videos, Chelsea Calder and Elisabeth Evans, are happy to talk with me.

Chelsea and Elisabeth met as roommates in the University of Michigan's Musical Theatre program, are both members of the Mormon Church, and quickly tell me that, yeah, for these purposes, Mormon names and Utah names are basically interchangeable. "For years and years, we would just kind of collect these names, me and my mom and my grandma and we just found it totally fascinating. And my family, my mom's family, we all have like really normal names," Chelsea says.

She points this out as evidence for why she's able to see how "Drenessa" is . . . not quite average. "And when we talk about the Utah culture, I mean, it really is very much the Mormon culture, the culture of the members of the Church in the State of Utah," she confirms. She and Elisabeth both now live in New York, so they feel that they have an outsider's perspective on the distinctive names they spoof. Which they swear are 100 percent authentic.

Elisabeth says they don't lack for material. "We have, like, a variety of sources from this newspaper article, from people we had met, friends of friends on Facebook and whatnot. And then once the first video came out, everyone just flooded our comments section with other names that they knew and we got all of our names from the second video or the comments and from other sources. Just yesterday a friend of mine sent me a picture of his nephew's class and all the names and like 75 percent of them were just outrageous."

Hilariously, they have no stories of blowback from the "Utah names" video. Rather than take offence, everyone whose names are spoofed just seems happy to be represented, even though the videos are clearly pointing out the ridiculousness of having brothers named Rhevv and Raccer. Chelsea and Elisabeth clearly have a lot of affection for the namers, but are very aware of how the names sound if you're not familiar with Utah culture. The names can be perceived as strange, and they aren't necessarily overtly religious names—some are, but there's nothing in the Book of Mormon that refers to "Tungsten."

Elisabeth breaks it down for me: "One category is names that are drawn from Mormon culture, from Mormon scripture or Mormon history, like Brigham [named for Brigham Young, founder of the Mormon Church] or Ammon."

Chelsea breaks in: "Or Christian scripture in general. Like Isaiah, Abraham, you know, biblical names and then names from Mormon history, and Mormon Scripture." Yeah, sure, Christian scripture—except one of the first names skewered in the boy version of "Utah Names" is "Ayebraeham." No kidding.

Elisabeth continues: "The second category are names that we would call traditional, but have changed spelling to make it unique, like you add a couple Ys or an EE or a K instead of a C or double K."

Chelsea: "So one of my favourites in this last one we were doing is Emily. We found so many spellings of Emily. One was Emmaleigh and another one was MLE, three letters. And then the last one was similar to the first, Emileigh." She can't contain a grin from playing across her face.

Elisabeth: "The third category are just like made-up names, names that don't exist; just making a name out of something that isn't supposed to be a name, like [the element] tungsten, is one of Chelsea's favourites. We found a lot of people have combined two names. Say your father's name was Jerry and your mother's name was Erica, and then you become Jerrica."

Chelsea: "A lot of things that are also objects. Willow, Blaze, Chevy, things that are not [traditionally] people's names. [I know] a family of Mystery and Secret, that's for real."

Elisabeth: "I remember one instance we had the name Trace, and then there was Dexana, who was the tenth child."

Right, of course. Because Mormon families—some, but not all—have a lot of children, and live near other Mormon families who have a lot of children—so avoiding repetition is exponentially more difficult than it might be elsewhere. Is this why Utah names are so . . . Utah?

Chelsea agrees. "Maybe they're making up names because they've simply run out of normal ones."

This makes sense, especially when the girls tell me that they think the origin of the "Aydens" actually comes from Utah. "A kid I went to high school with was called Kayden," Chelsea notes. "He was the first Kayden I ever met, and we're twenty-four and twenty-five years old now."

Elisabeth points out that the same can be said for the "Mac" trend: "Mackenzie, MaKylie, Mickendrie, Maclae. Like all of those ones. I feel like every high school cheerleading team is all Mac names."

But this well-established, very specific name trend can't just be due to people spinning off Michaela, can it? Something larger is at work here. Elisabeth thinks it's because Mormons often live in quite insular communities. It's harder to distinguish yourself when everyone is from the same type of faith and culture and family traditions, within a relatively small area like a single state—so different spellings of the most popular names are invented. But I come up short when Chelsea mentions a family who has a Cormac, a very Irish name.

She nods. "We did Thor [in the video] and one of the funniest comments was 'Oh, are the Mormons cool with like, Norse gods as their children's names?' But yeah, I think so. People are more apt to take names from cultures or different places [from] where they have lived."

Elisabeth says, "There was a girl that I met once, and she was named after a town where her father served his mission in Germany."

Aha. Members of the Mormon Church go all over the world to serve their missions—trips about two years long that young Mormon men, in particular, are strongly encouraged to take to spread the word of their church. It makes sense that since so many young people take these mission trips immediately before starting their families, influences from around the world might be imported into a family's names—and that those same influences might be softened or changed or Americanized, after a while.

Chelsea and Elisabeth seem amused and horrified by the choices made in the name of Mormon culture, but nonetheless defend the names' right to exist. The fact that names are sometimes reflective of a community isn't unusual—so is it any more unusual if the community is based around a faith?

Stacy Goldstein, a chiropractor from Ottawa, thinks the unusual is what makes it great. She grew up in what she calls a "traditional, but not observant" Jewish household, and admits that she never really liked her name all that much. "When I thought Stacy I thought blond, California . . . one of those books with characters named Candy and Brittany and Stacy. I always felt like it was kind of a funny choice for me, and even now sometimes I see it printed and I think oh, that's a funny name for me!" She laughs. "But my middle name is Joanna, and [Stacy's mother] chose it for Jo from *Little Women*, and I'm so much like that kind of character that I always thought I should be Joanna Stacy."

Stacy also has a strong connection to her Hebrew name, Tzipporah Shulamit, but doesn't use it day-to-day in the anglophone area of Ottawa where she lives. Still, when, as adults, she and her husband became Orthodox, she decided that her children would have Hebrew names, not Anglo ones. "Judaism really sees Hebrew names as being the real source of identity and spirituality," she explains. Her son Moshe and daugher Elisheva Leah (often called "Shevy") are young, but Stacy hopes they'll come to appreciate the significance and gravity of the names she and her husband chose—even though they don't use Hebrew names themselves.

Stacy and her husband, Michael, used the Jewish tradition of naming for a deceased relative, and in the case of her son Moshe, the connection to the great leader Moses is an added benefit. "We do hope that through the connection [both to his grandfather and the biblical Moses], my child will feel strengthened by the history of his name and encouraged to be a leader." However, Stacy lives in the real world and isn't trying to imply a literal connection to Moses—nor is she sure a spiritually connected name supersedes more earthly concerns.

"It's not to say it doesn't come with difficulty," she clarifies. "When I say my son's name is Moshe I get blank stares, and I'm thinking 'Well, this is pretty common, Moshe is Hebrew for Moses, who's a pretty well-known guy in biblical literature.'" She acknowledges that while the names are well-known in observant circles, her children may run into problems later in life, particularly because they don't have Anglo names to fall back on. She hopes they won't need them, but, "We talked about whether we would give them an easy English equivalent [name], and we felt like neither name was so difficult or so unique that it would be impossible. I guess I just want them to know where their names come from." I press her: what if, when Moshe and Elisheva Leah are older, they want Anglo names like their parents? Stacy is pragmatic. The names have lots of available nicknames—Moe, Ellie, Sheva—she goes on. But she insists she wouldn't be upset if they wanted to change their names, since part of having a spiritually significant name is having your own connection to it. "If my kids decide they need something that they feel a little more connected to, well, I would encourage them to find something with meaning."

Meaning. For some people a name that is "meaningful" is about the literal meaning of the name: "calm," or "laurel leaf." For others, it's about a name worn by someone who's had a huge impact on the world or the parents—a president, a pastor—even, as I heard recently, a sensei. But as I've pointed out, when the meaning of your name is not obvious, the name must stand alone. And it can and often does announce who you are up front, especially if it's a rare name with a particular culture attached. But there are hundreds of names that, while very obviously in regular use in English-speaking countries, are nonetheless not expanding to other cultures. They're the names traditionally associated with South Asian, African-American and African-Canadian cultures. "Black" names. Indian and South Asian names. Asian names. As in, never-used-for-white people names.

This bothers me.

I talk with another name enthusiast, the proprietor of the name website AppelationMountain.com, Abby Sandel. She agrees that what I've run into often in my name-advice-giving is true: culture is a very big deal. For Abby, most of the questions come from people going through international adoption. "Do we keep the birth name? How do we mix our family traditions in?" Then she very casually drops a bomb. "And race is huge!"

The idea that certain names are chosen by certain races, or are seen as only belonging to certain races, is not one you see in print very often, but it's something most people know if they stop to think about it: some names are only used within certain races, even if they're "culturally" North American.

I tell Abby that this hasn't come up as often as I might have expected. "You are one of the first people who will admit that."

"Well," she acknowledges, "it's a tough subject."

Yeah, it's a tough subject, and even referring to it as such is simplifying like crazy. One of the reasons, of course, is that people come to a discussion of race from different places, but often have similar ideas on what racially identifiable names are, what they mean, and why. When people consciously steer away from names that are not "Anglo" names, or are identified with visible minorities, they know there's implicit racism in that decision. Nobody wants to confront that reality, and fewer people want to talk about the brass tacks of why some names are considered for everyone, regardless of race, and some really aren't.

But Amy J, a blogger and event planner from Toronto, would. Amy is passionately honest about the racism associated with certain names, especially in the black community. "I think people are perceived or treated [positively or negatively] based on their names. Your name can be valuable currency." She admits that while she acknowledges the existence of "desirable" or "undesirable" names, she never had feelings about her own name, Amy, per se, "other than when the discussion of 'black' names [was] coming up, and being sometimes grateful and sometimes embarrassed for being grateful."

I ask her to clarify—does she mean "grateful" that her name isn't visibly, or audibly, black? She confirms that when people hear Amy, they assume she's white—and that there are benefits to that false assumption. In fact, we started talking because Amy tweeted about a conference for black women in the media, where everyone nodded knowingly when a conference speaker brought up a certain fraught topic. "It was part of the discussion around black women having a 'white' name and 'sounding white' on the phone, and then meeting the person and revealing the truth about their name/voice bias or imagery that they built in their head."

I have a sinking feeling that this is ridiculously common, but I ask anyway: "So if someone assumes you're not black, how can you tell that someone is surprised when you meet them in person?"

"It ranges from them being flustered to them out-and-out saying they were expecting someone else." Right. Because a black woman is likely to be called LaTavia, right? The assumption that people of colour wouldn't have mainstream Anglo names is both reductive and racist. White people can and do adopt names from all over the globe, based on a book they've read or whatever exotic vacation spot moved them. But it seems the expectation is reversed for those of other cultures—and black culture in particular.

This, of course, highlights something bigger than names—the idea that black "culture" predominates over any other cultural identifiers. I know myriad black and Indian and Asian people who are just as culturally Canadian as I am and just as entitled to any "Canadian" name—that is, any name that's capable of passing without comment. But of course, all of those names are of Anglo-European origin. If a name from a different origin is chosen, it seems like a bigger statement.

Amy knows everyone has biases about names, including herself. (She was taken aback when a fellow commuter—a white guy—told her his name was Tyrone.) But when her son was born, she was very worried about what to name him. "It was SO hard. This is something that he will be judged by. Studies have shown that [when applying for jobs, people with] 'ethnic' names don't get to the interview stage as [often] as 'Anglo' names do." She decided a name for her son that didn't say anything ethnic about him on paper, but felt conflicted about admitting that. "I see both sides. It's hard to fight the system [that discriminates against ethnic names], so any chance you have to level the playing field [by naming a child something "typical"] is your responsibility as a parent," she reflects. "On the other side—you should be able to name your kids whatever you want!"

Imagine this. That instead of being proud of names that express your heritage as a parent, you feel there is no choice but to stay away from anything that might reveal your cultural background, rather than conceal it. So you can give your child a traditionally African or African-American name, and possibly open him or her to discrimination—or avoid choosing a black name, with all that avoidance signifies. Either way, it's uncomfortable. No wonder the issue of ethnic-name avoidance is not coming up much in the name blogs. If you want to be different, you choose "River"—and don't ever have to confront any uncomfortable cultural questions.

But for many, the idea of leaving a culturally relevant name and a badge of culture on the cutting-room floor is unthinkable—especially since, in the case of black names, the names African slaves had were taken from them and often forgotten for generations. For social psychologist Dr. Askhari Hodari, reclaiming and celebrating those names is a necessary part of maintaining black culture—and it's also a joy.

Dr. Hodari, a professor at Stillman College, an Historically Black College University, or HBCU, in Tuscaloosa, Alabama, has always been fascinated by names. In fact, she collected books that included African names because they were so interesting to her—but when her friends kept "borrowing" them and not giving them back, she wrote her own: *The African Book of Names: 5000 Common and Uncommon Names from the African Continent.*

Dr. Hodari, who feels a strong connection to her African heritage, was given a more traditional Anglo name as a child, but, "My brother was born when I was about five and a half, and I just remember getting so angry that he had an African name and I did not." So much so, in fact, that Dr. Hodari changed her name, which was a kind of a mashup of her parents' Anglo names, as an adult.

Part of what we don't understand about African names, she explains, is that "In most African cultures the meaning is extremely important. I don't even think they worry so much about the sound or the length of the name." Obviously this alone can contribute to some cultural divides in North America, where entire name trends are born on similar sounding names—ask Ella and Stella and Eva and Ava what I mean.

But using African names in North America can be difficult—especially if they're adapted. "There is a lot of criticism here in North America, in the U.S. in particular, of what they call African American names. I'm not sure I really know what an African American name is, to be honest. But I know that when people say that, they mean names like Moesha, or Shakita or Tamika. I appreciate the creativity of the names, though I know they can get outrageous, at least in some people's perception."

But Dr. Hodari, who holds African naming ceremonies for clients who want to rename themselves or add an African name to the ones they already have, explains further how some of these names come to be—and why they're not just "made up."

"Most African names have some [syllable] like sha, la, pa. Those are sounds that come from the African continent and that clearly, black people like. I think the difference is that blacks in the diaspora and in the U.S. in particular may not know the meaning of some of the syllables that they have chosen." Which is why, perhaps, the name "Shaniqua" has become almost a punchline, mocked for its "silly" sound—even though chances are it began as three distinct and meaningful sounds—Sha Ni Kwa.

"But I also want to say," Dr. Hodari continues "That there are African American or black names in the U.S. where people are deliberately taking words that they do know and making a mash-up. So for instance, Niamoja is not a traditional African name. But we do know the word 'nia' means 'purpose,' and 'moja' means 'one,' or 'unity.' So I have a friend named 'Niamoja,' and she just took two African words that she knew and she made a name." That is, you can say the name means 'one purpose' if you want to, but it's not a recognized word or name, any more than, say, "HappyLunch."

Dr. Hodari, like Phillip Guo, encourages her clients who want to wear an African name in day-to-day life to choose something short, without a lot of syllables to distract people, like "Nia" or "Kofi." "Or Siri, the name of the Apple system, is an African name that means secret. I don't know if the people that named Siri know that, but I knew 'Siri' was 'a secret,' because I was already using it." Dr. Hodari emphasizes that African name culture is, to her, a direct reaction to names that were stolen during slavery. "I think people are trying to hold onto the ability to decide how their names will be carried forward."

The ability to decide how your name is carried on, and how it's seen and perceived. In some cultures, that's a straight-up luxury. So what do you do about it?

The Call-Back Gap

Unfortunately, cultural discomfort isn't in any danger of going away. But if you're coming from a place of privilege—and yeah, I think we're at the point where a generally easily understood and pronounceable name is privilege—it can be easy to forget that for many people, name stresses occur daily. Crucially, they don't always go away when someone becomes "of age," either. Schoolyard taunting can be the least of their worries.

Shelica Miller never expected to have trouble with her name. Growing up in Ottawa, she was the only Shelica anyone knew—which, she says, was great. Of course the school secretary, who had known her for years, insisted on mispronouncing it "ShaLIKEa," but, Shelica says, "I mostly thought, 'What's wrong with you? Everyone knows Shelica.'" Though she knew her name was unusual, she made a command decision to like it, particularly after her younger twin brothers, Sheldon and Shane, were named to "match" her. "They were like my crew," she remembers, which more than made up for the lack of any personalized hairbrushes or pencils.

Shelica's definitive positivity is no accident—she says she had to decide to see the good things about her name, because she was well aware there were people who wouldn't.

"It didn't occur to me until after I left school. I would apply for jobs. I'd be in these roundtable interviews and see how well I was doing [relative to the others] and then I wouldn't get a call. Because of my résumé."

Because, she clarifies, of the name Shelica on the résumé. She assumed it was an anti-Jamaican name bias—so she did an experiment to find out. "I put Shelley," she explains, "And . . . it worked. I got calls."

A shadow crosses her face as she remembers, clearly still conflicted about the unexpected problem and the arguably imperfect solution that was the only one she could live with. "I changed it back to Shelica because I have to be proud. I can't hide who I am. That's who I am. I'm the only one [except for a baby she met on a flight to Jamaica] for a reason. I have a special name for a special person, so I might as well show it."

Shelica's rationale for her "special" name is one that resonates with me, though I was never able to announce it as confidently. Then again, by the same token, I never changed my name on my résumé. It never even occurred to me to do so—which means I'm in a distinct minority where oddly-named people are concerned.

I received a letter for my name column from a woman who wondered whether she should rename herself. She had sent out hundreds of résumés with her traditional Vietnamese name, actually four one-syllable names, anglicized with a nickname derived from one of her surnames. She was qualified, but she wasn't getting interviews:

> During my job search over the past couple of years,
> I have found little success in securing an interview. I
> have seen studies like this one and this one that have
> demonstrated that when hiring managers have two
> equally qualified candidates—the first, a Westernized
> name and the second, an ethnic name—the candidate
> with the Westernized name was more likely to be
> successful. They even labelled this phenomenon the
> "call back gap."

After applying to hundreds of jobs (not an exaggeration), I couldn't help but wonder if I would be more successful if I had a different name. I know there are people who have their legal name and have given themselves a professional name, similarly to actors that have stage names.

I'd really like to hear your opinion on renaming yourself as an adult. Maybe there are existing schools of thought on this issue and I'm not aware of it. Is it a practice looked down upon? Are there risks associated with doing this, i.e., does it come across as misleading?

I debated, because, assuming résumés are equal, all an "English" name up front does is tell the interviewer they can be comfortable. They don't have to worry that this is someone they won't be able to communicate with. This is a terrible way to choose people to interview, but it's also kind of at the interviewer's discretion. Anyone who has been on the deciding side of a pile of résumés knows that trying to winnow sixty-five applicants down to even ten interviewees means some things get lost. Why subject yourself to the reject pile before anyone ever looks at your accomplishments?

So I told her to do it, knowing that I was maybe kind of contributing to the problem by endorsing this behaviour. But she can make more change from inside once she has the job . . . right?

Name censorship doesn't have to come from outside, either. Television and radio host Pay Chen tells me that she always knew her name was difficult. "When [adults] would say, 'What does it mean?' I didn't know what to say. Nobody asked Timothy what his name meant." But she didn't realize how ingrained her name worries were until she had her first on-air hosting position.

"I had a hard time saying, 'Hi, I'm Pay,' off the top," she confesses. "I think I always felt a bit of dread when introducing myself." In fact, her hesitation was audible enough to need attention. "My producer had me see a vocal/performance coach; I would speed through my scripts. And I remember her going through [my] tapes and saying 'You rush through your name,' which was true. It was like I wanted to get it out of the way, and you couldn't actually understand what I said. 'HiI'mPay'—one word. The coach said to me, 'You must introduce yourself clearly.' She made me practise a million times and I haaaated it. And she said I had to PAUSE after I said it. That was hard for me."

The name therapy, however tough, paid off (the pun is one Pay understands is bound to happen) and she sees a lot of upsides: "I can often call to make [recurring] appointments and just say 'Hi, it's Pay . . . [no last name]' Like Madonna. Cher. One name."

I agree with her; singularity is the gift that makes up for a whole host of name ills—even if it takes you well into adulthood to actually be able to appreciate it.

The Future Is Ferdinand

One thing I know is that the world's population is becoming more beige. Mic, a serious news website aimed at young adults, discussed the reality of our continual global interracial procreation. They quote scientists who posit that in a hundred years—maybe less—we will have "sexed ourselves into one giant amalgamated mega-race," which is something that's not a new thought, but is still hard to imagine, like the fact that the self-driving cars we've been promised for so long are finally here! This won't erase culture, obviously—the most common question I'm asked is how to serve the name needs of a baby who has four or more significant races, ethnicities, or cultures in his genetic inheritance. The future is coming. But the future is here, relative to even twenty years ago, and yet the cultural cherry-picking of names is still so selective.

There have been some inroads made, but the most accepted names from other cultures are still ones that sound familiar to North American/European ears. Actor Dev Patel, for example, has a name that sounds a lot like Dave. Would he be as successful if his name were Ratnapur? Director Ang Lee has the benefit of an easily understood name in English (and one that, as far as I can understand, he hasn't further anglicized), and that may make people who want to hire him more likely to feel comfortable picking up the phone and working with him. Aziz Ansari's name is traditional, but also short, easy to pronounce, and fun to say—all of which gives him a distinct leg up. Names matter in all walks of life.

I fervently hope our scope of names expands, both for altruistic reasons and because there are so many cool names out there. I want more people to use Vikram and Dagny and Rakim and Sugeewa. I want to discover, name by name, where we go from here. I know parents must choose names with their heads and their hearts, and I'm not going to have ten children to personally bestow names from a variety of cultures, but we can't let Angelina Jolie do all the work, can we?

5

CAIN AND ABEL, MARY-KATE AND ASHLEY
The Lasting Legacy of Sibling Names

A friend recently sent me a clip of actor Liam Hemsworth on the red carpet. The interviewer reaches out to shake his hand, saying, "Hi, I'm Chris." But in the din of the red carpet, Hemsworth heard something else.

"Did you call me Chris?"

"No, I didn't—"

"I'm Liam."

"Hahah, I know," said the reporter, who was very young and doing very well in what was about to be a tense situation. "I said *I'm* Chris." Hemsworth—Liam, that is, not his brother Chris—looked visibly relieved and embarrassed. One imagines it's a situation he's been in one too many times. Because the only name you hear as often as your own is your sibling's. For better or or worse.

From what I understand, I wasn't actually supposed to have a sibling. My parents were pretty set on having only one child—it probably seemed a relief after the homes full of kids they grew up in. But around the age of three or four, *someone* began whining that she wanted a sister. Someone who was probably given a falsely inflated sense of power—because very quickly after I commenced said whining, I was informed that there was a baby en route.

I assumed it would be the sister I'd ordered. In 1984 elective gender discovery was still very rare and we had no idea what was coming our way. I mean, I assumed I knew; I was blissfully ignorant that I didn't have the benefit of medical science to back me up. So I was unsurprised when one early Saturday morning, I woke up at my friend Melissa's house to be told there was a phone call for me. Labour had started in the middle of the night, and so I camped out in Melissa's blue canopy bed while we waited for the baby's arrival.

I gripped the phone. My dad spoke too loudly, ebullient from joy and lack of sleep. "Hello, my Du! You have a baby sister!" She hadn't arrived on my birthday as requested, nor, I would discover, did she arrive ready to play, where by "play" I meant ready to watch me lecture her all about Rainbow Brite—but she was a sister, not a brother. Just what I ordered. Next item of business?

"What's her name?" I demanded. I don't know if my parents realized back then how epic my interest in names would be, but they did know I had opinions about mine, and I think they'd deflected earlier questions of this nature by saying we couldn't name the baby until we knew if it was a boy or a girl.

"Well," my father began. "We're thinking of calling her Shannon."

And then I bellowed, because this was Not Fair, and I understood at age four-and-change that the arrival of a sister marked the beginning of a long life of Not Fair. Blame Judy Blume's *The Pain and the Great One*, maybe—I knew I wanted a sibling, but I also knew I was going to have to fight this person for everything I had. In this case, it was what I didn't have—a name that fit into mainstream 1980s North America. "You can't!" I cried. "You can't let her have a more normal name than me!"

As I screeched, Melissa looked over at me with the kind of disdain only a seven-year-old can display for a four-year-old. Our families met through her mother's job as daycare provider, but we had evolved into close family friends, and I was forever fascinated by the possessions of a "big girl." She had all the *Little House on the Prairie* books, a Michael Jackson button (which I inherited once she decided she didn't like him any more), and, most bittersweet to me, an array of awesome paraphernalia with her name all over it.

It seemed to me at the time that there was a whole industry devoted to the celebration of Melissa—her name was on everything! Buttons! Sweatshirts! Toothbrushes! If there was a novelty item, she had it with her name proudly marching across the back. I couldn't rein in my jealousy, which was exacerbated because most of Melissa's hand-me-downs came to me. Sooner or later I got all her dresses and Lego and My Little Ponies, but you know what never came? All those Melissa items. I mean, I guess they knew not to rub salt in the wound.

So already, at four years old, I knew that names were important. Not that I was so lacking for stuff—I had as many trinkets and gifts and toys as any kid—but my foldable travel hairbrush always said "Myrtle Beach, S.C." or "Niagara Falls." I wasn't part of the club. So my histrionics about "Shannon" were all jealousy—what if my sister got to have her name on a hairbrush? In the mid-'80s Shannon was not overly popular, but recognizable. She wouldn't be looked at sideways at piano lessons or soccer. She would fit in.

Not in my house, she wouldn't.

I felt powerful when my sister was ultimately named "Sheena," which qualified as Irish enough for my mother and not "common," though at the time, Sheena Easton was a popular singer, and the reference that people used to familiarize themselves with my sister's name when they heard it. It's not like she was Ashley (or Shannon) but ultimately the combination of being a second child who had slightly more broken-in parents with a slightly more familiar name set her

Here is a picture taken at the hospital after my sister was born. Melissa looking wise, my new sister looking irritated, and me after tearfully insisting I <u>was</u> big enough to hold her.

on a path to just be a lot more chilled out than I was about these things and a host of others.

Our Mythical Brother

However different Sheena and I were, it didn't stop us from becoming acutely aware that we were it for one another. We only had each other in the Canadian world that we lived in, full stop. Cousins and extended family might as well have been mythical.

Maybe that's why we created our imaginary brother, Niall.

As a kid, I had an intellectual interest in "where babies come from"—less in the mechanics requiring "the talk," and more in the idea that there was potential for "me" to have been someone else. This was so intriguing that we gleefully interrogated my parents about what would have happened if either of us had been a boy. The questioning was a full-time occupation one winter.

The answer to "What would my name be if I was a boy?" was "Niall" for both of us. Sheena and I debated this. On the one hand, Niall was an unheard-of Irish name that would, like our own names, never show up on a toothbrush or a door licence plate. On the other hand, it was charmingly close to Neil, which was very much in vogue and acceptable. It didn't exactly smack of normalcy, but it had the faint whiff of it. Would our fictional brother have met with approval or not? Sheena and I designed an experiment to find out.

When I was about ten, my mother, finally unpacking the last of the boxes from a move two years before, found a school picture from when I was eight that had gotten lost in the shuffle. I was in no rush for it to be found, but Mom found it charming. I can't explain it. In the cardboard-framed 8-by-10, I am wearing what appears to be a heavy bowl cut, which was an entirely unisex and acceptable haircut at the time. In truth my long hair was caught at the back of my neck with a medieval torture barrette known as a "bow" that little girls used to clamp on our fingers and occasionally style our '80s hair with—but it's obscured from view in the photo by the absurd angle the Josten's photographer always placed your shoulders at. I also wore a brown-and-black striped blouse that was likewise seen as eminently acceptable for an eight-year-old girl in the '80s. Unisex clothing back then was both actually unisex and utterly unremarkable.

The combined effect of the bowl cut and brown/black button-down was somewhat masculine—at least as much as a round-faced eight-year-old can be masculine. Sheena and I hung the picture, and when her new friends from the neighbourhood came over we told them the picture was our brother, Niall—and that he was away at boarding school.

They weren't dumb kids by any stretch, but you could see them struggling with the concept. "Niall" sure did look like me, but not exactly like me (my ever-present thick glasses, which I'd taken off for the picture, helped to separate us). Boarding school was exotic and ridiculous in our circles, so nobody would ever check. And the name? Well, nobody had ever heard it before, but the truth was most people, particularly kids, couldn't distinguish my parent's accents, jokes, and references anyway—maybe they'd been talking about Niall all this time. Every time the kids from the neighbourhood came over they'd stop to study the photo and ask us questions. When was his birthday? (May 16.) How much older was he? (Two years older than me.) Why didn't he come home for Christmas? (He did, but you were at your Nana's.) For a moment there, we really had them.

Not the actual pic, but the haircut that allowed me to convince everyone "Niall" was a thing.

Ultimately, my mother couldn't help giggling when interrogated about her "son" by deadly serious seven-year-olds from down the block, and the jig was up—but not before Sheena and I stopped to think about how "Niall" would have fared with his Canadian contemporaries. I think our initial assessment was right—both he and his name would have been a hit. The fact that, as of this writing, there's a Niall in one of the most popular boy bands in the world bears out the name's popularity.

Balance Above All?

Do sibling names have to "match"? Does it matter if one is more popular than the other or more palatable to the ear? For my money, the answer is absolutely. Siblings are grouped together constantly and, as I demonstrated above, they're constantly comparing what they have and who gets what. It can become very apparent if one child is Sue and the other one is Ariadne that there are different expectations of them or different assessments of who they are.

This doesn't just exist in the family unit. Teachers remember that James is Jason's brother, letters and invitations are addressed to both, and in every situation up to and including death (announcements), their names will be linked. It's not crazy to want them to sound balanced beside one another.

I remember hearing that an acquaintance was having trouble thinking of a name for her second child, and seeing myself as a superhero to the rescue, I thought "This is a job for a name therapist!" (okay, maybe not in so many words). I eagerly sent a Twitter DM (as you do), but her response was not as enthusiastic as I might have hoped.

"Oh right. You like names to 'match.'"

OUCH. No, I don't think names should match—I think they should "go." There's a world of difference. My friend David had a much easier time with his name than his sister, Maren. Those aren't names that "go"—that speak to a similar style of name philosophy. But I wince at the idea of "matching" because of how easy it is to take it too far.

I know of a family who had twin sons, Michael and Nicholas. You'd think then that there would be two

names—and possibly only two—that might be out of contention for their daughter, born later. But no. Nobody in the
family saw any irony in the fact that the daughter, Michelle,
basically wore the same name as her older brother. (I can only
assume that her middle name must have been Nicole.) I just
couldn't fathom that people hadn't thought about these things,
but I guess they liked the way the names sounded. A lot.

Once you have a sibling—or are one, for that matter—it's not
just your name that's significant, but the names that are said
alongside it. Name nerds are often wrongly mocked for their
interest in names, as though it's not a topic that deserves consideration. This is incorrect, of course. But if I were going to
pretend to be an outsider and find a reason why people make
fun of those who obsess about names, it might be because of
the use of the word "sibset" (*sibset* [noun]. A group of siblings.)

   Those seeking advice on baby name forums sometimes
don't ask for help naming children, but for help naming a
"sibset." I'm of two minds about this. On the one hand I think
there are probably way too many combinations of children
named Max and Ella or Will and Henry. This is what parents
are trying to avoid: names that don't sound too similar or too
well-used. Which is a valid concern, if it's the kind of thing
you get concerned about. I remember the thrill I got when, as
a young *Beverly Hills, 90210* fan, I learned that Jason Priestley
had a sister named Justine. Sure, Jason and Justine sound kind
of cute together, but—get this—Jason Bateman ALSO had a
sister named Justine. Clearly the way to have your children
become teen heartthrobs was to name them Jason (admittedly
a hugely popular name when both were born) and their sisters

Justine. I couldn't get over the coincidence! (I was ten, I hadn't been exposed to too many coincidences, perhaps.)

But it reinforces the point that similarly-named children are, if nothing else, sure their parents are spreading love around in equal measure, and maybe even building jokes into the mix. My sister's friend Christie Chuakay's middle name is Antoinette. Her brother's name is Christopher Anthony. She admits that even though she knows it's "so awkward" to be named so similarly, they kind of enjoy it. "It makes sense because essentially we are the same person," she says. "I'm a girl version of him. It's weird." In fact, Christie says it's a good conversational icebreaker that they can laugh about. People assume that they're twins and they get to joke that their parents really just liked the names.

I'm not going to lie—there's a bit of snobbishness involved in name nerdism. Okay, a lot of snobbishness. It's easy to scoff at names you think were not creative or exciting enough. But until I talked to Christie about the name she shares with her brother I never thought that there could be a benefit to a shared name. Christie and Chris feel like they're a duo against the world.

There is no shortage of siblings to interview about their experiences with names, but there are some situations you can't make up. I consider myself lucky to have a wonderful mother-in-law, and luckier that she comes with a bonus—an identical twin sister. They are as much in love with their names as anyone I've ever met, and maybe more, because each seems to loves the other's name almost as much as her own.

They are Joan and Jean, and they are a twin force. They are the kind of twins who will not see each other for weeks on account of travel by one or both—and then show up to see each other wearing the same outfit coincidentally. They talk three or four times a day—more, if you count Facebook chats.

One of the things most notable about them is how much they each use the other's name when talking to one another—more, I think, than "average" people do. Scene from a family Christmas:

"Well, Joan, I think it's time we got this bird carved."

"Okay, Jean, let's make sure we have all our platters."

"Joan, do you think it's big enough to fit both turkeys on here?"

"No. Too tight, Jean. We better get out another tray."

"Joan, do you want to tell them all to come in?"

I'm not exaggerating. I wonder if this is a twin thing, where the rhymey same-iness of the names makes them feel more securely together. Can't have Joan without Jean.

I ask them about it—together, of course: "When you were little girls, did you like it that your names 'matched'?"

Jean says she did. "Jeannie, Joannie, or Twinnies was what a lot of people called us."

But Joan remembers it slightly differently. "[People] would say there go the twins, or, hi twin, and if they got our names wrong, we would sometimes correct them or just say 'oh hi.'"

I love this. What's the point in arguing about what your name is? If you're part of the very specific two-person unit that Joan and Jean are, maybe the real truth is that both names (and the name "twin") belong to both of you.

Which means it's important that they're in harmony. Of course, there are always exceptions. I heard a story of a family who liked their children's names so much that when two tragically passed away, they had more children—and named them the very same names. Nobody wants to believe that children are replaceable, of course, but if your name is recycled from your siblings who died before you were born? You might feel like a replacement. (I have ghoulish thoughts about reused Christmas stockings and backpacks with the name labels still accurate . . . !)

But as jarring as that decision may have been, I kind of understand the inclination. If you chose the name you love best for your first child, why wouldn't you try to replicate that as much as you could for your second? That's what happened to Cole Bastedo, eighteen months younger than his older brother . . . Carl. He confesses some frustration at the names, which, let's face it, *really* sound like they go together. "I think when I was a kid I didn't hate that our names were so close as much as I hated how adults would get us confused. When you're a kid, adults are supposed to be these mystical brainiacs, but they couldn't tell 'Cole' from 'Carl'? It was my first inkling that adults, like kids, are mostly idiots. That being said, naming your kids Mike and Mick may not be the best idea."

Breaking Name Patterns

Of course, not all parents name their children similarly. For every "sibset" with names so close you do a double-take when you hear them, there are sibling groups where one is William and the other is Kelly. Where one is Joe and the other is Regina, called Diane (true set!). Or sisters like Anat, Ronit, and . . . Karen.

I had heard the story of this combination for some years before writing this book, and it was jarring enough that it stuck with me. That third name is a wild left turn. From the first two names with T-endings to one of the most generic of girls' names. Two names that are overtly Hebrew, and one that almost defies having a cultural origin these days (though it is originally Danish). A possible explanation is that maybe they are a blended family—a switch in parents or a stepsibling introduced—but this isn't the case. All three women share the same parents, immigrants to Toronto from Israel. What happened is both more mundane and more fascinating by a long shot.

I meet the sisters for lunch, and it's a sibling performance at which I am merely a spectator. All three sisters are straightforward speakers, but each has a different tone in our discussion. Ronit, who is forty-eight, is frank, almost gruff, yet utterly open in her discussion of every topic. Anat, three years older, is pragmatic and direct, the kind of person whose speech lets you know she sees everything in black and white. Why wouldn't you, when that's how you should see them? And Karen, the reason we're here? Karen, the youngest, is thirty-nine, bubbly and happy and, though she's a mother of three, still has the cheerful affect of a popular teenager.

The general topic of names sparks immediate banter, when Ronit drops a bombshell on her sisters—her actual first name is not Ronit. It's hard to believe they have never heard this before, but this is what I love about name therapy—there's always something hiding, that you didn't think was significant until someone asked you about it.

Ronit's sisters are shocked: "What does it say on your birth certificate?"

"Regina Ronit. [Instead of Ronit Regina.] I think [our parents] got confused. They didn't know how to fill out the form."

I love this, of course—the idea that there are secrets about our names that even our own family doesn't know. But the secret of how Karen became Karen is something they all remember, in various ways. Anat speaks first on the topic. She's the oldest, eleven years older than Karen. She remembers what happened, and I trust her, because she's the clearest speaker I think I've ever met. She answers every question with efficiency. Never stammers, never hesitates. You know how Bill Gates never says "um"? Like that.

"When we knew that our mom was pregnant, she was picking out a third name. She wanted to name Karen 'Limor.' And having struggled through life as Anat and Ronit, we thought we would save her from that hardship, and give her a normal name." She seems to regret the childish instinct to intercede on her sister's behalf in retrospect, or at least feels like it was a bit disrespectful of the intent—to give a beautiful, culturally based name. "We were younger and maybe not really grateful . . . for the Israeli names that we got."

Ronit doesn't share her perspective. "You know that show 'And I see Laura, and Tracy'?" Here we are again. Ronit is talking about *Romper Room*, which has apparently scarred an entire generation of uncommonly named kids! "You know how many years I waited to hear 'And I see Ronit, and Anat?' It didn't happen. Never got a keychain, never got a hairbrush . . . " See? The hairbrush!

Ronit is busy proving my point over and over again, which is why the would-be "Limor" is Karen. Now an adult with children of her own, Karen likes her name. To her, it sounds "light, you know? [Karens] are good girls." She liked knowing other Karens when she was growing up, and yeah—like any much-younger sibling, she got things the others didn't—like the coveted hairbrush with your name on it.

I can't believe this is how it all went down, and I tell them so. "Instead of saying 'Okay, we're going to have this little sister be in our club of odd misfit names,' [à la my screeching over Sheena's name], you sort of advocated for her. 'Well, it's too late for us but let's save our little sister.'"

Anat: "We did." (To Karen) "We saved you."

Ronit: "We saved you."

Karen: "I owe you guys everything."

Anat: "We did."

Ronit: "When you go to apply for a job—for a bank loan. When you go apply for school . . . the name means a lot."

And it's true that Karen's world is different than her sisters'. While Ronit maintains that she usually has to tell her name to people three times at a minimum, and Anat has had fights with her company's human resources department to assure them she's not a man, Karen is blissfully ignorant of a lot of these problems. She was gravely offended a few weeks earlier when someone at Starbucks misheard her name as Ken. "I got *Ken* in Starbucks last week [on my cup]. And I'm like 'Ken? Who's Ken?' And they're like 'Didn't you say Ken?' I said 'Do I look like a Ken?' and he goes 'You never know.'" Poor baby! That her name was once heard incorrectly! Anat and Ronit scoff with me. Karen will never know how we suffered.

But I can tell that, while Ronit's wounds are real (she made sure her children would never have to suffer any sort of similar fate), Anat is less concerned about these trivial mistakes and misunderstandings. Like I said, she's pragmatic. She doesn't see—at least initially—how a name can have this much significance.

"Do you think that your name affects your life that way?" she asks me. She's too polite to challenge me in so many words, but that's what the question is—can this possibly be so important?

"One hundred percent," I answer. "I really do. Do you think that you would be somebody different if your name were Melissa?" She looks doubtful. So I decide to push. "When you see your clients, don't they say 'Annette'? Didn't you say it didn't bother you when people mispronounced it?"

Anat agrees. "Yeah, I don't care about it now. I'm not sensitive. I'm very thick-skinned."

"Because your name is Anat."

"Sorry?"

"*Because* your name is Anat."

"Maybe." Anat is polite, giving me an out. But I'm very sure of what I'm saying, and Anat has said enough for me to think we've shared a lot of experiences where names are concerned. So I push further: "You had to advocate for yourself at a very young age. Think about even being in kindergarten and somebody says, 'So your name is what?' And you say 'Oh, it's Anat.' That's not happening to Bradley."

She looks at me. I'm either crazy or brilliant. "No."

"And so you learn to speak up a little bit more, I think."

"Well, maybe that's why I have a thick skin, because I've had to develop thick skin because I've had so many issues [with my name]."

I'm satisfied. I've convinced someone. But then it gets better. After a lengthy digression into past romantic intrigue, present handbags, and things that happen in Vegas, we talk about husbands, and then the talk returns to names.

When I ask the sisters whether Karen had a more Canadian experience than them growing up, the response is mixed. Karen says "Not really" at the same time the other two say "Absolutely." Anat and Ronit laugh at the idea that Karen's upbringing was anything like theirs, though they admit some of that had to do with parents who were more broken in by the time the third sister came along. Still, there were some unexpected . . . side effects.

"Like, you married a guy with a frickin' Hebrew name!" (Karen's husband is called Lahav.) "We tried to shelter you from a Hebrew name. You ended up gravitating towards . . ." Anat trails off.

"I over-identified with it." Karen muses.

"Yeah, you did."

Karen takes a breath. "But also because I felt like— well, you guys were clearly it, you know? You were Israeli, and it was a thing. But [people asked] are you Italian? Are you Portuguese? Are you this? Are you that? Like no one knew what I was. But the Jewish girls, the Jewish-Canadian girls very much [thought] that I wasn't a Jewish-Canadian girl. And so for me, that over-identifying was like 'Okay, well now there's no [question]. People are going to know that I'm Jewish, because I'm married to Lahav.' Maybe that's the thing."

I'm amazed and delighted. "You were looking for some Jewish cred!"

Karen has not a bit of hesitation as she agrees. "That's exactly what it was. Maybe that's why I named [my daughters] Shira and Talia and Dani." I've never considered this aspect. I remember pelting Karen with questions when she was naming her daughters, but never imagined she was securing their Israeli-Canadian identity in a way hers hadn't been.

Ronit points out that it was the opposite for her and Anat—they chose classic or "biblical" names for their children, but none that you'd assume were overtly Israeli.

I could keep talking, but the sisters have lives and appointments and school pickups. I thank the women for their time. Anat has been quiet in the last part of our discussion, and as I tell her it was a pleasure, she replies: "Actually you've got me in a bit of a tizzy, truthfully. Because I'm thinking I could have had a different life."

Ding!

But Ronit points out that, for better or worse, her name has made her who she is. She explains the standup routine she's perfected every time someone asks her about her name, which basically ends with "It's my parents' fault." I recognize the immediate name defence mechanisms, the jokes and patter, because I have a lot of that myself.

Anat is still thinking, though. "What kind of life would we have had if we had different names? That is just such a profound thing to think about. I mean, not that I feel so hard done by in my life, but I mean—"

Karen interjects. "With your super-pricy purse?"

Anat: "I got it at 40 percent off, all right?"

Siblings. See?

Fur Siblings

Of course, there are millions of people who don't have siblings at all, or who don't have children. That doesn't mean their journey with names is over. In fact, I'm starting to believe that giving a name is a compulsion, or an instinct, of adulthood. That's why there are people who name their cars, who name their homes and cottages, and of course, that is why the most interesting names you will hear in common usage are often bestowed on people's pets.

I didn't grow up with pets and decided this was a big resentment I needed to fix once I was an adult. As soon as I got an apartment of my own I went out to adopt a cat. The animal shelter had names affixed to all the cages, and you could tell that while some were there just to help potential adopters forge a connection with the poor animals inside the cages, others were bestowed with love. I spent a long time admiring a cat whose cage proudly read "The Attorney." I would have loved to take the Attorney home with me, but apparently I did not stand up under his scrutiny—his unflinching stare unnerved me. Instead I went home with a sweet young cat and, overwhelmed by choices for what to call her, accepted a friend's suggestion to use an author I liked for inspiration. The cat is officially Zadie Smith, after the author, but is called Zadie. I still think it's a pretty great name, given that I could have chosen "Mittens," but she cares neither for the name nor for the fact that I rescued her from a small metal box.

Dogs' names, for whatever reason, seem to be much more down to earth, much closer to human names. Author Mikita Brottman has an explanation for exactly why this is. "Dogs are increasingly part of the family . . . on the recent British census, many people put down their dog as their 'son.'"

Brottman is the author of many books, most recently *The Great Grisby*, a tribute to her French bulldog Grisby that also investigates the bonds between humans and their dogs. The chapter titles, each focusing on a different dog, are incredibly evocative: "Kashtanka," "Giallo," "Robber," "Wessex." In the book, Brottman says, "Rich insights can be gained from observing how people name their dogs," pointing out that some see them as substitute children. She points out that philosopher Arthur Schopenhauer named all of his dogs the same thing, "Atma"—the Hindu word for the universal soul. She also points out that while the presidential dogs of recent years have "boring" names, they weren't always so devoid of personality—George Washington had four, including "Drunkard" and "Tipsy."

Zadie, my cat, may not appreciate her name, but I also have a dog that my husband and I adopted shortly before we were married. After long and protracted discussions, she was named Libby, and she is the happiest Libby who ever wagged a Libby tail. Still, I know there are some people who are very against people names for dogs—Libby's buddies in the neighbourhood are called Lucky and Jacks, in addition to Dreyfuss and Alfie and Barney.

I ask Brottman whether naming your dog a "people name" is a faux pas.

"I actually write about this in [*The Great Grisby*] . . . Now is the first time ever that the same names are in the top ten lists for both dogs and human babies. Jack, Max,

Chloe, Sophia, Bella. So I guess our pets are increasingly part of the family."

The idea that a dog named Rumpus bounces happily at the dog park beside one named Wallace is hilarious to me. Are those who choose "people names" just using names they won't be able to use on children, or are they a reflection of the new reality, where pets are just as much members of the family as anyone else? If you meet a family consisting of Mom, Rowan, Eli, and Flora—who's the dog in this situation? The fact that it's no longer obvious is fascinating to me.

This is a departure from names like Noodles and Cinders, and those in turn might be left over from when dogs were either strictly outdoor visitors, or else highly pedigreed show dogs, whose very formal names, like "Playing with Fire V Gleishorbach," "Chidley Willem the Conqueror," or "Roundtown Mercedes of Maryscot," are usually chopped down to nicknames like "Chip." By and large, most of the people-named dogs I know or have heard of are named human names that are a little offbeat, as though the humans who name them know that "Ezra" on a dog won't raise eyebrows the way "Lord Chaunceleroy" might on a human.

At a certain point, a name doesn't exist in a vacuum. It's shaped and formed by the people around you and how they react to it—sometimes literally. Even as an adult, no matter how many times I say "Du-Ahn-A," with the weird flat middle A that only my Euro parents can really pull off with aplomb, the more people respond back with "Oh hi, Du-Awwwn-a." In fact, a girl in my eighth grade told me I should consider pronouncing it that way. So I veered harder the other way, now pronouncing my name with the flattest "DuANNNa." Still, when I introduce myself, people smile—if they haven't heard Johanna or Deanna—and say "Hi, Du-awn-a."

I asked Sheena if she'd ever had anyone mispronounce her name. She looked at me like I was a little bit silly and thus was to be pitied. This is a look I'm quite familiar with because she's been using it on me since the day she was born. She has very little to say on the subject. Her exact quote? "First name, never." I have no answer. She tosses her head, a little smug. She sees the Sturm und Drang over my name as a bit overblown. She never had problems with hers. The struggle is, therefore, not real to my analytical, scientific sister.

Me and Sheena, children of the 1980s.

6

IF IRIS IS IN, IS OSCAR OUT?
Why Name Popularity and Trends Are a Double-Edged Sword

Not long ago, some friends and I were playing old songs and wallowing in nostalgia. There are two essential parts to this game that everyone knows—trying to remember all the words to songs you used to know by heart, and trying to place each song in the era where it belongs. I don't mean what decade, I mean what era—or, let's face it, school year—of ours, specifically. Were we in grade 11, or 10? Which movie was this the soundtrack to? The easiest yet most cringeworthy way to pin this down is to discuss the memories and romances that immediately accompany each tune. I don't know why there's not yet a word for "the song associated with a certain crush you had."

We were past the number one hits from high school and deep into obscure tracks when one of my all-time favourites came on. SWV's "Weak." As the other four smiled, lost in their reveries, I said: "This is summertime, just before grade 11, sitting on my bed rearranging my school supplies."

My friends burst out laughing. I'll admit the association is not the immediate one you make with a song about a love so strong and sweet, "it knocks you right off of your feet," but I've never had any secrets about the love affair I had with school. Or schools, anyway.

Meet the teacher night!

I don't think my love of schools is solely about a "love of learning" or the not-insignificant fact that I'm a know-it-all. I relished being around so many kids my own age. When school started, I was an overprotected only child, so I got drunk on meeting everyone and on learning all the differences between kids in our classroom. My interest in names might only have been moderate before then, but when I arrived in a group of my peers, I realized definitively that it wasn't just that my name was less common than Melissa's, or my friend Erin's on our block—it was downright obscure.

I still remember it being mostly teachers and other adults who exclaimed over "Duana," usually not in a flattering way. My classmates didn't care what my name was, they just noted that teachers stumbled over it again and again. The kids didn't trip on it, because to a kid just starting school, any name is new. How do you distinguish that "Duana" is weird but "Alicia" isn't?

I also remember learning early that a name could evoke traits far beyond what the name supposedly "meant" in the baby name dictionary. The first person I met with a "new" name usually made an indelible impression on me. My classmate Tracy caught my interest early because the girl showed up to the first day of kindergarten wearing a cape, and since then, all the Tracys I've known have had a flair for the dramatic. While I'm sure there are very nice Bobbys in the world, the first one I met defined the name for me forever as "very short, very aggressive."

But I remember learning one thing at school most early and most often.

I learned Jennifer.

Before school began, I had a Jennifer as a babysitter. She lived down the street and she was nice enough, but we didn't have any particular connection. Jennifer talked on the phone and had boyfriends, and was very much not interested in discussing the exploits of Ramona Quimby with a precocious five-year-old who should have been in bed (and who, in retrospect, should have told her parents there were greasy fourteen-year-old boys in the house after they went out).

But once I got to kindergarten—*oh*. The Juggernaut of Jennifer became shockingly apparent. There was only one Jenny in kindergarten, but the following year, in a class of twenty-two children, there were five. That's 22 percent of the class with the same name, and my class was just one of many with the same problem. I didn't know it then, but the Jennifer onslaught during the mid-1980s was happening across the continent. The name, which sprang fully formed from the forehead of *Love Story* in 1970, didn't just seep into North America, it stomped like a dinosaur, trampling over everything in its path. By the time I got to school in 1985, Jennifer was absolutely everywhere. The actual overall dominance of the name peaked around 18,000 Jennifers per million babies in the 1970s—but given that roughly half of those babies were boys, it was actually 18,000 per 500,000 baby girls. Still just .036 percent overall—so how did it become such a phenomenon?

It wasn't just that there were so many Jennifers taking over the nurseries and schoolyards and shopping malls, although there were. It was that together, they formed a unit—almost a movement. Since there were Jennifers who fit every description: short and tall, intelligent and dim, only children and one of six—and since these Jennifers were present in every activity and every class, it seemed like "Jennifer" became a shorthand for "every girl." If Jennifer liked something, it was typical and normal and usual. If she didn't, that was typical and normal and usual, too. After all, how could so many Jennifers be wrong?

In that year of the five Jennifers, of course there were differences between them—but still, from the outside it could seem like an impenetrable wall of Jennifer. The teacher gave herself some crutches to get by. If I remember correctly, she instituted a lot of usage of middle names, so in the end there were a Jennifer Sarah, a Jennifer Lynn, a Jennifer Joanne, a Jenny, and a Jenn—two "n"s, not one. (I believe Jenn was in fact Jennifer Lynn number 2, and so the distinction of who got to be who was relegated to a coin flip. I thought of this years later when I heard that Matthew Perry and Matt LeBlanc also flipped a coin over who actually got to be called "Matt" in the *Friends* credits).

I was amazed by the Jennifers and their self-contained ecosystem, and of course I wanted to be a part of it— though I was aware, even then, that there was something not-quite-dignified about having to offer up your middle name just to be recognized as an individual—it seemed like a high price. Around this time I also began to realize that for some people, the middle name was an embarrassment. Like, what if your middle name was Enid? That would negate the cool of Jennifer right quick.

I don't want to say that Jennifers are all alike—the name is so common it's preposterous even to consider—but I will say that back then, at my school, there was, well—maybe an aura of what we would now refer to as *entitlement*. The Jennifers' collective sense of place in the world was so secure that they rarely had the kind of existential crises that plagued me all the time, even at five and six. If you were a Jennifer, you knew you belonged, regardless of race, creed, or socio-economic status. Whatever else was "different" about you, at least your name let you fit in, or go undetected until your other shortcomings were discovered. And wherever you went, you knew you'd find a Jennifer or seven to commune with. Even if they didn't wind up being your best friends, it could serve as a jumping-off point. What would it be like to have that level of comfort?

I was friendly with all the Jennifers, despite being patently not one of them. Jennifer Sarah and I played together, but we were too similar ultimately, and were always fighting and scrapping, so we stopped hanging out. You know who was happy about that? Jennifer Lynn, who wanted her best friend back.

But Jenn and I—by the fourth grade, Jenn and I had struck up a year-long love affair. Not with each other, though we did have a great friendship—but with the telephone. The hours I spent on the phone with Jenn, which amounted to me excavating and examining her popular-girl life, were my introduction to social anthropology, or the idea that those who can, *do*, and those who can't, sycophantically eavesdrop on what it's like to have a social life. I don't know why Jenn confided so much in me, at least originally, but I know why she continued. I was fascinated, and I never ran out of questions. I was a little elementary-school-aged Barbara Walters, and could probably quote her easily because I watched *20/20* every Friday, religiously. You know, like a normal kid.

That is, I watched it when I wasn't on long, oft-interrupted phone calls with Jenn. The phone calls were instituted out of necessity, since we'd moved two neighbourhoods over, and so the conversations Jenn and I might have had walking home from school or to the Mac's Milk had to be conducted on the phone instead.

We had a lot to discuss. She had a mean teacher; I was woefully behind on fashion. I can still hear her voice, half sympathetic and half exasperated, when I told her Melissa's hand-me-downs had finally netted me a pair of acid-washed jeans.

"Acid-washed are out, Duana. You need stone-washed now." How was I supposed to know? Where were these things written? Jenn wasn't just any Jenn—she was the relatively benevolent queen of our social circle and, eventually, of the school. She was at the forefront of everything, gave me a bird's-eye-view of what it was like to be "older"—at ten, she seemed impossibly sophisticated as compared to my not-quite-nine. Her social ease could have been due to her older siblings or network of cottage friends or any of the other ways we were different, but I could only see the idea that everything she had was wrapped up in having a name that everyone wanted. In my mind, being a Jenn set the bar of the life you'd want. My theory was proven when, in fourth grade, Jenn had a boyfriend—Anton. We all understood that this meant they held hands before school started in the mornings but never, ever talked to each other, while their various friends surrounded them in discrete boy-and-girl semicircles so they could still socialize despite having that one limb out of commission because it was fused to the opposite sex. So exciting! So adult!

But my childish idea of the ease of a Jennifer cracked a few weeks later, when she said Anton wanted to go to the movies with her—and she was hesitant. By this point I was already sneaking covert episodes of melodramatic teen television and voraciously consuming books that were way too

old for me, so I was seized by the most pressing issue. Would
he ask her to kiss him?

We investigated the issue from many angles, what she
would do if it were the case and what she could read or do
to prepare, and then just when we were reaching the summit
of the issue, one or the other of us was called to dinner. And
probably someone's parent saying "get off the phone,"
because the discourse of eight- and ten-year old girls was not
respected in the way it should have been.

But when we finally resumed our call later that night,
after dinner and piano practice and homework, I tried to
jump right back into the juicy problem she was facing. Jenn
stopped me. "I don't want to talk about that any more," she
said. "I was feeling really scared."

I was dumbfounded, and silent.

The idea that Jenn could be scared about anything was
shock number one. The idea that anything to do with growing up and being cool and knowing what to do with boys
could be scary was number two. I had no romantic experience of my own, of course, but I didn't expect to. Jenn was
entitled to know and experience all this stuff! It was her
birthright, by virtue of the name that allowed her to know
about popularity and boys and stonewashed jeans. (The
actual heart of the matter, that we were discussing this in
fourth grade and she had every right to be a little scared,
would not dawn on me until years later.)

I'm ashamed to say that was pretty close to the end of
my conversations with Jenn. We didn't drift apart immediately, and went through the motions of calling each other at
times when we knew nobody would be home to answer, but

the balance was upset. She didn't know everything about life and boys, and I could no longer use her like an encyclopedia, assuming she knew all the answers to everything.

Still, the name Jennifer retained a lot of power for me, and I was always surprised by its absence in pop culture. The younger daughter on *Family Ties* sported the name, but she was so clearly not a Jennifer while her older sister Mallory exuded everything that was *synonymous* with Jennifer, that I assumed the writers had gotten it wrong and were too embarrassed to change back. Jennifer didn't permeate the fictional world quite the way it did my real one, and so it seemed as though there was something I knew that had not yet made it to the world at large. (This is partly because adults tend to write names they know, which is why there were plenty of books about twelve-year-olds in the '80s with characters named "Debbie," despite my never knowing one in real life. It's also why I was infuriated to hear a radio ad in the summer of 2015 that involved two high schoolers back to school shopping—one of whom was named "Jen." As if! In 2015!)

The earliest tentpoles of my name therapy were constructed with the idea that everyone with the same name had something in common. I knew it wasn't all the way true, and yet at the same time . . . it kept coming true. I would feel a little worried for each new Amy I met, assuming her parents would be divorced like the Amy in Judy Blume's *It's Not the End of the World.* Then I'd chastise myself for being silly, and feel guilty for correctly predicting the fate of Amy's parents. Similarly and not coincidentally, I was gratified that the Nancys I knew were as knowledgeable, bossy, and ready to get into nitty-gritty subjects as the Nancy in *Are You There*

God? It's Me, Margaret (a book in which the characters assign themselves sophisticated, sexy names like Alexandra, Veronica, Kimberly and inexplicably, Mavis.)

As an adult I'm sure I have a more nuanced perspective on how different people with the same name can be. But as the Name Therapist I am honour-bound to ask the Jennifers—or at least some of their representatives—if they feel the same way.

The Jennifer Survey

Intellectually, I know that there are as many Jennifers in the world as there are recipes that try to make nachos a palatable dish. But I can't shake my idea that there are things all Jennifers have and know, like a secret code. Herewith the Jennifer Survey. I asked a nonscientific group of Jennifers from all across Canada a series of questions. Several dozen Jennifers replied, born between 1968 to 1983, which I think is about right. I personally know of one Jennifer born in 1985, but the sweet spot of the name is blanketed over the 1970s.

1. Why did your parents decide to call you Jennifer?
"My mom had an older niece named Jennifer that she saw before I was born and my parents loved the name."

"It was a popular name at the time."

"Having heard it 'around,' my dad liked the sound of the name. My folks looked up the meaning of the name [fair lady] and that sealed the deal. At the time there were no online surveys monitoring trends, and they had no idea it would become such a popular name. My mom liked Jillian, but my dad liked Jennifer more, and they felt that was the name that suited me best (especially after I was born and they got to know me for a few days)."

"Their favourite movie when they first started dating was *Love Is a Many-Splendored Thing* so they decided to name me after Jennifer Jones [the actress in the lead role]."

"They loved the name, and had no prior associations with it."

"Parents named me Jennifer because they thought it was a beautiful name, was a name that could grow with me and there were several nickname options."

"Initially, my mom wanted to call me 'Julie.' My father wanted to call me 'Jessica' or 'Frangelica'—partly named after his favourite cousin Frances and he liked the name 'Angela.' And I suppose the last three letters 'ica' [carried over from] his desire for 'Jessica.' He slammed the words together, and I am happy I didn't get named similarly after a liqueur! At birth, the doctor who delivered me asked my parents what they would like to call me, and my mother blurted out 'Jennifer.' No rhyme. No reason. No actresses or relatives came to mind. Simply 'Jennifer.' My parents agreed, and it stuck."

"Because they thought the name Amy was too popular (and apparently they have a twisted sense of irony)."

2. Did you like your name as a child?

"I didn't hate or love my name, it was pretty common. There were Jennifers in all of my classes. You get used to hearing your name and assuming [whoever was saying it] probably wasn't [talking] about you."

"I've always liked my name. As a child, I never recall having an issue with my name."

"Yes, I liked my name as a child. It was a popular name. It felt safe from any schoolyard teasing or bullying, or tough pronunciation compared to many other children's experiences at school."

"Oh yes!"

"I didn't mind either way. But as I started to become independent and wanted my own identity, I started to spell it differently. [Jenny] In grade 4, I dropped one of the 'n's and added an 'i' (instead of a 'y.'). It fully stuck by grade 6. My mom and siblings even adopted it! My sixteenth birthday present was personalized plates with "JENI B." It recently occurred to me that this is pretty awesome . . . that everyone changed along with me—no questions or concern! I definitely did it because I didn't want to be ordinary."

"I didn't like Jennifer because it was often used when my mom was being serious or angry with me, and it sounded very formal to me. But I loved Jenny and went by that for years, until I decided I'd grown out of it and told everyone

I would be Jenn (with two 'n's!) from then on (around grade 12?). So I really like that the name had three options, and I really liked that it was tied to the name Guinevere, as I'm a romantic."

[From a Jennie, NOT Jennifer] "I didn't, I always wanted my sister's name, 'Ashley,' and because there were so many Jennifers everyone always assumed Jennie was short for Jennifer so just called me Jennifer by default, annoying when it isn't your name. Sometimes people would even argue with me thinking I didn't understand that Jennie was short for Jennifer and that I didn't understand that my name MUST be Jennifer, it couldn't possible be just Jennie. I also got a lot of commentary from Jennifers that HATED being called Jenny, they would go on and on about how much they hated being referred to by that 'short form' and talk to me like I too would understand the frustration of being referred to the shortened version of Jennifer. I never knew whether I should just agree or explain that in fact my name was Jennie NOT Jennifer."

3. Did your feelings about your name ever change?

"I've always been okay with my name. I've never wanted to change it—I've joked many times about how common it is but it's MY name and I like it. My name was given to me for a reason . . . so as common as it is . . . . I've always embraced it."

"I used to always hate it when I was younger because it was so popular and as a typical teenager I was fighting for individuality, but now I don't mind."

4. What do you remember about meeting other Jennifers?

"Every year in school there was at least one other Jennifer in my class, so I was never just 'Jennifer,' I was often 'Jennifer H.' Then one year there was another Jennifer H., so I had to be Jennifer Ho. and she was Jennifer He."

"One year there were three Jennifers in my class."

"In the summers I guide for Wild Women Expeditions. The owner of the company's name is Jennifer, my trip logistics coordinator's name is Jenny, and I am, of course, Jennifer. It gets very confusing for the clients."

"In my grade 12 French class, there were nine Jennifers (across grades 11, 12, 13). I liked it because if Madame Pinault called for one of us, there was a good chance someone else would answer before me."

5. When did you realize Jennifer was a very common name?

"I moved to a new school in grade 5 and it was then that all the Jennifers started popping up. When I started playing sports in grade 6 and heard the opposing coaches calling out "Jennifer!!"—I knew I had to start using a nickname so I wasn't distracted from what I was doing from turning my head every time I heard someone say, JENNIFER!"

"I remember reading an article in high school stating that Jennifer and Michael were the most common names for the most years running. I remember feeling awesome and then ordinary."

6. How many were in your high school graduating class?
"Maybe two or three."

(Without "outing" either of the Jennifers here, this respondent is ten years older than the next one. What a difference a decade makes . . . !)

"I do remember counting them all at one point and it was around twenty. There were so many Jennifers at my school . . . I think in my high school one year I counted a total of fifty-two Jennifers. I remember that number clearly because I couldn't believe one name was so common that there were THAT MANY in my small suburban school and all of us born within a few years of each other."

7. Which, if any, of the Jennifer nicknames do you use? Why?
"I have always liked my name in full or abbreviated as 'Jen' with one 'n.' My thoughts towards those individuals or groups of 'Jenn,' 'Jenifer,' 'Jeniffer,' 'Genifer,' 'Ginifer,' etc. are that they are trying to [peel off] from the popularity of the name 'Jennifer' to make it their own. They also don't realize that 'Jenn' with two n's is ridiculous to enunciate the extra 'n' using the syllable 'nifer' part of the name!"

"Jenn. It used to be 'Jen,' but then a guy at camped signed my yearbook (or whatever the camp equivalent of a yearbook was) 'To Jenn'—and that was it. I had a crush on him for about seven days and he changed the course of my life. His name, unremarkably, was Kevin. No special spelling."

8. How do you feel about the name Jessica in relation to Jennifer? (*I wanted to know because Jessica took over the most popular name spot for many years after Jennifer retired. Many respondents had no opinions, or just thought it was a nice name, but one got exactly what I suspected was the case . . .*).

"It's like a bootleg version of Jennifer. Similar, but not quite the original."

The evidence is clear, right? Despite knowing and living all the pitfalls of their popular name, Jennifers tend to love their name and seem to take special pride in sharing it with 800,000 others.

I was a little knocked over by this, to be honest. It goes against everything I believe about a unique name making you feel individual. I hung on to the idea that a rare name was a special name, which would mean I would grow into a special person. It didn't occur to me until . . . maybe right now . . . that the whole special-name-equals-a-special-person theory was constructed by me, purely for my own ease of use. I mean, it did occur to me, but I quickly dismissed it, because if a super common name doesn't have a downside—if it only nets feelings of pleasure and inclusion, then what's the point of my struggle?

There is a point, right?

When Popular Is Unpopular

To be popular is to be well-liked. But to be common is to be well-used—or even overused. When I speak to people trying to name their children, everyone wants something "uncommon," and the idea that a name might be reused or overdone is upsetting to parents—just one generation after Jennifer was often given to multiple girls in the same extended family.

I started thinking about this phenomenon recently. The idea that someone else might share your name was anathema to me, but fairly basic for everyone else I know. And even though Jennifer is the known juggernaut name of the '70s and '80s, it was Julie that always seemed to me to be the quintessential '70s name. Julies were cheerful and popular and good in school.

I asked Julie Nixon Rensch, of Seattle, about this idea of Julie being the sweet spot of a popular name that wasn't a juggernaut. Born in 1976, she enjoyed the comforts of name popularity—which became conflated with actual popularity. "Sometimes there were other Julies in a group or class, sometimes not. Whether that was good or bad depended on how badly I wanted to feel special or included. At times it felt like we were all in a club. As in 'Only Julies can sit here' or 'I can only share my snack with you if your name is Julie.'"

The exclusion put Julie on the inside—and it also gave her a clear vision as to what a Julie was meant to be. "Being a Julie—you were expected to be good, follow the crowd, not a rebel. Very middle of the road. I don't feel that way about myself now, but I do feel like Julie is the dressed-down version or make-under of the much lovelier and more classic names of Julia, Juliet, and Julianne."

This is the crux of things. To Julie, her "popular" name feels a dressed-down version of these other names—all of which are in very common use today, while "Julie" is almost entirely extinct among anyone born after 1982 (and another name that went underrepresented in pop-culture until years after the fact—Julie Taylor on *Friday Night Lights* has a notably anachronistic name).

It's so clear to me that people who grew up with the extremely popular names are making sure their own children don't have names that could be shared with six or eight other kids at a lunch table (Julie's daughter is Mirabelle). All the people whose names were the touchstones of their day have, in my extensive but anecdotal experience, gone out of their way not to change their names or the perceptions of them, but to pass on virtually none of them to the next generation. When Catherine the Duchess of Cambridge and Prince William announced their daughter was named Princess Charlotte, I was surprised, to say the least, because Charlotte is already in (very) popular usage. That's not what we've come to remember from royal names of yore, and I for one was really holding out for something unusual—the kind that's so sophisticated it initially seems borderline unattractive. Remember the outcry over Eugenie?

But my bigger surprise was the reaction of parents on name and parenting sites who were not delighted to share a name with the princess, but dismayed. Where once it would have indicated that anyone who chose Charlotte had made a wise, sophisticated choice, now it just seemed that it wasn't so special any more. "What if people only ever say 'Oh, like the princess?'" one mother worried online. I'm consistently surprised at how clearly sharing a name has gone from a benefit to a detraction.

The pitfalls aren't just egotistical, either. One recent Monday morning, a colleague, Emma, came into work, equal parts amused and mortified at the events of the weekend. Her five-year-old daughter Tessa had asked for a playdate with Mimi, who went to the same school and daycare. Emma followed daycare protocol and asked the teachers for Mimi's parents' contact information, set up the playdate, and told Tessa it was all arranged. When Mimi and her mother arrived on Saturday afternoon, Tessa bounded into the room, excited— but stopped short as soon as she saw Mimi and her mother.

"Mommy . . . where's Mimi?" Tessa asks. Which is when Emma, dumbfounded, looks at her daughter, wondering what she's missing.

"Honey . . . this is Mimi," Emma explains.

"No, it's not."

It turns out that the e-mail address given to make the playdate belonged to the parents of the "wrong" Mimi, since there are two Mimis in the same afterschool program. This is amazing to me, because we've come full circle. From the ordinariness of multiple Jennifers or Michaels or Julies in a classroom, to not even considering the idea that there might be more than one Mimi in a group. To me, Mimi still sounds fresh and unusual, so after hearing the story, I asked Mimi's mother Sarah whether she was surprised that a name like "Mimi" was subject to a mixup.

"I was surprised but not shocked. In some ways I'm actually more surprised that people don't name their kids Mimi more often, because to me, it's, like, SO obviously the best name. I knew we would run into another Mimi here and there, at the very least as a short form for another name. My husband was quite surprised though when we discovered there was another Mimi, we had gotten used to her being the only one, I guess."

She admits that maybe in the back of her mind she guessed there might be a case of mistaken Mimis at school, but didn't want to assume. "When I told Mimi her friend Tessa wanted to play with her, she had no idea who I was talking about. Was I a much less involved parent than I thought? Anyway I asked her teacher, and her teacher said that Tessa's in another class. My thought at that point was, okay, the kids have some shared outdoor time, and Mimi could have been playing with her all year and not known her name (she is four years old after all)."

As it turned out, the girls were confused for a few short minutes and then ran off to play. I don't believe the mixup is going to be anything but a funny story for either of them, or their parents. But I love how names cluster in particular places, and how schools can expand your world from being the only one to being part of everyone.

Tips for Surviving Elementary School with a Weird Name

• When a new teacher or substitute is calling the roll, you know where you fall, alphabetically. The moment she pauses? Don't hesitate—jump in there and say "I'm here."

• If she looks at you with confusion, take it as an opportunity to say your name properly, correctly—before she has a chance to mangle it, or to use your "traditional" name, a fate that befell Philip Guo until he wised up and announced his English name right away.

• Listen carefully as a teacher slowly and carefully pronounces your name. Don't be fooled. Even if the initial syllables she pronounces sound nothing like your name, don't assume she's pronouncing someone else's. She's experimenting. Don't hesitate to talk over her if you even think she might say the name in a way that's wrong or embarrassing—better to be rude than to be stuck with the kind of nickname you've been all-this-time desperate to avoid. (It only took one teacher who pronounced my name Du-een-ah before the wonderful kids known as my "friends" immediately seized upon "Duweenie!" That one stuck.)

• If the teacher wants to call you by one syllable or your last name, do not protest. Do not insist that your name is actually Apeksha or Duana or Wallis. Take it and run with it.

From a letter I received:

> My name [Myfanwy] is Welsh and although I love it now, I hated it from the ages of about 7 to 17. I always knew when it was my time on roll call because the teachers would just stop and I would inevitably just call out the shortened version of my name. Even this would garner teasing.

Although the stress I experienced with my name as a kid was real, and other people's stories support it, I wondered if all of this was just so much elementary school angst. Was it really so important later on, if you weren't me? I wanted unbiased opinions and also ones where nobody felt pressure to agree with me as I poured a second or third glass of wine. So I headed to an institute of higher learning to see whether names and their influence last longer than the pride at a fifth-grade graduation.

The University of Toronto is an august and storied institution boasting over 47,000 students. I visited the St. George Campus in the centre of Toronto and asked the first fifty students I saw, all between the ages of seventeen and twenty-eight, whether they liked their names, and whether they felt the names had had an effect on their success up to this point, and whether names might have a further effect on their ultimate success or failure. I could give you the stats, just tell you that 70 percent of them liked their names and most didn't see a correlation . . . but then you wouldn't get to hear what their names were.

• Adelaide thinks there could be a correlation between
    names and success, just not *her* name and success. She
    doesn't think "Adelaide" gives her any advantage or
    disadvantage, but maybe if she had a different name
    then she would think so? (I hate to coin a term in this
    time of political correctness on campus, but is this
    Name Privilege?) Adelaide likes her name fine.
• Noah likes his name but immediately compared it to his
    twin brother Aaron's. He wanted to know all about what

I was writing, quickly became the interviewer instead
of the interviewee, and told me that clearly I was wrong
in my idea that names could affect anything, because he
and Aaron have had similar successes all their lives, and
they have different names. When I suggested that Noah
and Aaron are maybe the same type of name, and
therefore perceived in kind of the same way, Noah got
one of those slow smiles on his face that you see in
commercials where people realize they've won the
lottery. Though it's hard for me to believe people never
consider names unlike their own, I watched Noah's
mind open up in the moment, and consider his name
a whole new way. That's the point of being the "Name
Therapist"—showing people they have stories and
feelings about their names they never realized.

- Jessica dislikes her name, but thinks yes, maybe, it has some-
      thing to do with success, because it's easy to remember.
- Mohammed looked at me for a moment, deciding whether
      I was asking something other than what he understood
      me to be asking, then said he liked his name—but didn't
      think it had anything to do with success or failure.
- Ranja likes her name. She thinks there's no correlation to
      success, but likes her name because nobody else has it.
- Elijah likes his name NOW, as in not before—because
      people call him Eli, which means he's achieved his goal
      of not being called Elijah, and liking his shortened
      name, he feels, makes him successful. See? SEE?
- Peter thinks people take him more seriously than people
      with names like Dylan or Liam which he calls not
      grown up names.

- Tariro doesn't like his name. He thinks names do have an effect on success, but says he doesn't want to talk about why. I'm speculating here, but when a reaction is that decisive, I think it's fair to say Tariro has had some situations in which he thinks his less-than-common name worked against him.
- Eda doesn't like her name and thinks people give preference to names that are easier to pronounce.
- Kyle's parents gave him this name because it sounded exotic to them, as Portuguese people. He can't stop smirking as he tells me this, so preposterous is it now, in Toronto, in 2015.

And here comes the shift:

- Giancarlo loves his name! He loves it! But when I ask about its effect, he says that to have an ethnic name is perceived negatively in North America. He says all of this without prompting and I consider asking him to be my assistant.
- Asha likes her name because it defines her.
- James thinks names do have an effect, because "I know about *Freakonomics*."
- Roxy is tired of people asking whether this is her "real name." Yes, it is, and yes, answering that question all the time has an effect on her.
- Guarav knows exactly what I'm talking about when I say "Starbucks names."
- Thebana says her name doesn't affect her academically, but knows that in the real world, it could.
- And my favourite, Abdulrahman, says, and I quote, "Yes!

I love my name, it's amazing!" He is standing with several friends, and I ask each of them about their names (Abdul, Amir, Yousif, and Daniel) but it's Abdulrahman who is vibrating with excitement waiting for me to reach him. I wish everyone were that delighted with their name! When I ask him why, he trips over his words trying to say that it sounds wonderful, and that the meaning, "The servant of God, who is merciful" (Abdulrahman phrases it a little less succinctly), is also important to him.

So okay, meanings of names matter to some—but I want everyone to feel that way. Bouncing with excitement to announce the way they are labelled.

Still, it kills me that in my random study, the kids with names that have any resemblance to an "ethnicity" are aware that names mean something, and those who sport "regular" names seem oblivious, or to give it less credence. It's your name! How can you not have thought about what people's perceptions are? Or are you lucky enough to think the perception is entirely neutral, because there have been so many of you?

Teacher's Pets

Here are extracts from letters I've received at Duana Names:

Help! We are expecting our second son in early October. We had a difficult time naming our first son but once he was born settled on the perfect name for him, Mathis Alexander. You see, my husband is a teacher and I work with rescue dogs and have had the privilege of naming hundreds of dogs over the years. Between the two of us we have a very impressive list of names we cannot use.

Here's the caveat: I have taught at an all boys school for over a decade. I teach middle and senior school classes and have, over this time, run into a variety of young men both awesome and nightmare-ish. As a result the field is narrowed. There are some "no-go" names for me as a result (Sean, Michael, Sebastian. . . . Sean and Michael were brothers by the way <shudder>).

One of my favourite ironies about names is that the loudest complaints about names often come from the people who are exposed to new names, and name trends, on a very regular basis. Every teacher I've ever met has definite opinions on names—because when they're working in an environment where everything else seems very much the same year-to-year (classroom, curriculum, age of children), boring names can become exponentially more boring, weird names seem absolutely outlandish, and the biggest complaint from all teachers? There are precious few names they *do* like, because they're always talking about the ones that have been ruined by less-than-stellar students. In fact, the same names that could have offered constructive answers and good behaviour last year could be a nightmare this year. I can see how you'd have some PTSD and some trust issues, if year after year you hoped Gregory to be different than the Gregory before him, and year after year you were disappointed you'd given him the benefit of the doubt.

For example, Tim, a high school music teacher, says he

cringes when he sees a particular name on a roster: "Chase. Unquestionably. You're literally saying your kid is going to be a pain in the ass to pin down." In fact, Tim is biased in general against "word" or verb names, like Hunter—but he relaxes that rule for "virtue names" like Grace or Faith, because he thinks people talk to those girls about what those names mean, and so they're more likely to try to live up to them. It doesn't escape my notice that there aren't any virtue names for boys— something I'll discuss further in a later chapter.

Hearsay, of course, all of it. But no teacher I speak to tells me they don't remember names, or that they all blend together. Stacy, a middle-school teacher in a major Canadian city, tells me she never needs to spend time with another Matteo. As soon as she walks in the room, she's on edge— she and Matteo just don't mix.

John teaches grade 1—an increasingly unusual position for men. So his "trigger names" are about ten or eleven years "younger," in terms of popularity, than the ones Tim reacts to. "Lucas is a weirdo. I'm sorry. Every time. This one kid thought he was a dolphin. Like whoa, Lucas!" Then he makes a credible dolphin noise. The kind you know he learned from endless repetition—not by choice. John also believes Daniels are going to, in his words, "Wind up on the six o' clock news." He pauses, in case I don't get it: "With body parts."

There is hope, though. Emmas, John says, can always take care of themselves, and they're smart, to boot. He's never had an Emma in ten years of teaching . . . "whose reading wasn't far-and-away the best in the class."

And one teacher knows the anxiety names can cause in the classroom. From a letter I received:

As a teacher, I give a fair warning when I learn students' names. I announce that I'll pause before each name and if your name is often mispronounced, jump in and tell me how to say it. I also include a pronunciation guide on my attendance for a supply teacher. Having a name that represents family or culture is beautiful.

But teachers aren't the only ones who carry stereotypes of certain names. We all do it. Mikita Brottman, who wrote about dog names, also wrote a piece in the *New York Times* about what it was like to date three different Davids. The movie *Heathers* was a cult hit that operated on the assumption that all its viewers would understand and agree that every high school girl named Heather was sadistic and power-hungry— at least in the 1980s.

I'm not immune—I tell all these teachers *I* think that all parents of boys named Justin expected their sons to be the handsomest one in the room. That they chose the name because it was slick and trendy sounding, and parents rewarded the things in Justins that made it true. This is half speculation and half pop-parenting book, but is a Justin more likely to be rewarded for a daring feat at the playground than a Myroslav? Is he going to be encouraged as much in chemistry as in track and field? Justin Timberlake is the archetype for this role, *obviously*, but he's not alone. Justin Bieber, Justin Theroux—all have the attitude of privileged boys who have always been beloved. Would Timberlake have half that swagger if he were Lawrence? Elio? No—Justin. Easy to say and to understand, and, because it rocketed out of obscurity in the early '80s, it felt very fresh and young and trendy. Now, since the world has discovered Canadian Prime Minister Justin Trudeau, the name has the chance to really grow up.

Ve Ri Tas

In my humble opinion, there is nothing that sounds as important yet is as nondescript as the "Ivy League." I don't remember exactly when I became fascinated with the colleges of the academically super-elite, but it was right up my alley to become a fan. Not because I ever thought I'd actually attend Harvard or Yale—even as a tween I knew that kind of academic achievement required a little more focus than I was able to muster—but because anyplace that deems itself the best of all schools and has a whole world of paraphernalia to wear, and fictional characters who aspire to it, is catnip to someone like me who will watch and read and go to anything that involves a school and classmates. We call this the "Hogwarts Principle."

Pop culture fetishizes these schools, from *Good Will Hunting* to *Gilmore Girls*. If you consume them in bulk, as I do, you think, why sure, if I went there, I'd be an academic marvel! Who wouldn't, in those beautiful old libraries and dorms devoted to the exploration of ideas and the expansion of intellect? If only you were there on that grassy quad, watching the trees shake their way down through fall in New Haven or Cambridge.

. . . . Just me, then?

Not surprisingly the Venn diagram that is my interest in names and my interest in schools shows a wide overlap. I had originally wondered whether the students who attended Ivy League universities had anything special about their names. Whether students who attend one of the most highly regarded institutions in the world are distinctive in the names they were given, or whether the distinction is that the names were utterly traditional and uninteresting. What's the actual allure of a place like Harvard, beyond the promise of meeting a math genius from Southie? It's an incredibly selective institution (just 5.3 percent of applicants to the class of 2019 were accepted) and, of course, it promises an extraordinary education.

And then I realized I had missed an amazingly essential question. Who's *giving* that incredible education? Who is qualified not just to be at this institution, but to form the minds that come out of it and wear the mantle of having received one of the most incredible educations money can buy?

What are *their* names?

I decided to analyze the first names of 5,984 Harvard faculty members, a healthy but not exhaustive sample from a range of faculties including Medicine, Education, Humanities, Business, Engineering and Government. I wanted to see what I could discover about any recurring themes in faculty names, if there were any. Was there someone most likely to teach at Harvard?

The answer is yes. His name is David.

Of those 5,984 faculty, David is the number one most recurring name: 174 occurrences, to be precise. Michael is the next most popular name, at 114 occurrences. Then Robert, John, James, Daniel, Richard, Joseph, William (only 53 Williams—I was sure there would be more), and so on through the "typical" names dictionary. The first female name to appear is, sing it with me, Jennifer. I came up with 42 Jennifers—tied with Mark—and 41 faculty named Elizabeth. The next most frequent female faculty names were Susan, then Nancy, then Laura, with Lisa, Mary, and Amy next in line.

I am no statistician, but it's clear to me that the names of the faculty that occur most frequently are "traditional." That is, that they're most commonly used in English-speaking families, especially given that some of the faculty are likely tenured professors who have been with the university for decades, who were born in a time when a much smaller selection of names was in popular usage, and when most of the people who would eventually work at Harvard were born in the United States. Then there's the over-whelming preponderance of "David." Are parents more inclined to encourage a David to become an academic than they are to encourage an Ethan? David's usage peaked in popularity in the 1950s, so it's reasonable to assume the name is so prevalent at Harvard some fifty years later because it's biblical, popular in virtually every country, and is common enough not to have a particular image associ-ated with it. Obviously, the same can't be said for Ethan—at least, not yet.

But popular versus unusual makes me look twice in this sampling as well. There are 668 names that appear in the faculty list at least twice (Tiffany, Shiladitya, Deirdre, and Fawwaz are all in this category). But there are another 1,615 names that are unique, meaning that 27 percent of our sample size have names that are unique in their already unique environment. I'm not saying their unique names were instrumental in getting them to a place where they are qualified for the highly selective academic jobs they hold, but I'm not sure I believe that it hurts.

So what does it mean? Ultimately a popular name finds itself in fairly dense company—within a certain self-selected group. After all, none of the Davids wound up at Harvard by chance—it was a deliberate goal to get there. Which means that not all Davids dream of teaching at Harvard, but that people who dream of teaching there might be more likely to be called David.

But not for long.

Name demographics in the workplace, including academia, will be fascinating over the next few decades as baby boomers retire, and their jobs are filled by men and women from all over the globe, something that was so much less likely just a generation ago. It's entirely likely that this same analysis done on Harvard faculty in forty years will show Isabella as the most popular faculty name. Or Shrajeel. Or Nevaeh.

Ultimately, I'm a romantic where education is concerned. I think school is the first, if not the best, place to discover who you are—to find out that everyone speaks slightly different languages, and that yours might be classics or economics or basketball. I love the academic environment, even though you basically could paraphrase all the comments on my report cards as "A little less conversation, a little more action." But it's the first place where our name defines us not just as identification, but in comparison to everyone else. It's heady stuff. Whether you are the fourteenth Stevie or the first Verushka, staking your place is never more important than among your peers. After all, the more you identify with your name, the more you become it.

In the fourth grade, I revelled in units on medieval culture and prayed that some assembly or fire drill would save me from the daily indignity of flailing through long division. That year my name first became associated with a specific quality, Mr. Spurr, our "core" teacher, asked us one morning to write down ideas for the class Christmas play—yes, at a public school. We've come a long way.

I remember being a bit disillusioned by Christmas that year, and very aware that I was supposed to be caught up in the magic of it all. I was having increasingly demanding conversations with my parents about why, if Santa Claus didn't exist, people kept making TV movies about him. I'm not the first kid to get annoyingly forensic about needing "proof" of Santa Claus, but that "nobody believes but everyone's pretending" phase seems really exhausting for all involved.

That was what I thought about as I scribbled down my ideas, and I remember that I wrote them in play format. I don't think I was bold enough to name the characters—they were Kid 1, Kid 2, and so forth—but I'm pretty sure there was a "Christmases in Medieval Times" theme brewing in the script. The only line I remember verbatim is, "And since I'm eleven, I always have to put up the Christmas lights!" I had no idea whether or not these were the ideas that he was looking for, but it was a better assignment than a book review. I handed my notes to Mr. Spurr and put it out of my mind.

I found Mr. Spurr intimidating. He was a gruff man in his mid-fifties who didn't suffer the foolishness of fourth-graders lightly, and—crucially—he taught gym, which for years had been part of the reason I was afraid of him. Nowhere were my inadequacies more obvious than in the physical arena. I have joked about it for years, but my gross motor skills were so lacking in my primary school years that when I was about seven years old, the school called my mother and told her I might have muscular dystrophy. I couldn't manage to walk on a balance beam or even along a bench six inches off the floor. I couldn't catch a ball; I couldn't evade a ball coming at me.

As a result, I am the only person I've ever known to have participated in remedial gym classes. People think I'm joking, but I'm dead serious. They may not have been called that, but twice a week for a number of years, I met Mr. Spurr in the gym for extra lessons while he tried to teach me the most basic elements of physical activity. He was patient, but couldn't hide how shocked he was that his step-by-step careful teaching was not helping me to improve my physical skills whatsoever. Our relationship in those sessions was strained—I knew I couldn't make him happy, and I hated gym so much I couldn't even care.

So I cringed when, a couple of days after I wrote the Christmas script, Mr. Spurr called me to his desk. I didn't know whether there were going to be more gym classes scheduled or whether the jig was up with regard to counting on my fingers underneath my desk. I noticed he had a number of photocopied pages spread out on his desk. The first two had my rounded childish printing all over them.

"This is our Christmas play," he told me. "I think we should call it *Time-Travelling Christmas.*" I nodded, not quite sure what he was getting at.

He turned over a title page on his desk and showed it to me. *Time-Travelling Christmas* was on top, and below it read "Written by Duana Taha & Ken Spurr."

It was my first writing credit.

I suppose it could seem as though he did it out of pity, given that grade 4 was rough overall. But it didn't occur to me then. I never worried that Mr. Spurr might have done this out of concern that I needed something special, because I sure as hell wasn't going to get a place on the gymnastics team. It's conceivable that that was why he made that decision.

But when I took my script home—the same one that was photocopied for the entire class—it had the title page with both our names on it for all the kids to see. When I learned my lines, they were the ones I had written. And those two pages I wrote were, unchanged, the beginning of the script, and they were the ones we performed in the show. Afterward, the principal and other teachers said "Oh, and here's Duana, our writer!"

Duana, our writer. School is the place that defines us, and our names.

7

BE TRUE TO GERTRUDE
Starbucks Names, Identity Crises, and Name Pain

Taylor Swift was not around when I entered high school to remind me to "take a deep breath, girl." I would have appreciated knowing it was okay to feel so overwhelmed. I was elated to be accepted to my arts high school, and was expecting an environment like *Fame*, without the grit or under-age exposure of breasts. I assumed there would be a lot of earnest kids trying to follow their dreams and spontaneous musical numbers breaking out in the cafeteria. In reality, my high school was a laid-back, any-thing-goes kind of place for kids to figure out who they are, but compared to my mental picture it was *Trainspotting*. There was a lot of angst, eyeliner, and everyone but me had been issued a pair of combat boots along with the requisite ripped tights. The worst part about the whole endeavour was that as I walked around, shy and unsure of myself, I was aware that I was representing what "Duana" was to 2,500 new classmates. This was a whole world of new people who didn't know me, and I had the opportunity to define my name in a whole new way—to live up to whatever it was supposed to be—but I wasn't doing it. Instead, I was busy doing things I didn't know would become synonymous with my name. Like, somehow it escaped my knowledge that most other would-be young adults were making it through the day without spilling lunch on their shirts. Not me. I didn't realize I was making a reputation for myself. If someone said something disparaging about "that girl Duana" there was nowhere to hide. No doubt about which person I was (and no normality by association with a normal name to soften the blow).

Everyone around me seemed to know who they were, and who they were was very, very cool. I would watch, making no attempt to disguise that I was desperate to know how they did it. I shared a bus stop with an impossibly glamorous Nathalie. She had a fierce eyeliner game and a penchant for her hair cut in layers before that was cool, and I decided it must be the Gallic influence of her French-inspired name that gave her the confidence. I have no idea if this was true because we never spoke once in four years. A guy named James announced in a crowded hallway that he was so disillusioned with the end of *A Tale of Two Cities* that he threw the book across the room, giving us the impression that this particular brand of literary overwroughtness (and Facial Stubble as Emotional Depth) was what it was to be "James." Later evidence has shown me that I wasn't entirely wrong.

I was judging, I guess, but that wasn't a bad word yet in the 1990s, and besides, could you blame me? I was trying desperately to find out more about people. How they defined themselves.

New Year, New Name?

So why didn't I just not *be* Duana? Given that my name felt like a burden, I had realized around ten that maybe a nickname was the answer. Perhaps what I needed was a respite from having to define who and what a "Duana" was, and usually finding that the reality was far away from who I would have liked her to be.

So I decided to change my name. Instead of waiting for a brand-new environment to do so, I had announced to a classroom full of people I'd known for years that I would like to be called Dawn.

Dawn? I wish I were kidding. Dawn?

I know that we are supposed to be kind to our former child selves and that back-then Duana didn't see exactly why this was a losing proposition. But I know what I was trying to do. I was trying to mimic the kids who were called Maggie for Margaret, or Billy for William, and I couldn't find anything that went with Duana. I was trying, I realize, to mimic the immigrant method of choosing an anglicized name that somehow resembles their given name, in the way that Jaswan becomes John. But though Dawn had a tenuous connection to Duana, it was kind of airy and silly. (And it was patently obvious that I had just lifted it from *The Baby-Sitters Club*, which is an advertisement for onomatopoeia in names if I've ever heard one. "Dawn" was the hippie, California-transplant character who ultimately couldn't hack it on the East Coast. "Claudia" was the exotic artsy one. "Mary Anne" was good and wore braids, because you couldn't just name her character "meek and boring.")

Not surprisingly, my classmates, who had known me for years, did not accept "Dawn." I'd violated the first rule of having a nickname. You don't give it to yourself. My insistence on the "new" name faded after a few days, but the teasing lasted for weeks.

I always think of that experience when I remember a guy named Charles. At least, that's how he's known now. Charlie is a very trendy name for preschoolers and kindergarteners today, but growing up in the 1980s and '90s, Charles was virtually the only one we knew. He didn't go by Charles, though, or Charlie—it was Chuck. This stood out not just because it was not the trendy nickname of the time—that would have been Charlie, I think, since there would at least have been a refrence to the actor Sheen, but because Charles and Charlie and Chuck were all very rare when we were growing up. But Chuck it was, and it was difficult.

First, because "upchuck" was the acceptable slang term for throwing up at a time when "barf" and "puke" were words restricted to the no-man's-land of the school bus. There is nothing more thrilling to school-aged kids than teasing that can go on under the teacher's nose, without even lowering one's voice, and a lot of it went on in our middle school classroom.

"Oh man, I'm going to UpCHUCK" was a popular refrain. The inverse worked, too. "What's up, Chuck?" sounds innocent if you're a teacher not paying attention. If you're a kid already teetering on the precipice of the nausea that comes from a distinct lack of popularity, you know that such an innocuous question is just an innovative way to insult you. The extra sting is when the ammunition for harassment is built into your name.

Still, this *wasn't* the worst of it. The worst was the "Name Game." You know that song where you use your name and its first letter to customize the syllables of the lyrics? "Shirley! Shirley, Shirley bo Birley, Bonana fanna fo Firley, Fee fy mo Mirley, Shirley!" Endless fun. "Lincoln! Lincoln, Lincoln bo Bincoln Bonana fanna—" You get the idea.

But Chuck heard it more than anyone. Want to take a guess at why? "Chuck Chuck bo Buck, Bonana fanna fo . . ." and, after a furtive glance to see if there were any adults around, the song continued, to Chuck's consternation. What can you do when your name rhymes with "a swear word"? How do you counteract the fact that people can tell you to "f-word" off, basically, under the guise of a totally school-sanctioned song?

Chuck bore the songs and chants of "UpChuck! UpChuck!" with as much grace as he could—in fact, I remember him working hard to be calm, but it had to be difficult. Sure, anyone can be made a target, but there are no profanities that, off the top of my head, rhyme with "Kirsten." All kinds of kids can be dumped on—but "four-eyes" can get contact lenses, and the fat kid might slim down. What do you do when the insult is your name? When the problem is the only part of you there's no way to outrun?

So Chuck tried to change his name. As we got older, he made more and more of an effort to use "Charles." Mostly it didn't land, or, if it did, it was mockingly. "Chuck—sorry, 'Charles.' He thinks he's the dad from *Little House on the Prairie*." I'd love to say that the end of this story was that Charles made peace with Chuck, and that it taught me your name burden is as easy to slip off as a pair of shoes, but unfortunately, the truth is not so simple and also, not so flattering—to me, not to him.

Most of the kids in our small eighth-grade class were continuing in the gifted program for high school. But I was gunning like mad, instead, for the high school for the arts, north of the city. The polar opposite of the gifted program, the arts school demanded a commitment to one particular art for four years, and basically seemed to me to be a direct ticket to Hollywood—if I could just get into the drama program, surely the rest of my career as an undoubtedly famous actress would be a piece of cake. The school reportedly accepted just a fraction of its applicants, and each time someone commented derisively that "it sounds like you're going to the school from *Fame*," I secretly revelled in the comparison. I was going to go to *Fame*, or at least a suburban Toronto equivalent of the famous Fiorello LaGuardia High School for the Performing Arts. I was going to be famous. Leave everyone behind and start anew, with people who knew nothing of "Dawn."

Apparently, Chuck felt exactly the same way.

So when we started in our huge new school with all new classmates who didn't know either of us, Chuck and I wound up in a lot of the same classes. Each time—or at least a few times—when he introduced himself as Charles, I snickered a little or at least asked him, pointedly, "Don't you mean Chuck?"

I wish I could blame this on ignorance or a tone-deaf misunderstanding. But the truth is I was so out of my element, surrounded by kids who seemed older and more sophisticated than I was, that I needed any opportunity to feel like, no matter how low on the totem pole I was, at least I wasn't the bottom. So I put Charles there instead. Nice, huh?

I'm sure I wasn't the only reason that the name "Chuck" was mentioned in our high school. I'm sure Charles slipped up, and that someone else knew him from swimming lessons or something, and that in 1993, when 80 percent of my classmates were named Greg and Christopher and Lindsay, people snickered a little at the very formal "Charles." It wasn't *only* because of me. But I looked into the face of someone else with name pain, and I snickered. It was as if I didn't know what it was to be someone whose name was a cross to bear.

New (Nick)Name, New Life

While friends of my parents or other grown-ups had occasionally said my name was "beautiful," I was stunned the first time someone my own age asked me about my name and said "Oh, that's kind of exotic."

Pardon me?

But it kept happening. That name is "unusual," "amazing," even "enchanting." From people called Amanda or Erich. It was almost as if the positive expectation for my name was more important than the damage I was doing to it. Like I had a responsibility to my name to be more than just a standard geeky girl like the lead character in the film *Welcome to the Dollhouse,* whose pariah status, it's implied, is earned because she's just so . . . her. (This wasn't just an idle comparison, either. First of all, when I watched the movie at my house with a couple of friends, my mother passed through the room, looked at the television, and tittered, "Oh look, it's Duana!" Thanks, Ma. Then, to add insult to injury—the main character? The one whose lack of cool is the premise for the whole movie? Her name is *Dawn.* Memories of times I tried too hard were never far away.

Circa "Dawn." What you can't see is that my turqoise pants and shirt contrast with my fuschia purse and shoes. Sigh.

So, two revelations. One, people liked my name more than I did. That was great, but it meant that, two, I wasn't yet the person my name seemed to say I should be. So who did I want to be, exactly—and how the hell was I going to get there?

The people who were, in my opinion, defining the standards for their names seemed to have some qualities in common with each other. They all said smart things out loud and nobody rolled their eyes at them. In fact, their smart statements were usually followed by that brief pause that indicated everyone knew it would be lame to applaud, but they wanted to, nonetheless. Kezia was like this. One of the many Jens was like this. Sabrina comes to mind. Bev was like this, changing the name, for me, from a "mom name" to one that meant mouthy and sassy and smart. Chris and George and Ian—lots of boys embodied this self-assurance I coveted, and they didn't have unusual names to begin with.

But the more I watched Sasha and Nathalie and Ian and everyone else growing into people, the more I realized I wasn't living up to the exoticism or sassiness or individuality my name was supposed to impart. So I felt a failure as a Duana. Super.

I wish I could take credit for the solution that extricated me from this navel-gazing obsession, but I can't. What happened was that people in school started to call me "Du."

My parents quite frequently shortened my name to this one-syllable nickname, but I was surprised and delighted when people at school adopted it, because, as we've established, you can't nickname yourself. The short name felt like belonging, even if it was actually just my classmates saying the only syllable they could reliably be sure was contained in my name. "Du" wasn't sultry and international, necessarily, but she was talkative and opinionated and energetic, and those were good places to start.

Nicknames are an essential part of the name game, and are an established way to distinguish between the swaths of men called John. Particularly for men, nicknames are used to create a sense of intimacy, or at least, to create a little distance from a very formal first name. One of the best example of how nicknames can become as prevalent as names themselves is the fact that all stuffed toy bears are called "Teddy bears," after Theodore Roosevelt. A political cartoon in the *Washington Post* depicted Roosevelt showing mercy to a captured bear his handlers had captured for him to kill, and, struck by the image, a toymaker coined "Teddy's bear." The rest is history, of course—except that even here, there is "Name Pain"—Roosevelt hated being called Teddy, because it reminded him of his beloved first wife, Alice, who had used that endearment for him. He wanted to distance himself from it so he'd never have to feel the pain of it again. In fact, Roosevelt's name pain goes deeper—the loss of Alice affected him so deeply that he also stopped calling his daughter, who was named after her mother, by her name after he remarried. She was variously known as Baby Lee or "Sister," but never Alice any more. Nicknames are useful as an escape from all kinds of name pain.

But they're usually born of affection or tradition—a Tobias at a new job may find himself immediately called Toby and have no way to escape from it, or a group of cousins, when one brings home a girl he's dating called Jess, immediately formalizes it to Jessica because that's what their family would default to. My favourite third-person nickname story came from a woman in her forties, who nonetheless couldn't keep the derision out of her voice as she told me about an acquaintance called "*Raquel*," air quotes and heavy sarcasm hers. "She was nicknamed 'Kelly' for years, until suddenly she wanted to be taken seriously one year in her late teens, and she became *Raquel*. Please." Switch back from your nickname at your peril.

Nicknames were always a bit confusing to me growing up, though God knows I tried to wear them. Maybe the reason I don't love a nickname today is because of how poorly I executed trying to "acquire" one. But there were people around me doing the nickname thing to much greater effect. I should have paid more attention.

Johnathan Nightingale, Chief Product Officer at Hubba, a retail software company, has a serious job with high stakes—in fact, current estimates say there are half a billion users around the world. And Johnathan uses his childhood nickname professionally. The one he was given in seventh grade, due to a clerical error.

"Nightingale, Johnathan, didn't fit on a twenty-character attendance register," he remembers. The last-name-first system meant that only half his first name appeared on the page. "The teacher read it out loud as 'Johnath,' emphasis on the first syllable, and it stuck. I know I didn't hate it because I didn't resist when other people started using it. I adopted it pretty quickly."

This, to me, is the key. Johnathan definitely didn't ask for the nickname, or try hard to get people to use it—his lack of eagerness may be what made it so attractive to everyone else. In fact, it became everyone's name for him, not just his. "I had enforcers that I didn't expect to have. I remember a new kid joined our social circle. Maybe new to the school, maybe just new to us. And he called me 'John'—and the whole group lurched because nobody called me John. I don't care; I'll answer to both. But as far as that group was concerned, I had a nickname and it was Johnath. If you knew it, you were allowed to use it. You'd only know it by being around our group of friends, particularly digitally but in person as well."

Oh yes, digitally. The kids in this group were very into BBSes, short for (online) bulletin-board systems. You would get an external modem, which was a product that half the stores hadn't heard of at that point, "convert" your IBM-ripoff computer to Commodore 64 mode, and then log onto chat rooms with an online alias. While some people chose overwrought handles like "Extreme" or "Livewire," Johnath simply chose "Johnath." It worked out well for him, so he saw no particular reason to stop: "Every time you sign up for some new service or some new identity, first of all, Johnath's usually available because it's an uncommon nickname, which is nice. If you see a Johnath [somewhere online], it's probably me even if there's no identifying information."

The ability to set himself apart from a group, particularly online, is huge for Johnathan—which might explain why he brought his nickname into his adult life. He could have invented new digital identities. Instead, he used the name that set him apart—something his "regular" first name was never going to be able to do.

Stealth First Names

There are other people whose "regular" first names are similarly unmeaningful. For these people, there is virtually no connection to their names at all. They walk among us, barely batting an eyelash as you shout their given names. They don't care. I call them the Stealth First Names.

These are people who reveal, usually after you've known them for three to ten years, that they don't actually use their given first name, but go by a middle that you've been calling them for years—or even some sort of stand-in name. The part that makes this most upsetting to those of us who actually adhere to the name we're given? Usually the reveal happens in some sort of intimate situation—that is, when you're comfortable enough with a friend that they hand you their credit card to sign for the pizza, or you're in line at security for your first vacation together and idly browse their passport, and then: ". . . Who the hell is Elizabeth Stamatina Fey?"

Okay, so I haven't been in line for an Acapulco getaway with Elizabeth Stamatina (Tina Fey, to you) or for that matter with Vera Mindy Chokalingam (yeah, you guessed it—Mindy Kaling). But, though celebrities are major trendsetters where names are concerned, they are merely a symptom of this major epidemic, which, I promise, is happening all around you. J. Edgar Hoover or G. Gordon Liddy are names that nod to this effect, but most of the time it's in super secret. First names unused, lurking on government documents, making you feel like an awesome spy when you discover them.

Why have a Stealth Name?

I sat down with one of my first-known offenders to find out. I was really looking forward to my drink with Garrett. I had already known him for years when working at adjoining desks at an entertainment show one day, I heard him booking a flight over the phone. "James Garrett Wintrip," he announced to our travel provider.

I spun around in my cubicle to stare at him. Since when? Why? Who says? Garrett shrugged. My incredulous reaction didn't mean anything to him—he couldn't process my surprise and I couldn't understand his nonchalance. Nearly a decade later, I asked him for the full story—one he doesn't think is quite as amazing as I do. "My full name is James Garrett Wintrip. I think my parents liked both names but that they thought Garrett James sounded worse than James Garrett, which I agree with."

I will hear this over and over again—that "First, Second" sounded better than "Second, First."

But what follows is pretty amazing. "Did you ever meet another Garrett?"

"No. Well —" He hesitates, and I raise an eyebrow at him. "I was on Grindr once and I think there was a Garrett. I was just like, 'that would be weird.'"

Grindr, of course, is a "geosocial networking application aimed at gay, bisexual and bicurious men," or in common parlance, a hookup app. It hadn't occurred to me before now that you could search these apps by name.

We look at each other. I start to grin at him. I know Garrett, and I know that if you want him to be up for the next adventure—usually another drink or a cigarette, back when we were young and naughty—it has to be his idea.

"I'm going to go on Grindr right now. And I'm going to search Garrett," he said.

"Oh good. Now *this* is an experiment."

But Garrett actually prefers the search function on a different app, so we boot over to it. This app of course not only lists all the people with the name, but how geographically close they are to us. The screen fills with people all named Garrett—or using it as their screen name. It's a buffet.

Obviously, I understand logically that not everyone who has the same name is going to be similar, as The Jennifer Survey made abundantly clear. But as I scan all the Garretts, I find myself for looking for one who has some physical characteristic in common with *my* Garrett, something in a thumbnail photo on a tiny phone that indicates they have a similar wry sense of humor or outlook. Which is ridiculous—but unlike any given Jen, Garrett is the only Garrett I know, so all of his traits are more firmly tied to that name.

Garrett, on the other hand, is more amazed by the possibilities.

G: Oh my God. Can I pick my favourite one? Look at them all!

D: How does that make you feel?

G: Oh my God. (laughing) I love this!

D: Do you feel a bit narcissistic right now?

G: I don't even know how I feel. It's so weird. We should all get together.

D: You should.

G: Now I'm just finding the good-looking ones. Like I like *that* Garrett.

D: He's super cute. And that's a good picture. There are so many Garretts!

G: They just keep coming.

I actually have trouble counting how many Garretts there are, because they just keep loading and loading. Ultimately we are presented with over 200 Garretts, though of course not all of them are within walking distance.

Garrett promises to tell me if he decides to go on a date with any of them, and I keep asking him to do so. Who would have thought you could date your own name?

It's a phenomenon I hadn't thought of before, and that seems shortsighted. While more and more names are becoming used for both sexes, Adrian and Adrienne together, or even George and Georgina, isn't quite the same thing as Greg and Greg or Sarah and Sarah. Then again, maybe it's not happening. Maybe it's a taboo, or too silly to talk about, since nobody chooses a partner based on their name (. . . right?). I decide to ask Dean McArthur.

Dean, a social worker in Brooklyn, lives with his boyfriend, Michael, an artist. This is completely run-of-the-mill except for the fact that Dean is actually also a stealth first-name Michael. This probably doesn't affect other people the way it does me: I can't stop thinking about it. Luckily, this is one of the reasons that Dean and I are friends. He says, "I feel like it's a bit of a punchline or something to end up dating a guy with the same name as you. I think they have that on *American Dad*. So when people are asking questions about us as a couple I'll joke about it, but even though I'm the one joking about it, I feel a little weird, like I'm relying on something homophobic to make a joke."

"Like, you're pointing it out before someone else can?"

Dean explains. "It's just a bit . . . lazy. Like, yeah, a lot of men have the same name, because a lot of men have the same name. It's like when people tell me and Michael that we look alike, which my mom does all the time, I want to say 'Well, we're both men,' but other than that we don't really look alike. Also if you could magically turn heterosexual couples into the same gender there is no doubt that lots of them would end up looking the same."

What we're getting at, here, of course, is that there are just so many damned people named Michael. It was the number one name for boys for close to forty years. The fact that Dean himself is named Michael only reinforces the familiarity of the name. Dean says: "I have ambivalent feelings about the name Michael. I think Dean is actually really cool and unique and special AND associated with *The Gilmore*

Girls, but then I have this Michael in front of it reminding me that I'm kind of ordinary. Does that make sense?"

Yes, actually. In fact, ordinary is the word that often comes to mind. Stealth first names are generally given because they fit some sort of propriety requirement. Either the first name is there to honour someone— a grandfather or a saint—or the name "just sounded better" with the first name first, but never to be used.

This is actually what we usually do with middle names. We choose them for rhythm and flow as much as for strength of sound or meaning—and then we rarely use them again. It's such a waste of names (and some people feel so strongly about this waste that they don't give them at all, something I can't conceive of. Why choose fewer names when you could have more?).

But more and more I'm discovering that stealth first names aren't real first names because they wouldn't fit the "brand" of the person wearing them. The actress Karen Lucille Hale would seem to have an antiquated "mom" name if she used her first name. But Lucy Hale, her professional name, sounds entirely appropriate to appeal to her teenage demographic. Robyn Rihanna Fenty has less impact than simply being Rihanna. In fact, celebrities are the biggest source of stealth first names—Troyal Garth Brooks (Troyal!) is one of my favourite examples. In "real life," stealth firsts are often used because the preferred first name is either too formal, too common, or too odd. Interestingly, men seem to have first names that are "too common." Henry Ross Perot stands out more, to me, when he uses his middle name. So too do Joseph Rudyard Kipling and Keith Rupert Murdoch.

Women, on the other hand, tend to go by names that are less formal than the first ones on their birth certificates. I know a Josephine who went by Joy, an Adrienne who uses Elaine, and my friend Heather is actually first-named "Melanie" after a father's ex-girlfriend.

Most stealth-first-namers I spoke to, like Dean, Garrett and Heather, don't have any particular feelings associated with their stealth firsts, and why should they? They're never called by them, and don't have any negative associations to hide or positive ones to build on. Stealth first names are essentially middle names, just put up front. But there is another kind of "stealth" name to which people are far more invested, because the names are connected to a basic human need. Caffeine.

The Secret World of "Starbucks Names"

Names are my job, in a way, but my name comes up all the time for a reason unrelated to name therapy:

Coffee.

I love coffee so much. It's my favourite drink. I would drink it at every meal (and I have) if the health effects were not dubious and the caffeine content alarming. Brewed coffee, very hot, very strong. Black. I know this is the way and the light because I was brought up this way, where my parents regularly polished off two pots between them on a weekend morning, and where the commencement of my coffee drinking, around age twelve, was regarded with the quiet, misty-eyed pride a lot of people apply to their children's *actual* commencement. It is not unusual for me to wake up, have a coffee, and then purchase another as soon as I leave the house.

But now in coffee shops it's customary for the server to ask for a name with each order. This seems silly to me. I don't really know why it matters whether the coffee jockey I'm never going to see again spells my name correctly. It doesn't feel to me like they're neglecting our friendship. But they ask, every time. A lot of people, I notice, spend a lot of time correcting them. (Remember Karen who was horrified to be called "Ken"?).

So for ease of use, and to close the gap between me and my precious, I just use a quick, easy-to-understand pseud-onym—a "Starbucks name." Usually Dana (although if they mishear "Diana" I'll answer to that too.) In fact, Dana is my alter ego for ordering pizzas, getting help in overly-friendly electronics stores, and for sales assistants who want to cheer-ily write your name on your dressing room door. It is short, easily understood, and completely forgettable.

It's not my name. But it doesn't need to be, as long as I can remember my alias long enough to pick up my coffee. I would have thought most people would agree with me. But there are Tumblr pages called "That's not my name, Starbucks" where people post pictures of the misspelled names the brave baristas Sharpie onto each cup. People care—far more than I would have thought. You can divide pretty much everyone into two categories. Those who know what a Starbucks name is, and have one at the ready, and those who have never realized that such a concept exists.

The perfect Starbucks name is like a secret code: an easy, go-to name to import into situations where your actual name, and the explanation therein, causes more problems than it's worth to unpack the spelling of your name and answer the obligatory question about the origin or spelling that comes as a result. They range from in-jokes to the most oft-heard misspellings of a rarer name. My friend Paolo tells me, disgustedly, that his Starbucks name is "Paulo." Hilding prefers to use the name of whomever he's with as a Starbucks name. He orders first and when asked for his name, says "James," so that James, behind him, has to make up a name of his own.

I mean, it's fun. It's not a big deal. I could never understand why it matters if the barista gets your name wrong—although I did laugh hard at the story I read online of a man who told the barista his name was "Marc with a 'c'" and received a cup that read "Cark"!

Instead, why not just give them one that's hard to screw up? This is a policy that works for me and, as mentioned, one I field-test several times daily. So when getting a coffee with a friend in Los Angeles one day I was asked for my name and responded, as usual, with "Dana."

Jessi looked at me in shock. "What did you just say?"

"Dana?"

"Dana? Who the hell is *Dana*?"

A word about Jessi—she is a woman who uses this contraction of her given name (Jessica) all of the time, in every situation, and has done so for as long as she can remember. Professionally, personally—she is never, ever Jessica. The name makes her shudder—for herself, anyway, she's completely dissociated from it. I once heard her answer a question about the name on her driver's licence and even then she had to correct herself: "Jessi—uh, Jessica." So she understands about what one prefers to be called.

I'm nonchalant but defiant as I explain—it's too much work to spell "Duana" to every person I order a coffee or a handroll from. Why does it matter? Besides, the frustration of having to spell it is just not worth it. They're gonna mishear me, I'm going to correct them, and it's a disposable cup. Who cares?

"Okay, but—"

"What, '*Jessi*?' Are you going to tell me you know my pain?"

"If you're using a fake name to begin with, why not, like Esmeralda? Why not be Princess Destiny? If you're going to have a whole alter ego every time you get a coffee, why not?" She sips her tea, but she's still clearly confused. Like how could I possibly be neglecting such an opportunity?

I've learned that asking for a name and endeavouring to get it spelled exactly right is part of a Starbucks customer service mandate. But I've had my name exponentially longer than anyone in Starbucks' head office, and I know that whatever pleasure I get from Instagramming my correctly spelled name on my cup would not be worth the spelling and the talking and the explaining. Ironically, the names Jessi suggests are fun, but they're not any easier than my own name. The whole point of a Starbucks name is to be easy. The idea of experimenting with whether April or Aviva is easier to "get away with" doesn't appeal. I just want to get coffee with no questions asked. Is that so crazy?

Name Pain

Ironically, I'm at a Starbucks trying out different names when I meet a barista called Kendree. I know this is her name, of course, because it's written in bright marker on her nametag. As I take it in, I can see her face settling into a resigned look. She can see me looking at her nametag, and she knows I'm going to ask about her name. I know this face. I've worn it a million times. It's the one where you try to keep your face neutral as possible in the face of what's coming your way, which is sure to be insulting.

It's kind of amazing what people will say about the name you wear. I've been told that my parents must have been smoking something, that they obviously didn't like me, or that they must have gotten my name wrong. So I'm not surprised when Kendree tells me that apparently it's a Scottish/British/Irish surname, one her parents chose to honour that part of their heritage. She is regularly told by people that she's spelling it wrong, and has perfected the helpless smile of being unable to tell people what she thinks of their comments—at least, not while she's working. I wonder whether she has a Starbucks name of her own.

Name pain is particularly troubling because there are no self-help manuals on how to get by if everyone mispronounces or mocks your name. There are no manuals for rejoinders when someone in grade 11 pretends, loudly, that they think your name is "Do-ya-wanna." But most people whose names give them trouble have two choices. Either adapt the name, or evolve your thinking.

My father was the first to teach me about the "adapt your name" method. In fact, he used Starbucks names before anyone else I know—except in his case they were actually Random Electronics Store names. He never told anyone his real name, Gamal, when they wanted to act like buddies to sell him whatever counted as the gadget du jour. Why allow them to stumble over his name or condescend because they suddenly realized he might be foreign or try to bond with him over Malcolm-Jamal Warner? (Actually, my dad got a kick out of a famous guy "sharing" his name, albeit with a soft "j" where my dad has a hard "g," but he resented that someone *else* got to make it well known). He became "Jim" in those situations, and then, once the ruse was in place, why not throw in a couple of false details? Once he said he was buying a TV for his son to take to college. I can only assume he was talking about my long-lost brother Niall.

The other way to get through name pain is to evolve your thinking. My friend Lucky has had to do this many times over, not least a couple of summers ago, when the song "Get Lucky" was heard absolutely everywhere. At this point, I assume she's heard every joke in the book—so she's neither surprised nor bothered by any of them.

But real name pain—the kind where hearing your own name every day is a difficult experience—seems to come in two distinct types. The first is from people who don't feel in control of their names, or of what people call them. Ask a Beth whether she ever calls herself Liz, and watch her shudder. An Edward who introduces himself that way is necessarily annoyed when you call him Ted. Nor are nicknames the only places this happens. The thing about name pain is that everyone has an opinion on just about every name. This is one of the reasons I first understood what it

was to be the Name Therapist—everyone's experience
with their name is largely due to the way strangers react to
it. Do they smile and nod, or do they gawk? If they do,
what's your plan?

I once met a saleswoman who was chatty and personable, and who glanced at my credit card as I paid for my
I-shouldn't-be-buying-this pricey purchase. She asked me
about the pronunciation of my name, and when I answered
her she smiled and said, "I love unusual names!" Well, great.
So do I, and you just became my favourite person in this
retail mecca. What else do you want to sell me?

She was wearing a name tag that read Marijana. She saw
me looking and said, "I mean, because of my name, I think
about names a lot."

I nodded knowingly. "You probably get Mary-Jana all
the time, huh?"

But no, of course that's not what she was called.

"They call me *Marijuana*," she informed me, flatly. I
read her nametag again and realized. Marijana. Of course
they do—even though the actual pronunciation, "Mary-
anna," is not so difficult to imagine. "And then," she continued, warming to her frustration, "They get really super-rude.
'Oh, what the hell were your parents thinking? Oh, what a
terrible name!'"

The thing about terrible names, of course, is that we're
almost completely incapable of thinking our own names
are terrible. It's only in the context of someone else's opinion that they are awful, and then the name is reflected back
to you in all its unappealing glory. I was watching a Louis
CK (whose real last name is Seklay, speaking to a different

kind of name frustration) routine not too long ago where he told the story of a child who was bullying one of his daughters. To protect the kid's identity on HBO, early on in the routine, C.K. says he'll call the child, oh, I don't know ". . . Jizanthapus." Cue hysterical laughter, and me thinking that to the ear, actually, it's not that bad a name. Almost catchy in it's unusualness. Now obviously, by the end of Louis C.K.'s routine I'm going to find the kid repugnant, that's the point. But the name itself, until it's maligned, isn't that bad. (Someone pointed out that there are several unsavory slang terms in this name. Either I'm oblivious, or, get your mind out of the gutter!)

But it speaks to the second kind of name pain, where a name is considered to be "bad," like Chuck's, or like the name Cletus, which has always been associated with "slack-jawed yokel" in my mind. A character called that has appeared on *The Simpsons*, but I thought the association went back further. If it doesn't, it's certainly been adopted into pop culture, the way "Kleenex" means "tissue." You can talk about the buffoon who hit your car in the parking lot by saying, "Then Cletus comes bumbling over," and everyone will understand the point of your story: he was an idiot and you are clearly not at fault for whatever bruises either car sustained.

But one day a colleague began talking about his great-grandfather, a record-holder in the NHL. He called up his Wikipedia page and I noted "Cletus" was one of his middle names. I was surprised. "Yeah," said my coworker, smiling proudly. "I'm going to use that one [for a child] someday. Bringing Cletus back." His grandfather's illustrious career (Maurice Joseph Cletus Malone, better known as

"Phantom Joe," holds the record as the only player in the history of the NHL to score seven goals in a single game) had made a once-unthinkable name attractive.

But attractive is subjective, of course, and there are also those who split the difference when they realize a name hasn't been received as originally intended.

When I e-mailed Randy, who was recommended to me by a colleague, to speak about his name, his first response was "my name is one of my favourite stories," which, it's worth noting, is not the same as "I love my name." I was definitely intrigued, especially since not many of my interviewees have such perspective.

Randy's parents, immigrants to Canada, were expecting a baby in just a month's time when they went shopping at Eaton's. "If I was a girl, I was supposed to be Stella—" here Randy breaks off to make a gagging noise—"and if I was a boy, Jason." But things changed when his parents met the man who sold them their washing machine. "Their salesperson at Eaton's was a man named Randy, and once they got home, they decided that would be my name," Randy laughs. "I always wanted to, you know, go and comb the halls of Eaton's to see if I could find my namesake."

I comment that he must have been awfully influential, and Randy says that though he's often thought a lot about his name, he never pinned down exactly what it was about the salesman that had such an effect on his parents. His story would be merely cute if it ended there—but when has anyone's name story been finished the day they were born? Randy, who referred to his name as "unremarkable," was shocked when he moved to England for a summer and discovered that his name was actually quite remarkable: "In England, you know, they use *randy* to mean horny or oversexed." Which was a total surprise to Randy, who'd never heard the regionalism before. "It became this crazy conversation opener, and it got me into a lot of trouble and a lot of fun."

The balance of fun-to-trouble was tipped when Randy got a job in a bookstore, and became increasingly uncomfortable each time a customer learned his name, and reacted with shock or even a bit of pity—or thought he was "taking the piss," to use another British regionalism.

So Randy, spurred by a boss's suggestion, decided to change his name—at least within the confines of the British Isles. "It took me maybe ten seconds to think about [what name to choose], and then I said I'm going to be called Sebastian, because I love the band Belle and Sebastian. They're from Scotland and they were, I guess, foremost in my thoughts at the time. So I became Sebastian."

Randy didn't experience the difficulty I did with people accepting his name, though: "To this day, all my friends in England still refer to me as Seb, and they've kind of long forgotten that I actually have a real name."

To me, this story of a different name for a different time and place in your life opens a door that not all of us get to walk through. If nobody knows you by your "real" name, and everyone accepts the one you choose for yourself, are Randy and Sebastian actually different people? Randy, who now lives in Toronto but visits England often, says the answer is an emphatic yes. "Sebastian is just the more free and fun form of Randy. When I go to England, everything gets unleashed . . . it's just a different musical every night, three art galleries in a day, and the energy is boundless, and just . . ." He trails off, sounding wistful as he ponders the Sebastian side of his life.

"I think everyone turns into Sebastian when they're on vacation."

Love the Name You're With

My conversation with Jet Li Dotcom Clark is surprisingly frank and guileless. It's not that I expect him to be cagey, but he's only fourteen years old, and a freshman at Fiorello H. LaGuardia High School in Manhattan. I've met adults who are less articulate, especially since I'm asking him about a name, given to him at birth, that takes a couple of moments to sink in:"My name is Jet Li Dotcom Clark. Jet Li is my first name, Dotcom is my middle. Spelled out, D-O-T-C-O-M."

He is brimming with enthusiasm about the name, so somehow, I am too.

"Jet Li, my first name, was after my dog, and my aunt [The dog had been named Jet, and the aunt, Lee]. And Dotcom was because my parents met in the computer industry and my dad works [with] computer games and stuff. So that's where Dotcom comes from. I think it is cute."

Jet Li—who usually just calls himself Jet—understands why I wanted to talk to him for this book. He knows his name is more than garden-variety unusual. But instead of his name being the thing that makes him stand out, it's just the label on an intentionally unique package. "When I go to school, I wear what I want. I don't try to fit in with the norm. I don't try to pretend I'm someone I'm not. I don't try to do anyone else but me."

To me, this makes a lot of sense. You're never going to blend into the background with a name like Jet Li—something that Jet's parents obviously knew and hoped for—so why try? Why not lean in the other direction, and stand out? Still, while I am never more delighted than when I hear of a kid who feels like he's strong and able to be his own person, I want to be clear about which came first—the name or the attitude? How to phrase this for a teenager? I ask whether Jet thinks he'd feel as confident about all the aspects of himself—not just his name—if he were named Ethan, or Michael.

"No. If I was a Michael I'd be like the rest of everybody else. I'd be the same. I'd be boring and plain. And I'd probably dress in normal clothes and go to a normal school." Jet knows his own name is special, so he's confident that *he's* special as a result. "My name was just so weird and I had never met anyone with the same name. I always knew a lot of Sophias or Emilys. I always thought I was different. So knowing that, I didn't really care what other people thought of me. I still don't."

I hear everything Jet is saying, but there's a little part of me that thinks he had no choice but to feel this way; to assign meaning to a name like Jet Li, and not to see its possible negatives. That "I don't really care what other people think of me" kind of has to be your default in a situation like this, where you can't change what's unusual about you, at age fourteen. I suspect Jet Li knows, too, or will soon come to realize that there will be just as many successful and "unique" Sophias and Michaels, even if what makes them different isn't their first name.

But I have flashbacks when talking to Jet, because I re-member the feeling of being a young person and knowing that a lot of people, specifically adults, consider the choice your parents made in naming to be foolish. As a kid, I even remember the term "child abuse" being thrown around, as in "that name is child abuse." Jet knows this too, and he isn't impressed with the behaviour of adults, who are supposed to know better: "[A] teacher came up to me and he was like, 'Wow, your parents have a sick sense of humour.' And he walked away. He was really rude."

When I first interviewed Jet Li, I thought for sure I would be asking his parents about what they were thinking. What kind of people would give their baby son a name that draws so much attention? But I realized as he went on that it doesn't actually matter. The name belongs to Jet Li, and it's his job to make whatever he wants to out of it. In fact, I have to bring up the actor with the same name—Jet knows about him, of course, but he's not exactly a touchstone for fourteen-year-old Jet and his friends.

Jet's parents have their reasons for the name they chose. In fact, Jet says, his father wanted to go way more "out there"—options not chosen included a sequence of numbers and also the name "Cobra Commander"—but whether we think they did a good job or not, isn't the result the same? Jet loves his name. He thinks it's fantastic. In fact, the only time he seemed in any way surprised was when I asked if he could envision a situation where he might hide his name or not be proud of it. The idea was so anathema to him that I had to explain it more than once, and when I did, he was resolute. Absolutely not.

It might be easy to assume that Jet Li's optimism is childhood folly. That Jet will change his mind when he becomes an adult who experiences the pressures of the real world, and has to work within it. After all, that's what happens when you grow up. Or so I thought.

Enter Guybrush Taylor.

"I had to defend this name"

A thirty-something advertising executive in Chicago, Guybrush, emphasis on the first syllable, is delighted to talk to me about his self-selected name. However, when I ask about the name he was born with, he has a confession to make: "My name is not actually [legally] changed, so this entire thing is just like a huge favour that people are doing by just going along with it. Not that they know any difference most of the time."

Guybrush's story is astounding, mostly because of how simple it is. He started calling himself various names other than his given name Geoffrey, from the time he was a seven- or eight-year-old. His reasoning was simple: He would rather have *been* Batman or Ray from *Ghostbusters* than himself, and saw no reason why he had to confine his desire to be them to Hallowe'en. There were no representations in popular culture of Geoffrey, no superheroes or awesome adventurers bearing that name—so why not try to be someone else? Guybrush rotated through aliases regularly—trying to find one that felt like him.

"There was this computer game called 'The Secret of Monkey Island' in which the main character called 'Guybrush' kind of looks like what a pixelated version of me might look like. He was very, very funny, and just the personality was the same [as mine], and I thought, fuck, that's the one."

I *so* understand this sentiment. I remember when I thought that "Dawn" was going to be the answer to all my problems, and how distinctly it wasn't. Guybrush understands this, and commiserates. He realizes now (and did then) that changing his name to one he would share with a comic-book character wasn't the way to win friends. "In a junior high school, the geeks are becoming geeks and the bullies are becoming bullies and . . . nobody wants to hang out with the bucktoothed little redhaired kid . . . trying to call himself this dumb name, Guybrush."

So far, this mirrors my experience, but I press Guybrush for more details, because unlike me, he passed by the junior high school bullies and maintained his name into adulthood. He made it work as an actual name where most people might have admitted defeat and gone back to their given names after a few weeks. Guybrush chalks the success up to youthful hubris and stubbornness. He knew he had to convince everyone that this was the right name for him—which made his own belief in it even stronger. "My dad asked me a question that probably galvanized this entire process in my life. He said—and I don't think he actually meant to: I think he was actually trying to change me—get me to stop. He goes, 'What's the point? Like what's the point in changing your name to this stupid name?' And I said—and he reminds me of this probably once a month. My reply to him apparently was 'You can't change the world if nobody knows your name.'"

Right. *Right.* This is what I've been feeling over and over again. That your unusual name obligates you to do something notable. That you stick out for a reason greater than just your name. In fact, an unusual name can help the sticking-out be more bearable. Of course I'm not named like you people, I'm *different*. In Guybrush's case, it's just that the sticking-out happened first—by his own admission, he was the geeky kid who didn't fit in—and he chose a name that fit the person he already was. Which, in turn, allowed him to feel comfortable enough to be himself and find a place to fit in professionally and personally, while still standing out.

"I'm lucky to be in a place where . . . the friends that I have and the places I go and the things that I'm able to do are all a result of me finally finding a place to fit [as an adult]. And so because the name doesn't really fit—it's not entirely stupid, it's not entirely serious, it's not entirely local or exotic—you know, it's just kind of [undefinable], so in that case it's a perfect representation [of me]."

Guybrush's name is now a conversation piece, and if it's ever mocked, he hasn't heard it in his adult life. He tells stories of having gotten jobs because someone said, "We gotta hire this guy. We need a guy called Guybrush around." That's partly a function of working in creative environments where the offbeat, the ridiculous and the envelope-pushing are an essential part of the business. Guybrush maintains that it's a pleasure not just having a name that nobody else does, but also that nobody else could conceive of having (except the videogame designer). He doesn't feel pressure to live up to the assumptions of what a "wacky" guy called Guybrush must be like, because he sees the name not as a joke, but as an embodiment of the successful man he is now. Though he thinks the task of naming future children may be a challenge—after all, he knows how much weight names can have—he doesn't expect to choose something as offbeat as his own name.

Still, his legacy is intact in a way he never could have envisioned. When Guybrush worked at Taxi, an advertising agency in Toronto, he advocated for staff to have time off after big projects, and the concept, in that office, became known as "taking a Guybrush day." He left the agency, but years later came back for a brief project. During the orientation process, a human resources representative, not knowing the origin of the phrase (or perhaps having only seen Guybrush's legal name) explained to him the concept of "Guybrush days," straightfaced. It meant a lot to him, and he laughs at my suggestion that this is only the beginning of the name's impact. In fact, he feels a little pressure: "Well, now I've got to change the world, so I'm not going to lose this argument with my dad, basically."

You can change your name to suit the person you think you really are, or you can tough it out, hoping your actual self will prevail. This can all seem academic, but it can get real fast when your name gets a terrible association through no control of your own. There are many countries, like Germany, Sweden, and New Zealand among others, where it's illegal to name your child something "abusive or degrading", but what happens when your formerly fine name becomes synonymous with tragedy or scandal? A travelling-addicted friend named Katrina really-but-not-really says she thinks twice about visiting New Orleans since the hurricane. People who named their daughters Olivia, with fond memories of *The Cosby Show*, now omit that once-beloved program from the list of reasons they loved the name. But Katrinas and Olivias and everyone else attached to scandal just push through, hoping their personalities shine more brightly than their names.

This is the part of the book where I'm supposed to say that I met a boy and things were wonderful and "Duana" grew up. But I didn't have a high school romance. I was too self-conscious, I realize now, to let go and be totally drunk on someone else. I spent most of my high school years hanging out in the "music hallway" after school, pretending to do my homework between choir rehearsals but really just staring at couples. Wondering how they had found each other, and what they talked about when they weren't stealing kisses between working out answers to trigonometry questions. I didn't understand why some people had been given the keys, as teenagers, to like and understand themselves, while others of us were so bereft. I later realized that my biggest problem wasn't my insecurity, but my inability to pretend I didn't have any.

There are entire industries exploiting teenagers' insecurity, I now realize—but when I was that age, I thought I was making permanent, detrimental imprints on the name "Duana" that I'd never erase. I'm sure there are people from high school who still remember me because of some of the stupid stuff I did (if you're going to write a very, very unflinching and true 150-page novel about your high school friends that takes up the entirety of two Hilroy notebooks, you should a) not give it to people to read, and b) change their names. *Please*), but really, I was just reeling under the responsibility of defining the name. Still, like popularity, name individuality is a double-edged sword. Being able to define "Duana" was a huge responsibility. But it was also an opportunity, as I'd soon learn, that not everyone gets to have.

8

KAYLEY AS DESTINY
Gender, Class, and Naming for Success

One of the things that surprised me most as I escaped teenage angst and got a little older was that my unpopular opinions turned popular. Not so much in liking the right bands, which I will never be able to do, but the bigger stuff. The kind of things you think everyone is in agreement on, until you realize they aren't. I am, of course, talking about the F-word.

I don't remember the first time I said I was a feminist, but I think that's because I always remember the word having a positive slant, like it was a cool thing to be. As far back as I can remember, my cultural touchstones, from Lois Lowry's inimitable *Anastasia Krupnik* to Brenda Walsh in *Beverly Hills, 90210* to *Buffy the Vampire Slayer* (TV, not film, please) were open about the idea that strong, confident women were de facto feminists. It seemed so obvious in the 2000s.

I loved speaking up when things didn't feel like they were organically equal, volunteering to say the thing some other people didn't feel like saying, and generally "calling out" stuff I thought was ridiculous or unfair.

Not coincidentally, I didn't run into many situations where I thought I was being penned into a "girl role." I was, it seemed, either surrounded by too many women or too loudmouthed for that to be the case. Knowing, as I always had, that everything I was defined my name, both for me and everyone who knew me, I really wanted "feminist" to be part of the roster of qualities associated with "Duana"— partly because I assumed "smart," "socially aware" and other positive qualities were implied, attaching themselves to the word as part of a package deal.

But lots of names (and the people who wear them) never get to choose the qualities they're associated with. On one level, name association is highly personal. I have always found guys named Matt to be soft-spoken and sensitive, and while I'm sure there are dozens of stories to the contrary, my preconceived idea of who Matt is probably makes it so. Plus I have a lovely brother-in-law who reinforces this every day. Every Adam I've known is an enigma, someone who shapeshifts and doesn't stay the same for long; I've always felt like this is partly pressure to embody all kinds of traits, and that pressure comes from sharing a name with the first man ever. And while it's not always the most glamorous trait, I've never met a Cheryl for whom my overwhelming sentiment was not "that woman is *competent*."

These are personal impressions of course, but most people have their own. I've always made a habit of asking people the names of their childhood bullies and nobody's ever forgotten—or forgotten the association with the names, decades later. Mikita Brottman, author of *The Great Grisby*, had very specific impressions after she dated three Davids in a row—a coincidence she outlined in the *New York Times'* "Modern Love" column. I asked her for her overall verdict on having thoroughly field-tested such a name, and she agreed that she'd explored it enough that "It seems to be a good guy name," she told me. "Hard to imagine a serial killer named David."

But there are entire subsets of names that announce themselves before the bearer ever gets into the room to create a first impression. I always assume this is the goal with names like Liberty or Patience or Brock, which is not a "descriptor" name as such, but might as well be. Brock, the perfect marriage between Brick and Rock. We get it, he's a hard, unmoving guy. But beyond individual tastes and preferences, there are critical terms that come up in relation to names over and over.

They're usually related to sex.

The Importance of Being Britney

I don't know a lot of people who openly confess to visiting strip clubs, or exotic dancers, or gentlemen's clubs. But almost anyone you talk to on the street will acknowledge the concept of "stripper names," otherwise known as names you hear in the club—names of the dancers onstage. Crystal is the name I hear called a stripper name most often, but there are dozens of others, and qualities that help to identify stripper-name status.

Though this subset of names is sometimes referred to as "trashy" or "trailer park," the label "stripper" tells us that the name has four distinct qualities.

Taha's Tenets of Stripper Names

1. To qualify as a stripper name, a name must have been once popular for girls and, ideally, used to denote some indication of an association with class or money.
2. A stripper name often has a modified spelling. Ending in an "i" is a commonly cited trait of stripper names but ending in an "ee" sound also qualifies.
3. They are almost never "serious" names, nor usually among those names considered "classics."
4. They are often names for objects, or nonhuman things.

The stalwart stripper names, as seen in popular culture and on the front of establishments that advertise the women inside—Candace/Candy/Candi, Crystal, Nikita and her close cousin Nikki, Jade, Eden, Raven, Britney (of course), and then there are the ones that surprise me. Several Vancouver men in their thirties who swore they only had third-hand anecdotal knowledge of strip clubs (ahem) said that Natalie was a stripper name, and I was shocked. Natalie, to me, seems to signify a studious girl with dark hair. Since when did she get to be strippery?

One thing I know though, for sure, is that once a name's reputation drops as far as "associated with dancing on a pole," it rarely comes back up. The prevailing attitude in North American culture is that the worst thing you can be is a woman who takes her clothes off for money, and it's further extrapolated (if not always explicitly stated) that if you have a stripper name, there's a much higher chance that eventually, you'll wind up in that unfortunate situation. The term "trailer-trash" or "white-trash name" is sometimes used interchangeably with "stripper names," but we know they really mean stripper names because nobody ever lists a man's name in the mix. Oh, and then there's the unsavoury term "white-trash," created because, the offensive logic goes, other types of "trash" people don't get the "white" qualifier in front. It's brutal, but ignoring the fact that this word does come up in discussions of strippers or otherwise "trashy" names would be disingenuous.

A scene from the movie *Ted* echoes my thoughts here, the fact that it takes place between a grown man and his teddy bear (poor Mr. Roosevelt couldn't have seen this coming) notwithstanding. People who have never even seen the movie still reference its most memorable sequence. In fact, the reason I know about the movie at all is because of its almost clinical dissection of stripper names, although they use the "white trash" descriptive. One character entreats his buddy to guess the white-trash name of the girl he's dating, and Ted guesses: Mandy, Marilyn, Brittany, Tiffany, Candace, Brandy, Heather, Channing, Brianna, Amber, Serena, Melody, Dakota, Sierra, Bambi, Crystal, Samantha, Autumn, Ruby, Taylor, Tara, Tammy, Lauren, Charlene, Chantelle, Courtney, Misty, Jenny, Krista, Mindy, Noelle, Shelby, Trina, Reba, Cassandra, Nikki, Kelsey, Shawna, Jolene, Lurleen, Claudia, Savannah, Casey, Dolly, Kendra, Kylie, Chloe, Devon, and Becky. The punchline is that the girl in question has one of the names above, hyphenated with "Lynn."

So the joke is that there are *just so many* trashy names, I guess—and Ted can see trashiness in names that I would have assumed were fine. Like Serena. All the Serenas I know of are accomplished. Taylor? Has anyone told Taylor Swift? Claudia? Poor Claudia is a stripper name?

This seemed fishy to me. Who says these are the stripper names? Dudes, I guess. Who goes to the strip bars to become the experts in these names? Dudes. And who, in turn, make fun of these women, mocking both the names and the gotta-be-true-*sometimes* reasoning that they're just trying to put themselves through school? Guys, again. I'm not by any means saying all men are patrons of exotic dancers or promoting this kind of thinking. I'm just saying there aren't a lot of women offering counterpoint opinions or indicting "Beverly" as the ultimate exotic dancer name.

So my mission was to hit the strip bars. Find out exactly which of these names are actually making their appearance on the stages that attract so much attention and so much disdain. For my initial mission, I decided to take my friend Vera, who has been, over the past oh-my-lord-almost-twenty years, my classmate, roommate and coworker, and remains a close friend. She also doesn't let me get away with much.

I have never gone in much for the meanings of names, but "Vera" means truth, and it is so suited to her that I wonder what kind of vision came to her parents when she was born. Vera is truthful to a fault, a straight-shooter and an expert bullshit-sniffer. Given that I am a master embellisher, we have enhanced each other's understanding of how brains opposite to our own can actually function. She is so quick to call me on it when I'm telling tall tales that I try my hardest to make them sound believable, and I loosen up the mask of her cynicism by pointing out that nobody's actually as skeptical as she pretends to be.

Vera lives in Los Angeles, and was utterly game when I told her I was in pursuit of L.A.'s finest exotic dancers. We brought our friend Shernold, whose name is a treat of its own. ("You never heard this? My mother is Sherma, my father is Reynold.") This idea, to combine parents' names, is actually one that appears consistently in African cultures, as explained by Dr. Hodari, who calls it "an inside joke, in a good way." Shernold would be tickled to know she's academically verified.

At the first place we try to go in L.A., Cheetah's—get it?—the doorman greets us warmly, but points out that, for better or for worse, it's amateur night. He lets us peek in the door, and I see a woman with an incredibly muscular physique dancing onstage to a recently popular song that you wouldn't think she would choose, given that she's about fifty-five. She wears a one-piece unitard and boots that lace up to her thighs, and I have a *Flashdance* flashback immediately. She shakes her short blond hair, and I am struck by two certainties. This woman is awesome, and she is probably called Joyce.

Still, the goal here is authenticity, or in this case, "professional dancers." So we head to another, only slightly less storied locale—Jumbo's Clown Room. When I tell this story in L.A. later on, I will be told that this is not a real strip bar but a cool "hipster" strip bar, where those who are, I guess, so over strip bars can go, to discuss everything that's passé about them, while in a strip bar.

I'm joking a little bit, but when we get to Jumbo's, I'm not sure there's anything ironic about it. It's long and skinny and, crucially, there's a roster of tonight's dancers on the wall in neon crayon on a black-light board. You know what's *not* cool? Taking notes in the middle of a strip club. But I think we've established that for me, cool was never an option. I pull out my phone and take feverish notes. The roster: Tiffany Akiva Page Jenna Fiona Rev Juliet Zoe Priscilla Tiger Cherry Lux—wait a minute . . .

Oh God. They're not their real names.

Of COURSE they aren't. At least, not all of them. Zoe might really be called Zoe, but I'm willing to bet Tiger and Rev were originally called something else. Then I realize why. In a town where lots of people are trying to acquire "legitimate" performance careers, why would you strip under both your real name *and* your real face? *One* of them has to be hidden. Moreover, why didn't I realize this? What's wrong with me?

While I'm processing, Vera realizes something else— L.A. strippers don't get all the way naked—at least, not in places where they serve alcohol. Who knew this? There are many small bikini-type items and catsuits that are only nominally shielding nudity, but no toplessness. Or bottomlessness.

But what about the strippers' names? I'm mortified that I didn't realize how common it is for exotic dancers to use stage names, though I'll later discover it's not a universal practice.

But the realizations helps me refine my stripper name algorithm. Not all strippers have overtly obvious "stripper names," but they all obviously know they're expected to have, um, memorable ones. And a stage name is doubly important because this is not a place where you can be anonymous. The bar is about the size of a public pool change-room, and in about forty minutes' time, we will leave because a brawl threatens to encroach on our personal space. But for now . . .

I decide this isn't the place to ask women who are obviously trying for anonymity what their *real* names are—at least, not directly, since our conversations can be heard by just about everyone in the room. (When we arrive, the only seats available are at the foot of the stage, which later results in us being accessories in one of the performances involving a large quantity of Saran wrap, used in the most ingenious ways.)

Still, I know if anyone's an expert on stripper names, it's the women dancing. Nobody just happens into "Tiger" by accident. There's deliberate choice and calculation there—not just to have a name that's anonymous, but, let's be honest, to have one that will be appealing enough to the patrons to get them to spend more money.

So as each dancer comes offstage, I head over. To a woman, the strippers are sweaty and relieved to be finished, but completely friendly and open. I try not to sound too much like a nerd as I enquire, "How did you choose your stage name?"

The first, Juliet, says she and her sister used to pretend to be in plays, so she chose Juliet because it's beautiful, and she appreciates the theatrical connection. This bolsters my guess that show business is an end goal for many of tonight's performers. The next dancer, Akiva, has a similar inspiration—her name, which is often used for men as well, is based on a comic book.

Page gets really excited when I ask her, and explains that actually, there's a punk-rock fitness video starring a Page, and that she did this in honour of her because the woman's really awesome, and she tries to emulate her badass-ness in her act. Given that Page is also the dancer whose routine involved Saran wrap, I'd say badass is appropriate.

I am gearing up to ask the next dancer, Lux, about her name when she comes off the stage, and fervently hoping she's going to say it's from *The Virgin Suicides*—but I never get to do so. Because she comes down from the stage, get harassed by a patron, and immediately calls for: "George!"

That's the security guy. For what it's worth, he has two black eyes and he's tall and very skinny, so not every George is a royal baby, or a chronic *Seinfeld*-ian complainer. But I never get to ask him whether or not he feels like George fits him, because the fight that breaks out is so startling, and/or, the room we're in is so tiny, that Vera tells Shernold and me we need to *book*.

So we leave. I'm both a little more enlightened and a little more confused. Many dancers, and by extension escorts, use stage names, but in most cases they're names that *have* been used for real people. I mean, Tiger might be an exception here. And I'm sure there are people who use their real names when they strip—I'm looking at you, Fiona. But for the most part, these women are choosing stage names that they think sound like stripper names. But how did those names get to be the ones that are considered trashy? The answer is unfortunate, and unfortunately simple. Names that we consider trashy, or synonymous with strippers, are the ones chosen by people with lower socioeconomic status, whose daughters do often wind up in situations where exotic dancing is a means to an end rather than a choice. Those names are often names that *used* to be upmarket and now are not. Tiffany is the prime example here—the name was originally a surname, as in the surname of the jewellers whose jewellery empire was eponymized in *Breakfast at Tiffany's*. But for my money, the name changed when it was adopted for little girls as a way to impart some of Tiffany & Co.'s aura of wealth to a child. Then, when the pop star, Tiffany (her real name), whose brand was sort of "girl from the wrong side of the tracks," rose to fame in the 1980s with a series of performances at malls across America, the name became associated with the masses and not the upper crust. Subsequently, as the name grew more popular, it became a little more overt that parents were using the name to confer class on their daughters, which seemed to backfire as "classy" names became strip-club stalwarts.

For comparison, I investigated supposedly high-end escort services, which always seem to advertise their roster by first names. These names still definitely have a sexy factor—Paloma, Tatiana, and a lot, lot, lot of Evas—but they end in A and there's often an implication of an exotic, not-from-here locale. Natalia implies "elsewhere" in a way that Candi decidedly does not. Also, I suspect Veroniqua is never, ever spelled correctly. You know. On her invoices.

This stripper-name phenomenon affects all kinds of names. I always thought the "Paris" phenomenon was such a weird example here. Years ago, someone gave a very rich little girl the name Paris because—well, in this case, because her parents wanted to show off how much money they had, since of course I'm talking about Paris Hilton. But then she released a sex tape, and promoted gross conspicuous consumption, and then—*after* the sex tape and conspicuous consumption—people started naming their daughters Paris. Michael Jackson's daughter Paris was named before Paris Hilton became notorious, but the name had a popularity surge in the 1990s, dipped to a low in the late 2000s, and then, circa 2010 to 2012, enjoyed a massive surge again. This has to be related to the very famous Ms. Hilton. But why would you want your daughter to share a name with the most notorious of all the famous-for-sex-tape stars? Is it possible to have missed this pop culture phenomenon entirely?

Now, if those Parises born in the 2010s don't grow up to be pillars of society—and I'm not saying that's going to be the case, but *if*—then is the problem that a certain Paris took the name downmarket, or is the problem that she should have, in the first place, been named Abigail? (I'm obligated to note that her sister Nicky, born Nicholai Olivia, has been less notorious for many years).

Of course, the gold standard of stripper names, the one everyone mentions, is Crystal. I'm pretty sure the use of this name can be pinpointed to the early 1980s, Aaron Spelling and *Dynasty*, which I used to watch with my mother, faking insomia so she'd let me curl up with her while she folded laundry and watched the silliness on Wednesday nights. The female protagonist was beautiful and blonde and from what I remember, mostly hard done by, while simultaneously extremely wealthy. Her name was Krystle, so the special spelling trend was alive and well even back then. The character, played by Linda Evans, gave rise to all kinds of Crystals in the 1980s, but this alone doesn't guarantee it's a stripper name. After all, there are as many Jennifers who are CEOs as there are strippers.

Crystal, on the other hand, was quickly downgraded in public opinion as a "trashy" name. I don't know if it was the message implicit in the name—"crystal," as in tchotchkes, as in not-diamonds, or whether it was just that anyone who was named Crystal couldn't measure up to the glamour established by *Dynasty* and therefore fell shamefully short, but there is no name that garners a snicker as easily. Even Amber denotes some sort of depth, in terms of the precious stone, but Crystal? You can see right through her.

I asked a friend, Krystal, how she feels about this. Krystal is intelligent and accomplished, so I didn't assume the stereotype of the name as tacky or low-class would bother her. I was wrong.

K: I hate my name.

D: Why?

K: I think it sounds like a stripper. I've always hated my name. I feel like you [think of] Krystal as a stripper.

I shouldn't be surprised. Why would I be asking if I didn't expect to hear something along these lines? Still, it's what Krystal says when we're discussing her media career, which she loves, that really surprises me.

K: I probably wouldn't hire anyone with the name Krystal, to be honest. It's just so bad.

D: Come on! You wouldn't hire somebody named Krystal?

K: I mean, I wouldn't be prejudiced, I would meet them. But if I could choose just based on a name, I wouldn't choose [a] Krystal.

I can't imagine that this is a common sentiment. Some people must dislike the stereotype their name holds while still loving it because it's theirs. Unfortunately, Krystal isn't one of them, and it seems as though her family might feel the same way. She explains that the name was chosen by her mother, who objected to Krystal's father wanting to call the baby Vincenza, after his mother. "And my mom said no way in hell, I'm not doing that. And my mom's family is Scottish and so instead of choosing a family name or anything, I don't know, she just liked Krystal."

The name therapist in me notes that this is a name derived from a power struggle. Obviously, if Krystal's mother objected to a family name from her father's side, she couldn't justify one from her family. So the resolution was a name that, ultimately, meant nothing to anyone—including Krystal. "You know what, it's really funny—I don't really associate my name with myself, to myself. When I describe myself, I never say I'm Krystal or my name is Krystal."

She's gone through a series of nicknames and even debated being called by her last name. But nothing ever stuck, and like many of my interviewees, Krystal shares a common wound: "I'm noticing now that I see a lot of options for [products printed with] Krystal with a K, but when I was a kid, there were things, maybe a hairbrush or a doll or things like that, that my sister Amanda got and I didn't."

Even though I knew I was going to ask Krystal about having a stripper name, I was upset for her that she felt so dissociated from the name she'd had all her life. But then I had a revelation.

Many of the designated stripper names—Brandi, Amber, Candy and others—all of which I've heard used on actual people, not just in strip clubs—are words for things. That is, we know of Brandy, Amber and Candy as items—consumables, luxuries or other indulgences. There's no such *thing* as an Elizabeth—it's obviously a person's name. But a thing can be Tawny, or Amber, or Sapphire. Are these names stripper names because they encourage other people to look on them not as people, but as things? The idea that you can desire and lust for a Diamond or a Sapphire or even an Angel helps dissociate the idea that the name is for a person, and helps to create the illusion that the woman dancing in a strip club really is an *object* of desire, which heightens their "consumable" value, but makes people more likely to forget they're human beings.

But if my theory that the most successful stripper names are those that allow patrons to see them as things is correct, it doesn't explain all the other names that became "trashy" for no reason. It's seems to be a slippery slope. A once-acceptable girl's name is somehow deemed undesirable, and suddenly parents who choose it are criticized for not "aiming higher" for her. Even if Destiny lives her life beyond reproach, attitudes toward her name will assign her lesser value. As an example of how this can happen to the most unsuspecting name, take Michaela. If you've never run into anyone who wears it, it's a lovely, unusual take on Michael that sounded so pure back in the day that it was even given to the pure-as-snow lead character on *Dr. Quinn, Medicine Woman* on 1990s TV.

But as the name grew deeply popular in that era, some-one (or many someones) thought the spelling was confusing, since the name isn't pronounced "MICHAEL-a." So it became Mikayla. Or maybe Makayla. Or M'kaila. All of these are on record for what ostensibly is the same name. So choosing a name where the alternative spelling has become the accepted version, or one that doesn't immediately "spell itself," can be another one-way route to becoming "trashy."

Or, take the name Alexandra. For some it's a stable, staid name, and the nickname "Alex" imparts gravity and security. I know a lot of female lawyers named Alex. But while Alex says "Please execute my estate efficiently and forgettably" to some, Alexandra is sensual—even sexy. This is tripled with the nickname Lexi, which rhymes with "sexy." It's unlikely to be thought of neutrally—maybe it even unconsciously titillates our brains, whereas Alex is saved by also being a nonsexual name for men.

There are exceptions to every rule. Candy Crowley is a respected political commentator who was CNN's chief political correspondent and hosted *State of The Union with Candy Crowley*. She covered presidential elections for over two decades, and her incongruous "stripper" name appears not to have held her back at all. In fact, incongruous names in journalism seem not to be an impediment—instead they may contribute to making a person more memorable or recognizable. Cokie Roberts comes to mind—not to mention Soledad O'Brien. Turns out maybe Corky Sherwood-Forrest, a "joke" of a name on the journalistically focused comedy *Murphy Brown* wasn't such a stretch after all. In a career like newscasting, where, let's face it, almost everyone looks the same, having a name that makes you stand out can only be a benefit.

Of course, there's something very absent from the discussion here. About 50 percent of the population, to be precise.

A Stripper by Any Other Name

A name nerds trajectory is fairly simple. First, you become interested in names, and quickly realize it's not a popular or even an accepted hobby, and maybe you should keep your interest a secret. (Pamela Redmond Satran told me that she remembers getting weird looks when she told friends that she would like to "write names"—copying them down in a notebook to think about and consider. Dr. Hodari mentioned the exact same pastime, and both eventually turned their lists of names into books.)

Then you realize that names have distinct levels of appeal, and you wonder why. You dig further, beginning to investigate names in more detail. You pick up a few name books in the shop, maybe check out some websites. Remark on a couple of names to friends, see the experts respond to celebrity names or those in the media, and then all at once you realize the weirdness: the vast majority of name experts are women. People who are scholars in onomastics, or who give advice online, or who write columns, or have written name books, exploring the origins and culture of names—almost all women. They are quoted in this book and have, in some cases, made entire careers out of being name experts. They are excellent at what they do.

But it gives an odd and very inaccurate impression that names, or what they mean, or what they do, are a female concern. I can understand the origins of such a trend. In previous generations, in traditional family structures where Father earned the money and Mother raised the children, naming might fall under her jurisdiction. As an extension of the wife in this situation purchasing *Dr. Spock's Baby and Child Care* or *Heloise's Housekeeping Hints*, it stands to reason that she might also pick up a baby name book to discuss with her Dear Husband when he got home from a long day at the office.

But as we know, eight chapters into this book, it's patently false that names are only a female concern. Names concern everyone, but many name sites mention women and mothers almost exclusively and the comments there appear to be by women. It's obviously a holdover from the antiquated idea that the job of baby naming is for women, but it is frustrating.

What makes me even crazier are the exceptions. I discovered male name experts, of course—Dr. Mehrabian, who assigned numerical value to names, Dr. Evgeny Shokenmayer, who studies onomastics, and Dr. Cleveland Evans, who writes a column discussing the historical origins of now-popular names—but I was frustrated that many of the men who are interested in names are mostly interested in assigning them status and value. In fact, if stripper names are so abhorrent that you want to be sure you can avoid them or you'd

like to name your child based on your chosen occupation for
them or by your political affiliation, well, Mark Edmond of
Verdant Labs has created an app for that.

When we speak, Mark is in his Seattle-based laboratory,
and is amused by my assertion that a fascination with names
is a female preoccupation. But he admits that his interest in
names had to do with women, too. "When my wife and I
were pregnant, I found that there wasn't a lot of information
beyond basic popularity graphs, [and sites about] so-called
"meaning." So that spurred the idea for the app, Nametrix.
He continues, "Actually, one of the first concerns that came
to mind when searching for a baby name was that I wanted
to avoid a stripper name."

There it is again. Those persistent strippers! So pesky
how they just foist their names on unsuspecting babies.
Mark knew he was on to something, though, when he
attacked the problem with science. "It occurred to me that
I could figure out what names are stripper names via real
world data, not just anecdote. So on that hunch, I went
ahead and spent most of my free time for the next week or
two writing code to test the idea."

Mark goes on to explain the algorithm for Nametrix to
me, and admits that for the purposes of his algorithms, he's
conflating "adult" film actresses' names—he included performers who have been in at least one such movie—with
female strippers' names, in order to come up with what he
calls the "Stripper Quotient." Nametrix, which has been featured in the *New York Times*, on the popular website Babble.
com, and yes, on the Freakonomics blog, has become incredibly successful.

I point out to him that while of course there are real people named Sapphire and Crystal and Lola, the names are disproportionately chosen as stage names. Mark is unconcerned. "It's not so much that you were driven to the profession by your name or anything, it's just that a certain name might be favoured by strippers." Pulling his data from public places like published censuses and adult movie databases, Mark was able to run a variety of metrics to get a cross-section of results, which have made his app extremely popular.

Ultimately, even Mark gave his daughter a name that appears in the upper third or even quartile of XXX names— but one that he and his wife loved, nevertheless. He didn't want to tell me what it was, which I cannot fault him for, but I found it interesting that there's a bit of magical thinking afoot. Mark believes that stripper names are to be avoided, but he also believes that his daughter's unique qualities will supersede the "stripper quotient" he identified. Ultimately, love tends to conquer all where names are concerned.

But as Mark studied strippers, adult movie stars, and related pursuits, he realized he was only scratching the surface of the potential of Nametrix. "The biggest surprise was that you really can see correlations between names and professions, political affiliations, etc., with fairly straightforward analysis." Mark points out a graphic from the site, which plots names across the political spectrum. "You really can see how female names are primarily on the left-hand side of the Democrats vs. Republicans chart, and male ones are on the right." The most "left-wing" names, by a wide margin, on Mark's chart are Jasmine and Caitlin. The most "right-wing," out there all on it's own, is Duane. (Which, it seems prudent to remind you at this time, is not the masculine of "Duana.")

Mark is also delighted that he's discovered disproportionately high numbers of people with a small concentration of names in given professions. He lists lawyers named Cecily and Marshall, and graphic designers named Kurt, Vanessa and Jessica. But he cautions that this doesn't mean what we might think. "When people look at, say, the chart of the most disproportionately common names by profession, [they] will think the chart is showing them the most common names in those professions, rather than disproportionately common . . . so they'll say "Hey! I don't know any Mitzi accountants. Mitzi's a really rare name. This analysis must be trash."

But what Mark is saying is much more interesting. Not all accountants are called Mitzi, but *a high proportion of the few Mitzis out there are reporting being accountants more than any other job.* Isn't that amazing?! That there may be something about the name Mitzi that sends you in that direction? Look at the names who disproportionately report being librarians: Nanette, Margot, Julia, Abigail, Eleanor, Johanna. I mean . . . . sure. There are more Nanettes who are librarians than farmers? I buy that. And I love it.

Still, that doesn't mean you can make someone a venture capitalist just by choosing a popular venture capitalist name (Guy, Shawn, Nicholas, Alexander, Doug, and Joanna). There's still a lot of chance, or nurture, involved. Kayley may only be one part of a destiny. Still, some people choose to avoid the question altogether.

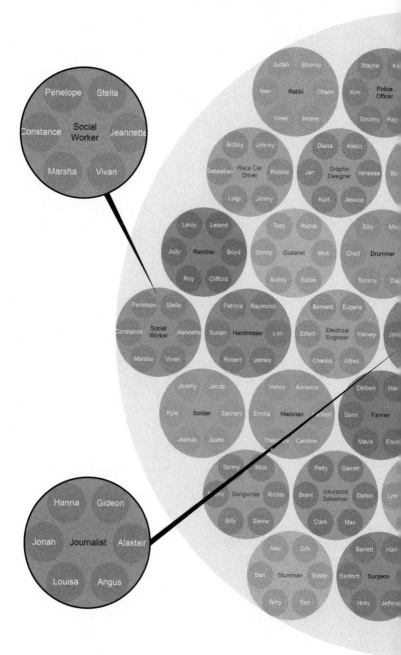

Top Disproportionately Common Names by Profession by Verdant Labs' Nametrix app

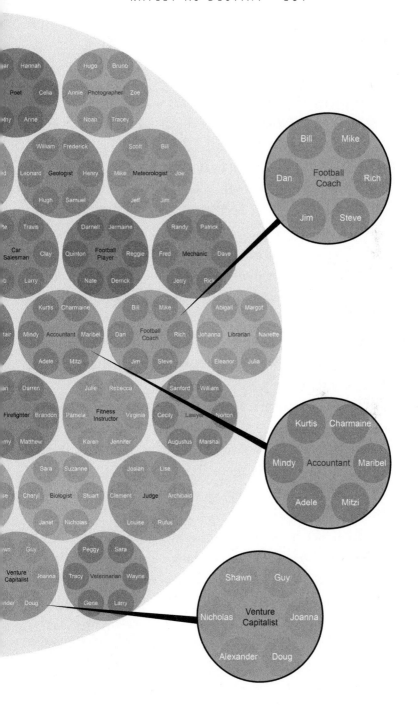

Girls Named Like Boys (Who Like Boys, Who Like Girls . . .)

You usually don't have to work very hard to find a woman who wears a traditionally male name or at least one that's unisex. Generations ago it was Hilary and Kelly that were borrowed from men—now it's much more likely to be Dylan and Ryan and Jordan, and the still-ubiquitous Alex. I have always been bothered by this phenomenon, because it seemed to me to be kind of . . . desperate.

Let me explain. As far back as I can remember, there were name aficionados who, when asked about names, said they'd love to name a girl George. Or James. Or, very often, things like "Will, but short for Wilhelmina. Or like, Henry, but her real name is Henrietta." I remember being kind of put off, and asking why? That is, why would you choose a gorgeous girl's name like Wilhelmina and then not actually use it? The answer was usually something along the lines of thinking a man's name was "stronger," or unexpected.

I was always incredulous at this reasoning, since it assumes that Doreen or Ariadne is wearing a name that's less "strong" because it's so obviously feminine. But rather than recite a stump speech about feminism in first names, I decided to talk to a couple of women who live it to see whether I'm off base.

Evan Statt is a seventeen-year-old student from Bel Air, California, who is interested in theatre and photography. She is poised, beautiful, and articulate—and relishes the opportunity to share her thoughts on her name. "It's just cool. It's not boring and it's original for a girl. I have never met another Evan, not even a boy. I've definitely had one of the best names in my school." Not only does Evan like the name now, but she kind of always has—proving that she had the self-possession as a kid that I barely manage to pull off today. "I [always] thought I was pretty lucky to have such an unusual name for a girl. I wore the name proudly. Oftentimes I would have to repeat my name when introducing myself because no one seemed to understand it coming from a girl."

I asked her mother, Lisa, why she decided to go with such a distinctly not-girly name. As usual, the name of the mother, and her feelings about it, will be revisited on the daughter. "I had always been fine with my name growing up but as time went on I became very conscious that five out of ten girls in the room were named LISA! I guess my parents thought that Lisa was a cool, pretty name and that they were being original. But so did every other parent in the mid- '60s! My sister is named Wendy, and the names Lisa and Wendy are soooo of that time period. I always had about four other Lisas in my circle growing up which meant . . . Lisa P., Lisa F., Lisa C. etc. It's like an epidemic! As an adult I still encounter Lisas all over the place and when I get introduced to another Lisa for the first time I say to myself . . . 'Oh, another one.'"

As a name therapist, I've heard over and over that being one of the crowd was a downside to a popular name. Not a huge, crushing disappointment, just a nagging reminder that you might not be that special, namewise, and that a common name meant seeing yourself coming and going for, possibly, your entire life. Lisa had this in mind when she thought about her baby. "Picking a name for your child is daunting. The name means so much . . . it represents my own creativity and I felt like, this is my one chance, I might not have any other kids, so get it right! Evan is a family name. I was very

very close to my grandmother and her sister. They were the Evans sisters—it was their maiden name. I liked the fact that it was unusual for a girl to be named Evan and I wasn't going for the 'girl with a boy's name' idea."

Evan seems to know that her name causes some people confusion—it's just that she takes it all completely in stride. "I'll say when introducing myself, "Hi, my name is Evan." The person I'm speaking to will just say, "What was that?" I have to repeat it a lot. An Italian woman who works at a restaurant we go to in Brentwood thought my name was Heaven all the years that I've known her since I was little. We just discovered this a few months ago when we heard her say my name. She wrote my name in a text to my mom and wrote 'Heaven.' My school bus driver for two years called me 'Yvonne,' my housekeeper calls me 'Even,' like even and odd, my whole entire family from Scotland calls me Avan, and sometimes I even get Evian, like the water!"

Can you hear the enthusiasm in her voice? Is it just that she's young and the exhaustion of correcting everyone hasn't worn her down yet? Obviously my jawing about a boy's name not contributing to a girl's strength isn't bothering Evan, whose self-possession leaps off the page.

Still, in a culture where we underline gender and sex with heavy pink and blue lines, I figured there must be some difficulties.

I asked novelist Curtis Sittenfeld, the author of the acclaimed, bestselling *Prep, American Wife,* and *Sisterland,* about her experience of the pitfalls of being a well-known woman with a man's name. She gives an example: "My parents tell the story, which I faintly remember, of when I was in first grade or something, I didn't get invited to a birthday party that all the other girls got invited to because the parents viewed [my name] as a boy's. And then I think at the last minute the parents realized the mistake—I kind of have a memory of this, but maybe I made it up."

So, okay. Not quite a wound that cuts deeply for Sittenfeld, who admits that she comes by her name honestly, if somewhat stealthily. "So my real name is actually Elizabeth Curtis Sittenfeld, but I'm maybe the seventh or eighth Elizabeth Curtis, starting with my great grandmother. It's not a direct line down, it includes aunts and cousins and that kind of things. So, to sort of distinguish me, so the story goes, when I was born my parents decided to call me Curtis, rather than Elizabeth."

I ask her whether she thinks growing up with what was then considered a male name was unusual, and she assures me that she still thinks of it as a male name, even among all the Ryans and Devons whose names are currently on the "girl" side of the commemorative keychain rack. I posit that constantly repeating her "boy's" name as a girl must have given her a certain amount of grit—not unlike the title character in Johnny Cash's "A Boy Named Sue," whose feminine name was engineered by his father as a strength-builder in the absence of the father himself.

Sittenfeld thinks she didn't come to that realization until quite late. "My first job out of college, I guess I was twenty-two—I was a reporter at a business magazine, and people often assumed I was a male." In fact, her literary success has not changed the possibility for her name to give utterly the wrong impression. She points out that one review of her first novel, *Prep*, made a very clear point. "It basically said, this is a book . . . set at a boarding school. It's about a young woman at a boarding school by a man who's clearly never set foot in one. I just thought it was so funny because obviously it's your prerogative to not like the book, but one, I am a woman, and two, I did actually go to boarding school."

In fact, even the names of the boarding school students drew attention. "One thing that was funny to me is when *Prep* was published, I think some people interpreted the names as satirical and they're actually not. They're supposed to be real, to realistically reflect what kids' names are at a fancy boarding school. There's a lot of name silliness in that community. I definitely choose names carefully, but [they were] also somewhat as a product of preppy culture."

Preppy culture, of course, is part of what it all comes down to. In *Prep*, the main character has an androgynous-to-male name—Lee—while her classmates are called Conchita and Aspeth and Cross and Darden Pittard (which, the book taught me, is an assonant name, where there are sounds that repeat—in this case D*ar*den Pitt*ard*).

Sittenfeld, who lives in St. Louis, agrees that it's partly her unusual name that gives her both an ear for her characters' names and a skeptical opinion of the real life names she hears. "If you go to a playground, kids have what seem to me, very self-conscious, unusual names—I mean not themselves, but as if their parents have self-consciously chosen them. And I feel I have a slightly uncharitable view toward that. I feel it's sort of revealing of the parents' aspirations to have these special children and there's something a little silly about the whole enterprise to me." She points out that her own children have what she would call "pretty common names. I think they have pretty names, but definitely names that you've heard before. I kind of feel like 'Oh, got over the special name thing, thirty years ago,'" she muses.

Sittenfeld knows that names matter, and concedes that, whether it's because of her own name or not, the names she chooses for her characters are deliberate. They matter. Specifically because of what they signify: "I think that, definitely, the names in my books are supposed to signify class. I mean, in some cases, obviously the class of one character is more relevant than others' and so somebody possibly could have just sort of an unremarkable name and they're an unremarkable middle-class person, but yes, I definitely think the more important class is, the more the name matters."

Sittenfeld's work walks these lines pretty directly. *American Wife* is a fictionalized account of the life of a woman who eventually becomes the First Lady of the United States, and whose life bears more than a passing resemblance to former U.S. First Lady Laura Bush. Though the characters in the novel are destined for high station, their names are resolutely down to earth. This is a question of cause and effect, right? Did George and his wife, Laura, get elected because they seemed unpretentious, or did Sittenfeld name her fictional first couple Charlie and Alice because the names were similarly unpretentious? It's a glorious name-centric Möbius strip, and Sittenfeld agrees. "As soon as I have a character who is born in like 1946 or something, I'll look at what were the popular names in that year."

And, of course, what names would be demographically appropriate. As Sittenfeld's character Lee Fiora knows, class is all around us, whether we acknowledge it or not.

Head of the Class

It's right there, isn't it? As soon as we talk about trashy names, or stripper names, we're also talking about the people who choose them. There's no doubt that there are some names that are much more prevalent in higher socioeconomic circles. There are so many reasons to cite the excellent name work in *Freakonomics*, but probably my favourite section is the one that lists given names for babies along with the average years of education for the mother who gave it. So like, Meredith scores high—her mother was in school for an average of 15.57 years. Phoebe's mother is almost as educated at 15.18 years. Sunshine's mother has a little less education—on average, 12.03 years. And the name Lizbeth is given by mothers who have an average of just 9.66 years of education. I'm scanning through the corresponding boys' list and note that Abdulrahman's mother has 14.08 years of education—another reason for my joyous friend from the University of Toronto to love his name. The highest names I find on the boys' side are Finn at 15.85 years and Deniz, at 15.65, the lowest, Jesus at 8.71.

Your name speaks to your class. For a long time, that meant only names of well-worn European extraction were appropriate for upwardly mobile parents to lay on their children. We know, by this point, that your name alone isn't your destiny, but it has significant impact. This is why, for decades, one of the more derisive criticisms lobbed at a name was that it was "made up."

But there is a name craze that—as of this writing—shows no sign of ending, and is rendering the "made-up" criticism obsolete. The trend focuses on the names that a lot of people call "the Aidens." It's not just about the popularity of the name

Aidan—partly because the alternative spelling "Aiden" over-took it. Both names were in the mid-hundreds in popularity through the 1990s, and then, seemingly out of nowhere, jumped to the top fifty. Actually, Aiden was more popular than Aidan, significantly. Then, as Aiden rose in popularity, people started choosing to juuuust twist the name a little bit. Cayden. Brayden. Jaden—yes, Will Smith, I'm looking at you. All of a sudden these were boys' names popping up everywhere.

It's hard to understand why, exactly, except that they must have sounded new. There is a certain brand of baby namers, who rose at the same time as Internet blogs and "personal brands"—who don't want to use a name anyone's heard before. Which I am supposed to be all for, of course, in my efforts to keep everyone from choosing the same six names. And I am, in theory, but this isn't like deciding to name a child Eberhard. I'm talking about a name that's liter-ally never existed before—and now is exactly the same as every third little boy in the town. How can Cayden seriously be considered a different name than Drayven? They all rhyme, and they all have origins in the 2000s. Jaden. Brayden. Braylee. Caydee. Brinlow. I am not making a single one of these up, but someone else did. Also it's worth noting that many are seen as unisex, or can be easily twisted to become unisex. Don't you dare confuse Caedyn with Camdyn.

These names are definitely a phenomenon more popular in middle America, though there is significant representation on the coasts, and for the first time I can remember, the "made-up" syllable names have buoyed "real" names back to popularity. People who can't bear Jayden but think the sound is fresh are turning to Nolan or Damon or Eamonn.

It says a lot that the "Aiden" trend is the worst example I can find of "bad" male names. Despite my grumpiness, the "Aydens" will grow up and chances are some of them will become heads of corporations and presidents. There is nothing in the mechanics of having a common name, even a created name, that is an automatic indicator that you're not of the same station as someone else. As long as you're a male, and your name isn't stupid, you're fine.

Still, there are enormous penalties placed on having a name that's "stupid." Baby name books, now evolving past simply being dictionaries, file certain names under "just don't," while the Internet delights in finding the stupidest names it can and making fun of them. Nowhere is this more prevalent than in the Urban Legend category. You've heard them—names so ridiculous that you have to read them over and over again to make sure you got the references in them. The problem, of course, is that most of them are made up. Despite the fact that the name Shithead (pronounced "Shi— THEED" if you're believing the urban legend, which you shouldn't) was disproven by *Freakonomics* years ago, I still met a teacher who insisted she had one in her class. People love to tell me, as soon as they hear about this book, about people who called their babies Happy and Sad, or SaturDave. Mostly, as baby names so clearly reflect on the parents, nobody wants to be seen as having a terrible name or one that indicates a low class. However, the lines are getting ever more blurry.

If we can identify low-class names, can we identify high-class ones? A very posh and exclusive U.K. boys' private school, in the 2012–2013 school year, boasts plenty of international students and parents of every impressive job description. But though there are some unusual names—the school has several Zains and every permutation of Matthias, Matteo, and Mathieu—there are also more than a few Davids, Michaels, and a heavy handful of Olivers and Benjamins. And yes, Jaden is here represented too: class, however overt, doesn't preclude trendy, and trendy doesn't limit itself to what's currently acceptable. I have to admit that this tickles me a little. I love many of the "classical" names, but I don't think we need to be creating new ones, and I kind of love that while there may be names that denote a lower socioeconomic status, it's no longer as easy to imply a high one just with a name. I also love that today's wealthy don't have to play by stodgy society rules in order to be in mixed company.

In fact, there are many, many name rules meant to be broken.

That's Not My Name

Sometimes the biggest name pain—there's that term again—comes from names that are so unpopular they're notable—even if, in and of themselves, they're not objectionable. I thought again about virtue names, and how they're not assigned to men at all. We talked at the top of the chapter about Brock or Stone, and there are other men's names like Frank and Ernest that have certain associations—but somehow the women's names seem to lead to more pressure, or more scrutiny, or more . . . something.

Charidy Johnston tells me that the *more* is actually attention, and it's not ideal. "Most people look at my name and they think that I've misspelled my own name. I mean,

Charity would have been a weird name anyway, but the fact that it's *Charidy* takes [the weirdness] one step further."

Charidy's mother chose the name while she was pregnant, after watching a Christmas special with a leading character named Charity. "I'm sure it was one of those terribly sad little matchstick girl sort of Christmas specials," Charidy laughs, "and she says she chose to spell it with a D because she liked it better."

An unusual spelling of an already unusual name is twice the burden to bear, though Charidy remembers her initial reaction to people's comments about her name was one any owner of a virtue name might have: annoyance. "I always get 'Oh, does that mean you're very charitable?' It's no longer hilarious. It wasn't hilarious when I was five." She recognizes that a name that "says" something the way hers does prompts a certain expectation in people, and though she tries to be nice, she doesn't feel burdened to embody charity (or Hope, her middle name). Still, she feels like her name brings her a certain amount of scrutiny that she could do without. "I consider myself a fairly ambitious person, [and] in those moments when I am trying to be taken seriously and I am meeting someone for the first time, I have to say 'I'm Charidy.' It can have that connotation that's very girly and young."

I just can't stop thinking about Chastity.

For the most part, I think parents have the best of intentions in choosing names, but I can't imagine what the benefit could be in growing up with a name that is a synonym for sexual abstinence. A person called Grace or Faith or Serenity has at least a fighting chance of embodying the qualities their names impart sometimes, but a person who is called Chastity is almost certainly not going to be chaste her whole life, so I'm not sure why a parent would choose a name that is necessarily so oppressive.

It's worth noting that one of the most famous bearers of the name was born Chastity Bono, who is now known as Chaz. Many people who identify as transgender choose names that have little or nothing to do with the names they were given at birth, but in this case I note a link between them. I also would never presume that a name had anything to do with Chaz or anyone else realizing that they identified as transgender, but I do think it would have been an extra-hard cross to bear as a teen and young adult, to have a name that was so overtly about sexuality while dealing very privately with the discovery of your own. Then, of course, there's the unique joy of getting to choose your own name to signify the person you know you are, and the decision of whether or not to tip a hand to the name you held at birth (sometimes called a "deadname" in the trans community). When Caitlyn Jenner announced her new name after her high-profile transition, I was struck by how youthful the name seemed compared to the relatively out-of-use one she had worn as a man. Though Caitlyn is sixty-five and not likely to meet a lot of contemporaries who share her name, it's so fitting that someone beginning a new life would choose an equally new name, generationally along with every other way. It must be a lot of fun—and a lot of pressure.

To this end, I spoke with A. Gapin, a software engineer from Jersey City. I enjoyed reading her blog, which covers her experience being a runner and being transgender in equal measure, and she thought long and hard when she was choosing the name she would be known by after her transition. It wasn't an immediately obvious choice. "When I was twenty [twelve years ago] and first starting to seriously think about transition, I wanted some way to conceptualize that in my head. I wanted that way to put a name to that identity (like I mentioned before) and even just a name to use online. But I really struggled with it. I didn't come up with anything I really liked. I think the biggest thing was that I didn't really know myself yet."

This is an idea that resonates with me over and over. We talk about people who change their names because their given name didn't "feel like" them, but what about someone who doesn't know what "they" feel like? It's just so much wandering in the pages of name books, waiting for something to feel right.

For A., it took awhile. "I used Samantha when I was younger. But I never really felt like it fit for me." In fact, it took nine years, and a series of "trying on" names, to find something that worked. A. says that, though she was obviously thinking of names for years beforehand, she didn't officially tell anyone she was transitioning until after she'd chosen the name, which, she points out, was not without its difficulty. "It was fun and exciting to finally start to get to explore myself in a way I never let myself do before. But having the pressure of CHOOSING a name that you'll go by for the rest of your life can be kind of stressful! Few people actually do that."

Added to this of course was the pressure to choose a name that not only denoted what she wanted, but felt significant enough to be the one. "One of my criteria was that I didn't want a more gender-neutral name or one that was as simple feminization of a male name." However, while she was deciding, she says, and going through transition, some friends and family simply called her "A," making it easier for everyone to leave the old name in her past while alleviating some of the pressure to find the perfect new one.

Ultimately, the name she chose is Amelia. Though she says there's no real-life person who inspired her to choose the name, she does admit an affection for Amelia Pond from *Dr. Who*. "There was something about her character that I identified with," Amelia remembers. "She took charge and was pretty badass."

"So those were traits that felt like they embodied 'Amelia' to you," I suggest. Amelia agrees, maybe a bit surprised. I find this a lot in name therapy. Often people tell me their stories, but are surprised when I point out what they've already intimated. Names are a lot more evocative than we give them credit for. In fact, Amelia says the experience helped her to find human qualities in names themselves, separate from the traits they might acquire from specific individuals. I remark that it's a neat concept, to look at an adult who has traits and characteristics, and to try to assign a name that fits her.

"Yeah," Amelia agrees. "It's a way to tie together all a person's complex identities."

I love this idea, that a name is an identifier for all the traits a person has. It speaks to the African naming ceremonies that Dr. Hodari holds, in which someone is named after a momentous occasion in their lives. I love too that adults might get to choose their own names—another reason I was always so fascinated by the concept of saint's names. But most names are chosen by parents for their children when they're just a few minutes old, or even before that.

And so begins my greatest name experiment yet. . . .

9

SILAS IS A CARTOON PIRATE
Finding the Baby-Name Needle in a Self-Important Haystack

When I say I didn't dream of growing up and being married and having a family and a Barbie DreamHouse, I mean I didn't. I didn't dislike the idea or long for it. I didn't *assume* that it would or wouldn't happen. I just figured it wouldn't, because I wasn't focusing on it.

It wasn't like I had been told I was destined to be alone, or that I was worried about becoming a nun by default. I just never thought I would be the person who signed permission slips, or debated about whether quitting piano lessons is a valid reduction of stress or a failure to commit.

In my twenties I was happiest careening around with my ever-growing group of friends, deep in denial that we would ever get older, despite how many of us were beginning to murmur our ages instead of announce them outright. Dating happened sometimes, but it was more of a vehicle for disaster stories I could cackle over with my friends. I knew that no stranger could ever make me laugh, or *get* me, the way the people I worked and played with already did.

And then, you know, things happen.

Sometimes you meet a guy and you make a joke, and instead of looking at you strangely or smiling patiently while mentally writing a tweet about the situation, he one-ups it. Sometimes the most ridiculous embarrassing propositions, like a follow-up call to a first date, don't feel awkward but sort of like you're entering a life already in progress, one that you were supposed to have arrived at a little while ago. I don't know what romance looks like in your life, but in mine, it involves an Oreo CakeStix bar being held for ransom in a Houston hotel room, and a photo of it in an e-mail sent to my inbox to be opened when I awoke.

Making our two lives into one we would do together was pretty blissful. It still is. His name is the most common name for men of his age by a long, long shot.

I've thought enough about names that I assumed that, when and if I did have the great love affair, I would meet someone with, at the very least, an unusual moniker. Maybe a Crispin or a Magnus, or a Vincenzo. It seemed that since I was an off-centre sort of person, I would likely meet someone equally off-centre, with a similar perspective on how we came to be so amazing and unique.

I did meet that guy. And I wish I could say that the fact that his name is Michael never gave me a moment's pause, but in truth, I just thought, well . . . there are a lot of people named Mike, and I had preconceived notions about what that meant, mostly based on all the Michaels I'd met before.

It's not that they were so objectionable, but I did kind of wonder whether the truly common name allowed any man who wore it to be truly unusual.

That's patently unfair, of course, but it's not without some cause—Michael isn't just a popular name, it was the number one most popular name for boys in North America from 1961 to 2004. There are forty-three years of Michaels in the top position. His mother says she named him because "there were three nice Dr. Michaels" at the hospital where she was a nurse. Did you catch that? Three *nice* Michaels, and, one assumes, many others who were only regular.

But you don't choose who to fall in love with and you definitely don't choose them by their name (because who dreams, for instance, about loving a Gord? Or a Chloris?). And so you go about your days, being happy and suddenly having plans to go out every night, and one day you realize your plans for every night now involve only the couch and

Me and Mike in NY, 2009.

that neither of you could be happier about it. That's the first stage of descent. The second stage is when one of you brings up the idea of getting a dog and the other one doesn't recoil. (We'll discuss that cat you also managed to acquire at another point.) The final stage is something that must be chemical, where you realize simultaneously that one of his jokes was kind of a dad joke, that you are now significantly older than when your parents had their last child, and you start realizing that after spending your entire adult life trying not to get pregnant, maybe you . . . should.

Here We Go

To say that we were surprised to be pregnant is disingenuous because we are grown adults with a healthy understanding of human biology. But stuff can happen a lot faster than you expect, considering the "people in their thirties should panic about having kids" rhetoric one hears. The idea that what starts off seeming like a medical condition will turn into a person takes a while to wrap your head around. Enough has been written elsewhere about that—I won't waste our time here.

But of course, being me, I did immediately begin sifting through piles of names once I knew I was pregnant. I'd never actually bought baby name books, partly because they're a strange-looking purchase for a single person (how would I explain that I just wanted to read them all?), and partly because I judged their value on whether or not they contained my name. Instead, I would skulk for hours in the baby aisles in bookshops, trying my best to memorize page after page of names and scoffing at the books that listed variants of names as individual entries instead of pointing out that, for instance, Rachael is just a variant of Rachel. But now that I had a legitimate reason, the sky was the limit. As I gorged on websites and popularity tables and yes, even purchased books made of actual paper, I felt like there was an embarrassment of riches I wasn't exactly primed to spend. I found myself jealous of my grandmothers who had eleven and seven children respectively, and probably sort of knew from the outset that they'd have several. Given that "several" was never an option, the importance of the name we were about to give was huge.

To me. Let's be honest, partly this was about me, me getting to name someone, more than it was about the person we were going to have and raise. Like I said, at the time it seemed such a remote idea that it would actually turn into a "baby." Not that I had a kid just to name it—but it was the easiest concept to grasp on to early in the game.

When the reality of the situation sank in—there is a person coming and we will be the ones to decide what the world calls him or her—I had immediate likes and dislikes, though it is absolutely true that since I didn't think I was going to have children, I didn't have names pre-picked out. I started to ruminate and came up with some immediate winners. I think a daughter called Jacinta would be inquisitive but love to laugh. She'd be strong, but fair; the kind of person who would be able to cut a school bully down because it was the right thing to do, but who wouldn't be sanctimonious about it.

I told this to Mike, idly, while we were on the couch, at a loss as to what we were supposed to be Googling in this new quasi-parental state. He was firm and not chatty about it as he told me no.

The fact that he said no was surprising. The fact that it was one word was exponentially more so. Mike and I are talkers. We discuss everything, and by discuss I usually mean loudly debate as we try to sway the other to our point of view. Usually we're racing to see which of us can make the other laugh first, but still adamant about "winning" the discussion. Given that we both prefer fifty words where five would do, I was very unfamiliar with him shutting down a discussion this way.

So when all rational discussion fails, I go to my other go-to method and pester (there's a reason I related to Ramona the Pest). "Do you want to tell me why? Like, if we're going to do this together we need to be better at discussing what kinds of things are bothering us, do you not think so? I'm just—I'm feeling kind of shocked that you would even shut me out like this when we're going through this massive thing together and you can't look up from your iPad?!?"

I elevated things a little quickly, perhaps. Hormones.

He looked up, finally. With a calmness that told me he was actually serious about this and not just arguing for sport, he announced: "I had a . . . romantic entanglement named Jacinta. I'm not naming our kid that."

You know, it seems like solid reasoning to me.

Being Modern

I have to point out here that Mike is astonishingly sentimental. I never met a man who has kept so many objects because of the place or time that he got them. He has flags from mountaintops he climbed—he would want me to point out it was *Mount Fuji*, not just any old mountain—and ugly *Simpsons*-inspired clay mugs made in grade 6 art class. He has every Apple product ever made, and probably still has a click-wheel iPod somewhere in his closet.

He's also sentimental in areas that don't involve Steve Jobs. We got very tense before our wedding because we couldn't agree on a song to dance to, and eventually, last-minute, chose one. I worried it was going to feel like a random choice but in fact, Mike liked it so much he plays it for us at every opportunity. It's called "Shbop Shbop" at our house, but most know it by "I Only Have Eyes for You."

And so he was sentimental about not finding out what flavour of baby we were going to receive until it was actually born. He wanted to continue the magic of not knowing, of referring to it only as "the manatee" (one of the animals described in the fetus-growth apps to help anthropomorphize the clump of cells). I disagreed. Basically I wanted to be one of the popular kids. All my friends had found out the sex of their babies and swore the knowledge cemented the "realness" of the pregnancy. It also doesn't hurt that the sex is usually learned during an otherwise long and boring stretch in the middle of the pregnancy where you become more acutely aware of how much you miss wine and sushi.

Maybe I was just frustrated because Mike was senti-mental about everything under the sun, except for names. How could he not see the import of this decision?

But in the throes of discussion, try as he might to understand, Mike had no idea why I want to give our child an unusual name. Mike was called exclusively by his last name in high school. He had two other close friends called Mike and will tell you the notorious tale of "the three Mikes in New York," given the slightest provocation. (The story—supposedly—is that on a school trip, three of them shared a hotel room with someone who was not a Mike. Suffice it to say the three Mikes got into trouble with contraband, which they swear did not belong to them, and they were escorted home early. The non-Mike classmate escaped unscathed.) While he does roll his eyes at the name's frequency, Mike likes his name, and he knows he shares it with a community of others. And he's heard me complain about the trials of my unusual name so why go that way with a poor defence-less baby?

I have since learned that it is fairly common for one partner to chase the other around with lists of names that wax and wane constantly, and for the other partner to constantly say no, without offering alternatives. But I didn't expect it in *my* house. There's a great degree of egotism in what I'm about to say, but—I am a professional namer! I've been naming fictional people and other people's real people for some time. I'm qualified to do this, more than most, and yes, *yes*, that means my opinion should count for more than the average person's, or in this case, the person I'm married to who doesn't think about this half as much as I do. I would let him remodel our house, if he were an architect. Obviously, he should let me name our kid!

But I get resistance to Barnaby. I get resistance to Persephone. When I suggest Malachy, I get the kind of look that says, "I took wedding vows but they did not include having to accede to Malachy." I don't understand, truly, how he doesn't see the beauty in these names. How he doesn't understand how lovely and unusual they are, and why that makes them *more* desirable in our current day where unusual is at a premium.

But he's not just debating with one other person, he's debating with me and with all the names I hoped I might have been named, and with entire dictionaries' worth of names that said something about the type of person I hoped our child would be.

I was very aware that the name was a key ingredient in the recipe of the child we were making. To massacre the metaphor, all the ingredients were added already so we were now at the labelling and branding stage. We knew that Lyle or Bethan or Sage or Chava says something about who a person is, especially when read on a birth announcement or in an elated, sleep-deprived text. They say you never get a second chance to make a first impression, but if someone knows your name before meeting you, you have already made an impression. Even though I've been entirely honest about the strife my name caused me, I can't imagine the number of opportunities I might have missed out on if my name were Dana. I think again of Guybrush remarking on people who hired him because "we should probably have a Guybrush working here" and feel like I've met those people. Often I got calls, professionally or personally, because people read "Duana" and were generally curious enough to find out what kind of person went with that kind of name.

The Playground Myth

One of our biggest points of contention was whether or not an unusual name would be eviscerated by a kid's peers. While I still don't recommend naming a child Pubert (one of my great joys is remembering how that throwaway joke in the 1993 film *Addams Family Values* made my friend roar with laughter for at least ten minutes in the theatre), there are precious few other names that will be so outlandish they'll reliably be made fun of. We live in an increasingly multicultural society, and kids don't necessarily know that Erica is more "normal" than Kaavya. Because it isn't. And where in previous generations a name might seem silly or awkward or made up, today's trends make that idea almost quaint (sure, I might dislike the name Brayden, but there's strength in numbers and he's in pretty consistent company).

Here is the list of finalists in the 2014 Scripps National Spelling Bee, where children generally range in age from eleven to fourteen (the official rules say they must be under fifteen and not have passed the eighth grade). The finalists come from all over the United States.

Neha	Jennifer
Samuel	Charles
Victoria	Vanya
Eileen	Sai Wishud
Chythanya	Kate
Amy	Maria
Ankita	Mary
Isabelle	Alexandra
Amber	Audrey

Tajuan   Paul

Alia   Yasir

Gokul   Tejas

Ansun   Tea

Shayley Jae   Sumech

Jacob

That list right there? That is a namer's dream! Look at the mix of names! Who is going to tell Tea or Ankita that their names are more or less normal than Tajaun or Jacob or Mary? Nobody, because to make fun of someone for being different, you need the rest of "everyone" to be the same. The group is homogeneous in its variety. The idea that you could be mocked on the playground for your name was incredibly real, once upon a time, only a generation ago—but name homogeny seems to have ebbed away in the amount of time it took us to go from carrying ten songs on a device in our pocket to carrying 10,000.

Don't misunderstand me: some kids are still mocked mercilessly at school, but most of today's classrooms lack the density of repeated, popular names to make just one the standout for its oddity. This also goes back to a point we've seen earlier—it's not kids who know whether names are unusual, for the most part. They are as likely to meet a Thessaly as a Tim. It's adults who titter and squeak and respond to the names so allegedly outlandish.

Once I became pregnant I was reminded that my family was name-obsessed, too. Even though my sister had a more recognizable name than I did, she had listened just as closely when my mother weighed and discussed all the names of the kids we went to school with, praising rarity and beauty above all. Both my mother and sister began sending me daily lists of names they'd come up with, satisfied if I liked the names and offended if I didn't—or worse, bitter, if I said another baby I knew had just been given the name. I realize now that their "interest" was closer to a passion, and that this is clearly a genetic trait. My father didn't participate in daily discussions but I do remember an occasion before I was pregnant when he listened to Sheena and me discussing names we liked for hypothetical children, and he told us whether or not the child would get an inheritance based on the proposed name. You probably had to be there, but I loved that he cared that much. For what it's worth, he liked Nina. And Julian.

Mike's parents, on the other hand . . . I don't think we ever got a recommendation from either of them. They liked talking about names and knew they were interesting to me (both Mike and his brother Sean would have been named Jodie had either been a girl), but they would never dream of pushing us in a particular direction. This restraint is something I'm unfamiliar with, but apparently some families practise it regularly! Imagine!

A Partial List of Insults Lobbed at Proposed Names in My House

Him: "That guy runs the AV cart in high school." (Declan)

Him: "Sounds like a cartoon pirate." (Silas)

Me: "Do you want her to be boring?" (Charlotte)

Him: "All I think about is *Archie* comics." (Veronica)

Me: "I don't understand why you haven't read anything since 1996!" (Scott)

Him: "We're *not* Russian royalty!" (Anastasia)
Me: "I'm sorry, do you have an Etsy store I don't know about?" (Henry)

As the nameless baby continued to loom, Mike and I ignored the impending issue until one night when, driving around trying to find parking before a movie, he remarked that his grandmother Alice was excited about the baby. I took this in and wondered if he was hinting for Alice to be a baby name. He swore he wasn't, but wondered whether it would go with any names. As a middle name.

The air doesn't often get thick with anticipation when you've eaten every meal with someone for years, but there was a lot of significance riding on Mike's next question. "What would be your favourite name, about now?"

I thought about sandbagging, hedging or lying, offering a sacrificial lamb so that when he inevitably rejected it, I could come back with something else. But I was tired, and probably mentally lazy, as evidenced by the fact that later that night, we went to see a superhero movie and I fell asleep twice. I was straightforward.

"I like Daphne."

Again, we're not really prone to silences. I'm preparing all my mental arguments as we drive, getting madder and madder because why can't I have a daughter who's not called something as plain as Ann, or whatever other typical name he thinks is safe? What's wrong with having something a little unusual? Not that Daphne is unusual, it's probably jumping up the popularity ranks as we speak! Which is going to be our fate because you won't go for Cosima . . . !

"I love Daphne."

"You do?"

"Yeah. Really."

"I do too."

"Okay!"

I think for a lot of parents, once they've had that discussion where they agree, that's it. But I couldn't leave well enough alone. I felt like I should use this area of consensus to push further into rarer options that we hadn't considered, so that we could be sure that we were really choosing Daphne because we loved it the most out of all the names, not because it was the first one we could agree on.

And there was another problem.

The Secret Revealed

In some ways, I am the worst. Tina Fey defines this quality, in reference to herself, as not knowing how to react when people show pictures of their pets, but I am the forgetful kind of worst. Like I might bail on a dinner with friends because I have to work late, and then remember weeks later that it was supposed to be an unofficial birthday celebration. Or I might casually bring up my interest in school rankings and real estate and, unable to disconnect my mouth from my brain, confirm to a friend that her house is an area that is considered "not-yet-up-and-coming."

But the worst way I'm the worst is that Mike and I pretended not to know the sex of our child.

We didn't intend to find out. "One of the last surprises" and all that. As I said before, Mike is ridiculously sentimental.

But as it happened, we had the world's least engaged or personable ultrasound technician at "that" appointment, the one where you see everything. Long before we got to the question of what was between the legs, she turned her monitor away from me and barked at me to lie back down. I didn't want to see the sex of the baby, but I didn't even get to marvel at the tiny knees and ears and backbone. I think she was probably having a hard day and needed to exert some power somewhere, but it meant that after a lot of discussion and expectation of seeing the ultrasound onscreen, I felt like I got nothing. Plus I had a strain in my neck and shoulders from craning to see what I could before she sternly told me to lie back down. Several times.

I was determined not to be a stereotype of a pregnant woman, but I couldn't believe the giddiness and anticipation I'd felt about seeing the baby, sex be damned—and how roundly it was thwarted. I had been on a business trip that morning and the excitement got me through the rigours of travelling! Mike raced through the city from work in order to be there! Then we couldn't even look at our little biological product together? I was gutted. I offer that to explain what happened next.

When she asked, with zero interest, if we wanted to know the sex of the baby, we said, "Maybe." At that lukewarm response, she didn't tell or show us, and instead wrote on the printout she handed us, and went off, I assume, to disappoint other patients with her bedside manner. We traipsed off to a contemplative brunch.

We had agreed that waiting to find out the sex should still be the plan, but now we had actual, tangible proof in my bag, on a paper we were supposed to give to my obstetrician, so we couldn't trash it. We could find out the answer to the big question without even getting up, and the temptation proved not even too much, but almost too silly. Why not look? But we said we wouldn't. But what were we saving it for?

I think we lasted half an hour. We opened the single sheet of paper and confirmed what I already suspected. "Likely male."

Daphne flew out the window, and a whole new set of names started marching through my head, demanding to be considered and crowned the winner.

I don't think it's crazy to say that I'd thought of boys' names less, cumulatively, over the course of a lifetime. As a woman thinking about girls' names, I projected them onto myself. Who would I be as a Darcy or a Philippa or a Nawleen or an Anaïs? But I didn't have a relationship with boys' names that was as intimate. I couldn't as easily picture the kind of experience a boy with a certain given name would have, or what would distinguish an Elan from an Egon—at least, not without more work. It was more challenging, but also more exciting. There was a whole new hemisphere of name possibilities in front of us that I hadn't considered, and we only had five months to decide.

And we weren't telling our families what we were having, which was a decision they'd all loved.

In retrospect, I don't think Mike's family would have minded one way or the other. "Keep it to yourself if you want, that's fine, good for you." That's their attitude. My own family would have seen it as "taking the fun out of it." We've never been short on opinions in our house. So Mike and I were keeping it tight. This meant that for fear of osmosis and social media, our friends were also in the dark. However, some of them strongly suspected we'd already found out, and barely kept the veil on humouring us. My closest friend, Lara, had known me for fifteen years at that point, and every time the question of the baby's sex came up she didn't comment, just watched me intently, waiting to clock any signs of my slipping up. I know she knew, and it's a testament to her indulgence of me that she never pointed it out . . . especially since she was pregnant with her second daughter at the same time ("Yes, of course we planned to be pregnant together, doesn't everyone?" *Of course* we didn't plan it!! What is wrong with people?), and probably had extrasensory intuition about my not-that-great poker face. She was also up front about her choices for baby names (Lara's well-named daughters are Simone and Estelle), so my holding back was even worse.

But, though I felt bad about the lying by omission, I felt somehow good about the privacy it afforded us. It gave us—particularly me—time to think about who our son was going to be, and who I was going to be with a son.

Because, of course, everything they say is true. As soon as you find out the sex of the little manatee who's in the process of growing himself, it's much more real. You can project forward to when they're two and five and twelve, and imagine in more precise detail what that might look like. Would it involve trombone or swimming or theatre or physics or large purchases of stocks we have to trade for him? What things are eliminated? Who is he not going to be, because he'll be our son and not our daughter?

One of the things that was most important to me then was that he understand and be sensitive to the fact that as a white male, he was landing at the very top of the privilege pile. I now realize it was preposterous to put that kind of expectation on a person who, at the time of this writing, thinks it's most fun to squeeze spiral pasta through tightly clenched fists that are also clenching his hair. But at the time, I gave it serious consideration. Was the kind of son I hoped to have an Ethan? A Montague? Could I ever get the name Otto to look appealing to Mike, even though he thought it was twee and ridiculous and the absolute definition of pretension?

Branding Up Baby — Realities versus Regrets

I know everyone debates baby names, and I think it's clear by this point in the book that the name indicates a set of expectations and desires the parents have for the child. The debate comes in deciding which name indicates those desires and expectations.

There are various ways to deal with the inevitable conflicts. A friend of mine told the story of how he was named on the way to his christening at three months of age. He always told it like it was a joke—but often enough that you knew it wasn't. Another friend said her mother declared, two weeks after living with her daughter Christina, that the baby wasn't a Christina at all but an Ingrid. The name was changed and everyone was much happier.

And then there are the more creative solutions. Media executive Tina Apostolopoulous was born to parents from different cultural backgrounds who couldn't quite settle on her name. The result? They called her Tina—and Trina. She has two names: Tina, used by one side of her family, and Trina, used by the other. "I kind of say that Tina [unofficially short for Constantina, after her father, but Tina on her birth certificate] is the Greek side, who's more 'business,' and Trina is like, more casual and social, when I'm at home, that's my Filipino side."

It's a pretty magic solution if you can get it, but let's face it, most people can't find two similar-but-different names that satisfy their unique cultural influences. So families use traditions and initials of relatives or other parameters just to give themselves some way to eliminate some of the names on the table—and still some people get it wrong.

Abby Sandel of AppelationMountain.net is a name columnist and enthusiast who changed her name as an adult, because the one she was given at birth didn't fit. She explains why her given name was so close but so far. "I was born Amy in 1973. It was the second most popular name for girls born in the U.S. that year, and by a quirk of geography, it was VERY popular in our part of Pennsylvania. I was a really early reader, and I found my parents' baby name book on the shelf. I read it cover to cover, stunned to realize that I didn't have to be one of four Amys in my kindergarten. I could have been Hepzibah!"

This is what kills me. I didn't have the same experience as Abby, obviously, but I was equally aware that there were other names out there that I could have been called, but wasn't. Some kids aren't bothered by having a common name, as we know, but for Abby having a popular name didn't work. "I was sort of a weird kid, and having an ordinary name felt . . . wrong."

Amy legally changed her name to Abby when she was twenty-nine, and had been informally using Abby for some time. She says the change was relatively gradual. "For awhile, I tried signing my initials—AB (for Amy Beth). In my high school yearbook, my page lists me as Amme [a creative spelling of Amy]. Anyway, A.B. led to Abs, which led to Abby. It's really jarring to change your name, and hard to explain, so I knew that I needed to find something I loved, without going too far from where I started." She notes that an uncle of hers was the first to point out that she should be called whatever she likes, but her parents took a little longer to come around. I'm not surprised, since it's such a hard thing to name a person. It would be brutal to have that person admit that no, you didn't do that great a job.

Some parents settle on a name months in advance of the baby's due date. For them, the desire to name the child in utero and spend the rest of the pregnancy that way helps the baby's impending arrival feel more real. "Brixton is the size of a watermelon! Only three more weeks!" For others, the idea that the name might be used widely before the child has arrived safely, been swaddled in one of those iconic striped hospital blankets and photographed intensely by an Apple product is anathema. But once a baby is here, he or she is here. Stamped it, no erasies. But a lot of parents admit to me, usually under the guise of letters guaranteed to be printed anonymously, that they have baby name regrets. They second-guess themselves.

Parents who say they have name regret often admit they felt they had to "get to" a decision due to time pressure. Either they chose a name seconds after the pregnancy test's stripe turned pink and never thought of anything "better," or the name is hastily thrown on the birth certificate in the hospital a few exhausted hours after birth, since the precious important decision of what the baby should be called is now standing in the way of the sleepless, sweaty family getting home.

The baby name industry is a huge one that should be able to surmount all these problems, but I'm reminded of what Jennifer Moss said—parents get stuck on certain ideas.

But baby names have evolved immeasurably since the advent of the internet, and ours is the first generation to fully take advantage of the idea that names can come from anywhere. Having said that, there are still trends, and in the last decade, the biggest trends in baby names come from the East Coast. More specifically, from the zenith of all things cool and trendy, the place that first announced itself as the cooler alternative to living in Manhattan, the anti–*Sex and the City*—the reason we eat kale by the bushel! It's all because of the rise of Brooklyn. The place, not the name.

Hudson, Who Lives in Park Slope

For the uninitiated, Park Slope is the preeminent "family" neighbourhood in Brooklyn, full of anxious, educated parents who only want everything that's most enriching for Amos and Arabella. Most famously, a few years ago on a "Park Slope Parents" message board, there was a posting about a "boy's hat" that had been found. It made headlines because the seemingly innocuous message led to threads and subthreads and name-calling and hurt feelings related to the following: How do we know it's a boy's hat? What defines a boy's hat? Do we need gender constructs anyway?

Of course that's an extreme stereotype and not what Park Slope is actually like, but—the people are pretty focused on their kids.

So I head off to Park Slope to find out whether the names are really that far ahead of the curve. We rent an actual Park Slope brownstone (the owner's effusive and welcoming grandchildren are called Akira and Enzo), and head to the playgrounds. I expect to hear a lot of mothers beckoning Cortland and Townsend as soon as I hit Prospect Park, but somewhat disappointingly, the names are fairly on-trend with the rest of the continent right now. Every name you think you heard at your grandparents' retirement community is in active use. Franklin and Emmeline and Dorothy and Joel and Evelyn, which is the one I truly can't get over. Intellectually, I can see that it follows the trends—from the white-hot-eight-years-ago Ella and Ava to Eva and Evvie and Evelyn—but personally, it has always felt old-lady to me. But then, that's what's popular. Sophia was the number one name in the country from 2011 until 2013, but a lot of the Sophias in Brooklyn are already rounding their eighth to tenth birthdays. They were ahead of the trends. They made the trends.

I meet Alexis Soloski at the Third Avenue playground in Prospect Park, and the ease with which we start a conversation proves she's a kindred spirit. Soloski, a drama critic for the *New York Times*, says she and her husband tried to look for a name that would give their daughter a lot of options. "I really wanted something that would make her strong," she says of daughter, Ada. But this is where Brooklyn's high population of artists can work against it—lots of people tend to have the same idea, as Soloski discovered when she ventured out onto the playground. She was surprised and a little nonplussed to find other Adas in her daughter's cohort, given that she had thought it was so rare as to be obscure.

In fact, the more time I spend in Brooklyn the more I'm anxious to find a new name—anything new. Is everyone called Sidney and Victoria in all the major cities, forever and ever, amen? Is the most subversive thing you could possibly do, namewise, naming your daughter Karen?

Brooklyn parent and professional nanny Susan Spratt-Waschler says she was fascinated by names because she didn't like hers as a child. While she says she didn't consciously set out to choose a trendy name for her son, "We wanted something unusual, that meant something."

"Something That Meant Something"

This is the thing I hear most often about baby names, that people want them to mean something. Not just that they love a name, or even that it has some cultural heritage. Parents are trying their hardest to find something the child can draw strength from when he or she learns about the person, historical or fictional, that the strength is coming from.

However, what inspires one person can inspire many, as we see in two literary-inspired names that have captured the imagination of this generation of parents. One is Holden, the pouty protagonist from *The Catcher in the Rye*, and the other is Atticus, the stalwart and true lawyer in *To Kill a Mockingbird*, who defends a man most would like to see jailed. This noble task, and the way it inspires his 10-year-old daughter, Scout, inspired Spratt-Waschler and her husband to choose the name for their son. "We thought that it would be helpful for him to learn . . . you know, that kind people matter and that books matter."

Yes, books matter, and characters inspire us, but the key word there is *us*. There are lots of people choosing Atticus, something that takes some parents by surprise. "I had no idea that this was a name people were choosing." Susan and her husband, Jacob, loved the name for what it represented, just not what it ended up representing—that they were very much of their time. "

"We were going to see our pediatrician. . . . My son was . . . over a year old, and the nurse called 'Atticus?' So we get up to go into the exam room, and there's another woman with a baby in a carrier, and she goes 'Wait, which Atticus?' I was floored. I had never thought that there would be [more than one]—it just never occurred to me."

I wish that everyone who is reading this could hear the dejected tone Susan is speaking in. She's genuinely heartbroken and, I get the impression, has told this story many times, never quite getting over it. Leaving aside the obvious—that Atticus Finch is one of the most famous lawyers in literature and certainly one of the most discussed and quoted, so his popularity isn't that surprising—I'm sad that the name has lost some of the happiness it once inspired in her. And once the floodgates opened, they didn't stop:

"As soon as we announced it, people were like, 'Oh, did you read that baby name book, *A Is for Atticus*?' and I was just . . . what? No!"

The book in question is subtitled *Baby Names from Great Books* and may explain why there are a LOT of Attici. Really. I met two when I was visiting Brooklyn for research, and know two more through friends of friends. I *like* the idea of naming a baby after a literary character, and so did Spratt-Wachsler, but if you need a book to tell you which character to choose, then maybe the gravitas and the import of the tribute is going to be diluted?

But I am so charmed by Susan that I have a new perspective on Atticus—I can see it's not a striving-to-be-literary name, but an honest expression of wanting to do something with a child's name that the parents can feel proud of. An often-repeated audio talisman that proves they're passing on their values as well as their genes.

All of this was thrown into confusion in the summer of 2015, however, when the long-awaited (and arguably fabled) sequel to *To Kill a Mockingbird*, entitled *Go Set a Watchman*, was released. The Atticus Finch character, so beloved in *Mockingbird*, expresses prejudice and racist beliefs. Suddenly, for many parents, a beautiful baby name choice was stained with an unthinkably awful association. In fact, one couple, David and Christen Epstein, changed their fourteen-month-old son's name from Atticus to Lucas, admitting to *People* magazine that, "When the new book came out, we just felt like, this does not at all encompass the values we want for our son to have and know . . . and we felt like our son was young enough that we could change his name."

The amazing part about this, to me, is that there *is* a baby boom of Atticuses. Presumably, all the "good" Atticuses growing up would dilute the unsavoury associations of one

Mr. Finch, especially since they're brought up by such socially conscious parents to begin with. But the association was just too much to bear. One person you don't like, no matter how incidental to your life, can taint a name forever. Tell me again the name of your childhood bully? Did it take you a second to remember it? Yeah, I didn't think so.

Dr. Albert Mehrabian's research says we like the names we hear most often, and that the less we hear a name the less we like it. So maybe it's impossible to like an out-of-fashion name until you had some reason to. This is why grandparents' names work—the names that sound foreign to most of us are sweet enough when you've heard them said lovingly by your grandparents for years.

Still, I wondered whether there were untapped pockets of name ingenuity—or if the global village we now lived in had equalized name trends to a point where Brooklyn no longer had quite so much of an edge. New York couple Jennifer Raine and Adrienne Davis say it wasn't so much that they were trying to be trendy with their daughters' names as that they were trying to be thoughtful. "I didn't want our daughter to be one of seventeen Sophias or Olivias in her graduating class," says Raine, who reflects that she experienced something like this as a Jennifer. She felt that New York name styles still follow the trends, of course—but feels the cultural mix of New York results in aging-hipster names like Solomon and Esther and Hazel on children just learning to toddle being mixed in with Diego and Ysabel. But they see "more kids in Canada who have names reflective of their culture—that it might be more acceptable here to name a child from his original culture rather than having to go with Kevin."

Is There Only One "Right" Choice?

A few weeks before our baby came, we went on a trip to New York, still undecided about the name. On the way out of the Museum of Natural History, after visiting dinosaurs and whales and cutely musing that "we'll bring our baby here," Mike sat down on a bench, because there was a brass statue of Theodore Roosevelt seated in the middle. Mike is not really one to get starstruck or overly excited about what or who he sees. He's not an Instagrammer. But he had to get a photo with one of his all-time political heroes. In the picture, he looks as giddy as a little boy.

I don't know which of us first suggested "Theodore," but afterward there was no swaying Mike from what he considered to be the greatest name ever created for a little boy. In the final days I rallied with Duncan, with Damian, with Archibald, with Etienne. Nothing came close enough to perfect, or made Mike even consider changing from Theodore. It wasn't that I didn't love the name, I really, really did—but it wasn't as unusual as I had hoped my son's name would be. It had been relatively obscure until recently, and in fact I'd loved it for years, but was it lacking a shock factor? Not beauty or style—I believed it possessed both of those—but a shock, an impact, the furrowed brow of "I've never heard that before!"? These reactions were daily occurrences for me, and I had gotten rather to like them. I know that would be the case if we named him Diarmuid (Dermod)—but is that a good enough reason to choose Diarmuid?

I wondered. I thought about the number of people currently naming their babies Leo according to current trends, and knew Theo couldn't be far behind. But what I couldn't deny was how good it felt to say the name. The phrase "my son, Theodore." The parade of nicknames. I wasn't opposed to Theo but figured I could flip everything on its head by calling him Rory as a term of endearment. In all the ways, I knew that it was perfect—it was pleasing to my ear and I could picture the little boy it would belong to, and the grown adult, too. In fact, I had used it in some of my scripted writing, long before the idea of an actual baby was on the table. It felt like exactly the name we would choose . . . and we did.

Theodore Angus Alastair arrived promptly six days after his due date. Despite the heavy-in-the-middle double-A names (one I had to have, and one was a last-minute inclusion to honour Mike's grandmother Alice, who passed away a few days before Theodore was born), we called him Theodore and have loved it. Although it is routinely shortened to Theo by others, we fall more and more in love with the full name every day and its three syllables seem homey and sweet, not too formal or whatever it is people think when they look askance at us and say, "But you don't call him Theodore, do you?"

I did, however, learn that certain things cannot be helped. For example, the nickname Rory didn't stick. I don't commit to it as much as I should, since I'm so entranced with Theodore I don't need to, and Mike never defaults to it—which means only our mothers bravely soldier on. Even better, Theodore is now old enough to mispronounce his name, which comes out as something close to "Dadure." He's very proud of himself when he says it, and can identify his name on the cubby bins at his daycare, and obviously, he's the most special and incredible and destined-to-do-great-things of anyone I've ever known. Obviously.

To date we have not met another Theodore, but I know it's coming. More than one acquaintance has mentioned that they have a friend who called their son Theo. I know he's more likely to be called by his full three syllables than some of those Theos, and that he will meet them eventually, and that probably I will wince just a bit.

But in the end, I realize he doesn't need the ridiculously obscure name I had, because he will have a different life than I did. He's surrounded by two sets of family who love him to distraction and are knee-deep in spoiling him, including my sister, who crowed with victory after we told her his name (she was very worried we might choose Cyrus). He's growing up in a neighbourhood where I've known the parents of his friends since before he was born. Perhaps most importantly, he was born at a time when we celebrate the differences we used to seem afraid of.

It doesn't escape my notice that that's exactly what happened with my own name. The label that was an albatross then became kind of training armour, and then became something I value more than I expected was possible. A lot of power for a five-letter-word. Which is what we hope all names are. A just-right label that helps us, and our children, take on the world.

10

ALL ABOUT EVE, GWYNETH, AND MILEY
How Celebrities and Pop Culture Shape Names

I have to admit that my life as the Name Therapist is, largely speaking, a very sweet gig. People don't realize how much they reveal to me when they discuss names; their relationship to their own can reveal how they feel about their personality, their family, and even their place in the world. They're fascinated when I tell them this, even though in truth, people are also largely fascinated because they're talking about themselves. Still, that's one of the reasons I love talking about names. It's where nosiness and narcissism come together in the most beautiful way possible.

There is, however, a drawback, in that there aren't many professional opportunities for name therapists. You can study onomastics or linguistics, but there's not really an academic field where "letting people explain how their names shape them" is considered an essential skill. So, since naming is about choosing a label for a person that you hope will fit them, I chose the next best job: making people up from scratch. There are two ways to do that, too, but since I have neither the temperament nor the ethics-free doctors to become a mother of dozenuplets, I chose the only other reasonable path. I make people up on TV.

As long as I can remember, I've nursed a persistent, pervasive television addiction—mainly because TV wasn't allowed much in my house when I was growing up. The distinction between me and kids who did watch TV was mostly defined by me always saying "Huh?" Mainly, I never understood catchphrases. I always knew I was missing *something* when people said things like "Take off, eh?" or "You got it, dude," but it was hard to pin down exactly what. The cruellest example of this was actually taking place in my own home. My parents were, for some reason, very fond of saying "Give it to Mikey, he'll eat anything." You know, the slogan from the Life cereal commercial in the 1970s. Which I had never seen, so I didn't get the joke. But they'd go on—not to mock me, just to amuse themselves. "He likes it! Mikey likes it!" I'm telling you. *Very* cruel people.

Television deprivation started to get harder to bear around eight or so, when people discussed Doogie Howser or Carol Seaver and laughed about their hijinks "last night." The more of their adventures I missed, the more it seemed like I was missing out on actual, albeit fictional, friends— which explains a lot about why TV seemed so attractive. Watching was verboten, of course, except for certain times on weekends (my parents' restriction was more about volume and "school nights" than content)—but I developed sneaking techniques. Oh, did I.

I could watch a show when I was home by myself, if I could convince my parents I should be allowed to stay home by myself, which was very rare. Then I had to watch the show early enough that there was time for the TV to cool down, because if a parent touched it by chance or by suspicion and found it still warm, the jig was up. I always wanted to watch at friends' houses, who didn't understand why I was so boring.

The most secure but volatile TV-sneaking manoeuvre involved the family computer, which lived in my room. The Commodore 64 was a keyboard, and a regular TV served as the monitor. One day, while inserting a game cartridge, I realized there was a switch that could flip the TV from "computer mode" to "TV mode."

Then I heard voices. Oh, blissful over-air reception!

I'd spin the TV dials until I managed to actually receive some snowy, barely visually discernible television. The audio was usually perfect, but because there were no visual cues to help me with the story, I would turn the volume up loud enough that I could follow what was going on. The caveat was "not so loud that my mother could hear the TV sounds," which was a hard setting to find on the dial.

This method was high-risk, high-reward—but I will always remember it because it's how I discovered *Beverly Hills, 90210*. I was ten, and my life was forever changed. The first episode I saw was the infamous sleepover episode, and I noticed right away that there was name incongruity. In the early '90s, everyone on television was named Kelly or Stacey, so "Brenda" was an anachronism. But the show explained it away—only folksy parents like those from Minnesota would name their boy-girl twins matching names like Brandon and Brenda, which were clearly parent names.

I was fascinated by the actresses' names. Shannen and Jennie and Tori—the spelling of each just different enough from the usual to be special. Maybe these names were different because they were destined to be distinctive. Famous.

In fact, the more television I consumed, the more names I memorized, analyzed, and weighed. Was that a name good enough for a "star"? "Mary Kate Ashley Olsen," the name of the youngest daughter on *Full House* was a fascinating moniker—why would you choose to give you child so many different styles within one name? When I discovered it was actually twin toddlers playing one girl, I was both disillusioned and fascinated. Then there was Mayim Bialik playing Blossom. Mayim! That was a TV name for sure, and there were more: Tempestt, on *The Cosby Show*, and Jaleel on *Family Matters* and Mark-Paul and Tiffani-Amber on *Saved by the Bell*) and Soleil-Moon (Punky Brewster, whose real name was Penelope). These were unusual to say the least, especially in my neck of the woods where even a girl called Marcella had a "rare" name. And yet the people who had them were successful in Hollywood! Ergo, maybe my ridiculous name and I would be a perfect fit in Hollywood! Science!

As a tween, I was pretty sure this "research" meant that I was going to be an actress. I didn't realize until later in high school that I wasn't good at it, which I knew because every classmate I had managed to be less self-conscious onstage than I was. I might have had more success if I had aimed at "funny," but it was the '90s, and ethereal, confused girls were the ne plus ultra of what acting was supposed to be about, at least in my Very Serious drama school.

So I wouldn't be an actress. But "the business" still seemed like the right fit for me and my odd name. I naïvely thought it would be all fun, all the time, to be a writer, a producer, a director. I've never been so grateful for naïveté, because while the TV business is patently ridiculous, I was basically not wrong—it is mostly fun all the time.

My first internship in the industry was at age seventeen on a tween music-video show. I spent my university years working whenever I could on short, live-event productions and had the time of my life on *etalk*, a prime-time entertainment show that gave me enough stories and celebrity encounters to dine out on for years. But I always knew I wanted to be working in dramatic, scripted television, where I could make up people and adventures and complicated lives. And then I could name them.

Making Up People from Scratch

A decade or so ago, it seemed nobody knew what a "writers' room" was, but today the term is understood as the boardroom where caffeinated writers make big creative decisions on a scripted show. Usually "the room" is full of endless stories about stupid things you did in high school or stupid things you should have done in high school. Also musings about lunch.

The most surprising thing to an outsider, though, might be how seriously all this make-believe is taken by grown adults. Yes, everyone knows that writing TV isn't curing

cancer—but as you craft Machiavellian plans for the characters you get to play with every day, you develop strong feelings for them, and live and die by their wins and losses. It's
kind of like being a sports fan. The fact that the characters
are fictional is entirely incidental. Writers want to put them
through the wringer and also protect them.

All writers feel deeply about the characters they've
given birth to—the difference is that in TV you're sort of
giving birth to them in a group in the room, and that generally you develop the character's personality first, and find
out what they look like much later. This slightly backwards
process makes character names epically important. I've
worked in the story rooms of many shows, but spent years
on the incredibly long-running *Degrassi*. My mark on the
show is, I think, entirely proportionate to the amount of
time I worked there—except perhaps where names are concerned. As we made up new characters every season, I always
had strong feelings about their names, and I'm proud that a
lot of my pitches stuck. But while lots of writers love names,
they definitely don't have universal impressions of them.
When you're trying to find consensus on who it is you're
writing, anything that gives you common ground, like a
name, becomes extra important. So I sat down with some
friends to find out whether there are hard and fast rules.

"We Laughed at the Choice That We Made"
I conducted a mock writing room in in my living room,
with wine. The players, Vera Santamaria, Matt Huether and I
all worked together on *Degrassi* under showrunner Brendon

Yorke in various capacities in various seasons, and we named a lot of characters together. Some very memorable:

> **Brendon:** I always hear your voice saying this name, and I think it's the mom was calling the kid by all four names. I can't remember. But you just made it up on the spot in the room and we used it.
>
> **DT:** Oh, Fiona Celestine Arabella Coyne
>
> **Brendon:** Yeah. "Fiona Celestine Arabella Coyne, you get in here right now." It's like holy, how did you do that?

I remember that one—knowing the very particular people who would choose those names for their daughter. For me, that's character work—it helped me understand who the parents and the kids were (Fiona was played by a fantastic actress, Annie Clark, and through her, the character became fully realized and memorable. All the careful naming in the world is worth nothing if your actors aren't fully committed. Then, in the summer of 2014, an artist called Skylar Spence released a song called "Fiona Coyne." It was inspired by the character, of course, but the name of the song gives me a little thrill).

Still, one of the hardest lessons I learned in the writers' room was that names aren't character shorthand for everyone. In fact, the others mocked the "ridiculous" names I pitched for characters, and I didn't mind that. I didn't agree that "nobody has that name" (or I did and that was the point) but I wanted to find the perfect name and we were all giving birth together.

What I couldn't understand was circumstances where they didn't argue back. I could totally understand not liking a name, but not caring what name was chosen? That was anathema to me. So we went back to basics. We all agree that names with a particular vintage attached are a helpful shorthand to understanding who a character is.

> **Vera:** Sometimes a name can help you when you're writing. So I like to give a clue, like if it's Janet, then I know it's a mom in her fifties.

> **Brendon:** Yeah, like if you're talking about moms or you're naming someone who's our parents' age then it's going to be Joyce or something, you know.

> **Matt:** It's all Debbie.

> **DT:** Debbie, Joyce, anything ending in a "een," Doreen.

But characters aren't always named thoughtfully. It can be, uh, spontaneous:

> **Vera:** When I'm writing, I almost feel like the name is like something I get caught on so I just name the character something dumb.

Brendon: You have to, or you can sit there for twenty minutes.

Vera: Yeah, and then I'll just breeze right through and then go back later on maybe. But I'll name them something dumb first off.

Brendon: And then sometimes it sticks.

Matt: This is from a later season, but [in 2011] when we named Zig, that's one of my favourite naming things, 'cause we couldn't name this kid and we put a series of names on the board and we looked at it for days and we had to name the character before the next morning when the script's published. And we were sitting there at the end of the night, and we're like, I don't know, Zig. And we left and then [the script was] published and we came in and we looked at the board the next day and just laughed, we laughed at the choice we made.

Brendon: 'Cause it's ridiculous.

Matt: And it turned out to be awesome 'cause again it's one of those names where there's no other Zig anywhere, right?

In fact, some of the most memorable character naming moments for me have been somewhat accidental.

That is, sometimes the name doesn't reveal its full power until later on:

Brendon: I think I named Jane.

DT: You had named her Karen.

Matt: Karen?

DT: 'Cause he wanted to name her after Karen O from Yeah Yeah Yeahs.

Matt: She was Kate when I got there, she was named after Kate from *Lost*.

Brendon: That's right!

Matt: And then Paula [Brancati] was cast, and Paula kind of looked like Kate from *The Drew Carey Show*.

Vera: So we had to change the name, so we found a different name. . . .

Brendon: Yeah, yeah. And I liked just the, like, plain Jane, you know, like a sort of a blank slate of a person, yeah.

Matt: So Jane is an interesting case, that is where we were using a name and then we were going to play the name against type.

Brendon: Mm-hmm.

Matt: We were going to say this is the most plain name and—

Brendon: And she's a rocker.

This character was my favourite, because she had two names. After Jane had been a character for roughly sixteen episodes, we discovered that Jane is her middle name. The character disavowed her real name, Anastasia Valieri, after some trauma with her family, and becomes "Jane Vaughn." I came up with all this backstory in a script I was assigned, and couldn't believe I got away with keeping it all . . . using her names as signifiers of where she'd been and she thought she was going. The idea that you can tell so much about a character by what they choose to do with their name is why I love names, but also why I love drama and fiction.

In fact, I'd argue that sometimes names are the reason why television drama is so memorable. "Who shot J.R.?" is specific and memorable because there weren't any other J.R.s, before or since *Dallas*. I asked co-creator and executive producer of the *Degrassi* franchise, Linda Schuyler, about some of the various series' more memorable names, which are often generated by the writers' room, but sometimes have other inspirations. Linda feels a strong connection to the characters on the show (we were both delighted over the "Fiona Coyne" song), and points out that sometimes the actors informed the characters, and their names. When the show moved from its first incarnation as *The Kids of Degrassi*

Street to *Degrassi Junior High*, "Amanda Stepto came for her audition, with her hair spiked out to *here*," Linda laughs. "And she kept it that way for the show. She did it herself, there was no hair people who did it, and [so] she was called Spike."

The Spike character got pregnant and kept the baby, and the storyline was the one that first brought Degrassi international attention, and the beginning of the rabid fandom that exists to this day. The show was (and is) memorable for its real-life situations and unflinching honesty about teenagers' lives, but it doesn't hurt that the character in question also had a super-memorable name.

Schuyler points out another way that names contribute to the show's success. Viewers everywhere feel connected to the characters due to a deliberate choice: nicknames.

"[Degrassi is big on them because] I think that's what happens when you have a good friend, it's sort of an endearing thing to have someone with a nickname that speaks to their personality. JT was always JT. In the old show, Wheels was [a nickname for] Derek Wheeler." The nicknames, combined with the commitment to diversity—characters from different ethnicities often sport names from their cultures—give the show realism that grounds its drama.

Sometimes though, truth is better than fiction. You can't talk about *Degrassi* without talking about Drake—who used to go by his first name, Aubrey. Without digressing into a subplot about rappers, which is not my game, Drake has been accused of being "soft"—mainly because of his teen-television-show past or the reputation of "Toronto the Good." But as a rapper, he uses his middle name. About as unpretentious as you can get, considering a lot of his contemporaries have a lot of very made-up monikers. It's just fortuitous, and it speaks to the Drake brand. He doesn't hide anything. However, I don't know what he would have done if his middle name had been, say, Morley.

In fact, names in teen pop culture are particularly influential. For about two years, I got letters from people worried that other people would think they chose their baby name from the *Twilight* series. I can sort of understand this philosophy around Edward and Bella, the lead characters (though I think the book's Bella was named according to real-life trends, not the other way around), but I couldn't believe there were people worried about naming their children Alice or Esmé—names that had endured for decades—because someone might think they read a vampire book.

However, Dr. Cleveland Evans thinks there's not enough attention paid to names in pop culture. A professor of psychology at Bellevue University, he also writes a column about the history of various names on Omaha.com, and yes—he's written a baby name book, and yes, it's because of *his* odd name.

Dr. Evans is frustrated by fictional names. He thinks that far too many characters on TV wear names that are too young for them, because the most popular names right this minute weren't popular when that character was born. Maybe this is the problem I had with *Family Ties'* Jennifer!

But his real bugaboo is with *The Fault in Our Stars*.

"The two teenagers, in a cancer support group, boyfriend and girlfriend . . . are Hazel and Augustus." He pauses to let that sink in. "I mean, there is almost nobody at that age named Hazel and Augustus! That should have been Hayley and

Austin, you know? But, he names them Hazel and Augustus, and then they became this hit movie, and that helped those names come back up [in popularity] again." He's half annoyed at the anachronism, and half marvelling at it all. "There's this Hollywood feedback loop where the avant-garde picks up on a name, and then Hollywood names a character that, which causes the whole general population to then pick it up further. . . ." Dr. Evans and I could go on, but he has to finish his column for next week. It's on Quentin, the name in the next John Green book and movie, *Paper Towns.*

Even if your interests don't lie in teen melodrama, there's no denying that Hollywood has an enormous influence on names, and it gets bigger every day. Memorable characters are usually memorable because of their first names—in recent history I can think of Rust Cohl or Buffy Summers, or "Platt" from *12 Years a Slave,* whose name is not even his, a poor substitute for Solomon Northup, the real name he's not allowed to use. Then there's Fat Amy from the *Pitch Perfect* films. Who knows or cares what Fat Amy's last name is? You know everything you need to know about her from her name, right up front. That's the goal of a first name, and if you get the right one, you can become the only one.

Of course, like anything in Hollywood, there's a great degree of luck involved. Susan Lewis knew that some people change their names in Hollywood, but she never planned to do so herself, until two things happened. She landed her first official union acting job—and then discovered she couldn't join the Screen Actors Guild unless she changed her name, since the union doesn't allow two performers in the union to have the same name, as it gets too confusing.

"It's a very big deal for an actor to land something [signatory] with the Screen Actors Guild. I remember they called me and said 'Yes, we'll approve this contract, but you have to change your name . . . so I had to come up with a new name within 48 hours.'"

She'd been known up to this point as Susan, or Susie, to friends, but when faced with the idea of a name change, she used science . . . in a way.

"I was very inspired at the time by Carl Sagan, and a friend said 'Try Sagan—as a first name. That way you can keep your same initials.' And there was nobody that I knew of named Sagan, and I thought it was kind of cool. I called SAG and said 'My name is Sagan Lewis', and it has been ever since."

The name changed everything, almost immediately. "Sagan is more serious," she says. "I got more laughs when I was Susie, I was cast in more comedies!" But not long after she choose her new name, she landed a regular role on the '80s hospital drama *St. Elsewhere*. As far as Sagan was concerned, the name had done very well for her, but she couldn't have predicted what happened next. Her fan mail (which, in true '80s fashion, really was mail, delivered in bags from the studio) commented favourably on her name. People liked it, and a few even said they were using it for their babies. Sagan remembers being flattered, and even sending baby gifts. But it wasn't until much later that Sagan realized the impact of her chosen name.

"I was at a fundraiser in Arizona. I met a young woman named Sagan. When I asked how she got her name she sighed and groaned, 'Oh, just from some old actress on a TV show called *St. Elsewhere*!'" She hadn't come to the fundraiser to see her namesake speak—since she didn't know she existed. Later,

Sagan, with the help of her son, found an entire community of young women, usually born between 1984 and '88, who were named after 'some actress.' There's a website, "A Sagan By Any Other Name," where virtually all the respondents agree that their parents named them after Sagan Lewis (or, occasionally, after Carl Sagan). Lewis also heard a young woman in a restaurant called by the name ("we were at one of those Benihana-type restaurants where strangers all sit together at a common table"), and discovered that she was named Sagan, "after the actress Sagan Lewis"—but was shocked to learn that "the actress" was the woman in front of her! In fact, the two Sagans became friends and pen pals. Meeting her namesakes has become a kind of bonus in her life. At a lecture she gave in Omaha, NE, organizers announced they had a surprise for her—and four women in the front row rose, revealing they were all named Sagan! Sagan Lewis is the unwitting inspiration of a "Baby Sagan"-boom, and now even tries to keep track of the Sagans when she meets them.

What's most interesting to me about this is that with singular, "Hollywood" names, people who choose them aren't just reacting to the rarity of a name. Sure, Sagan is a cool-sounding, unusual name, but was there something about the actress that inspired these parents in particular? Speaking with her, I couldn't get over the warmth and intimacy she was able to convey to a stranger, even taking into account her day job. Ultimately, people choose names based on a feeling, and choose "Hollywood Names" because they like the feeling the person onscreen gives.

Sagan thinks the name confers an air of respect, and that there's "integrity to the sound." Perhaps that's the reason, then, why it feels like Sagan is a "real" name, not just a stage name. "I am Sagan, but I love visiting [memories of] Susie Lewis," she laughs, "She was a spunky little thing." Though Sagan may think Susie had more spunk, Sagan clearly has something equally as important—resonance.

Name Up in Lights

When we talk about celebrities and "stars," we tend to say they're unusual, special, that they "have something." I always thought part of that something is a great name. A great name isn't necessary for onscreen success, obviously—there are many very famous and successful Jennifers, for example—Lawrence, Hudson, Lopez, Garner, Ehle, Aniston. But distinctive names can give an up-and-comer something extra. Like Gwyneth, for example. Before, say, 1997, Gwyneth was not what we'd call a household name. In a time when Lisa and Kelly and Alicia were seen as the ultimate in femininity, Gwyneth was clunky and consonant-laden and awkward. But, when Gwyneth Paltrow became the hottest new actress in Hollywood, she was the only Gwyneth. Suddenly the name was synonymous with a certain slender, sophisticated, early-Oscar-achievingness. *Gwyneth.* Having an unusual name is at least part of the reason she was able to supersede her famous father, Bruce. If she had been called Jessica or Amanda we'd have to ask "Jessica who?" as she was rising, and her last name would be the answer—and the defining feature. As it is, however, Gwyneth, the name, becomes the prevailing characteristic of her own person.

There's no shortage of names like this in entertainment, either; the question is, of course, whether it's cause or effect. Elvis Presley was not a huge star *because* of his name, but the fact that he wasn't called Bobby was part of what propelled him to one-name fame—and let's face it, Elvis is a great-sounding name. I also think using one name creates intimacy. Ann-Margret. Cher—hell, even Sting. If you're on a first-name basis with a star then there's intimacy there, which works well if you are said star, who wants your fans to feel like they know you intimately.

Then there are the performers who are so famous that they barely need a last name. There's only one Charlize. There's only one Beyoncé. There's only one Pharrell. There's only one Miley. Sure, they have surnames, but who needs to use them? Are you really going to get Beyoncé confused with anyone else? There used to be only one Demi (Moore), but then a second Demi (Lovato) rose to fame and now is arguably more recognizable than the first one—something that seemed unimaginable ten years ago. A single distinctive name doesn't make you successful, but it sure doesn't hurt. Madonna dropped her surname early on, but I mean, come on. The woman's name is MADONNA. Her sisters are Paula and Melanie. Is it any wonder that she's the one who found international fame and acclaim?

Also, one-name celebs generally make themselves that way. I've nursed a talent-crush on single-name celebrity, Retta, for years. She played the utterly cool Donna Meagle on *Parks and Recreation*, and explained in an interview on female pop-culture-focused HelloGiggles.com that she dropped down to Retta from her full name, Marietta Sirleaf, because an announcer at a standup night wasn't able to get his mouth around her whole name. As he struggled with pronunciation, she decided to shorten it on the spot, and became "Retta" ever after.

It's a ballsy-as-hell move. It announces that she's *that* important, *that* memorable. Why should she need a surname? It's one of the magnificent parts of being in film and TV, because it's a legitimate choice to make as an entertainer. Conversely, accounting firms are not as cool with you just going by "Greggy," for example. I always think about Miley Cyrus, who was born "Destiny Hope," but was nicknamed "Smiley" as a baby, because she was so visibly happy all the time. When she was a toddler and began to say the name, it came out "Miley." All of which would be just a cute anecdote if she didn't use it professionally, make millions, and then legally change her name to that mispronunciation of an affectionate nickname. She'll forever be the only Miley, no matter who else imitates the name. No wonder there are so many people trying to recreate this "effortless" phenomenon. . . .

Creating Cool Names If It Kills Us

Most of the names I've listed above, particularly the single-name celebs, are seen as very cool. Trends can change, but there aren't a lot of red-carpet regulars named Priscilla or Edith or Ernest. Cool names carry so much currency in the entertainment business because in L.A., virtually everyone is trying to sell an image of being cool and hoping they're making it. (Look, even the city has dual identities: Los Angeles and L.A. The two labels couldn't be more different.

One is long and florid and, tellingly, is almost never used by anyone who lives inside the city. "L.A." is short, colloquial, accessible. Make up your mind!)

So, cool names are on everyone's mind—and everyone's lips. L.A. parents play it cool, but talk to any of them for five minutes and they'll tell you which celebrity's kids go to their school. Maybe it's that extended exposure to celebrities' "real lives" that provokes a move towards "cool names"—if you know your kids' classmates are called Willow and Jaden or Pax or Sparrow, there can be pressure to be more distinctive and original than simply choosing Emma. There's a generalized understanding in Los Angeles culture (and New York, too) that a lot of people who live there ran away from boring or bland backgrounds to this more creative space, so they could make it big and have creative, unusual lives. While they don't necessarily have names that say up front how unusual and artistic they are, they're going to double down on making sure their children's names are as stuffed with sophistication and cool vibes as possible.

Screenwriter Kayla Alpert thinks this is the quality that most defines an L.A. name—specifically, the names people who moved to L.A. try to give to their children. We talk at the Grove, the outdoor mall in L.A. where everyone tries very hard to seem like they're not. This aspiration of chill is what leads L.A. to be associated with names like Dweezil and Cricket and Bodhi. Kayla, a fellow name nerd, thinks it's a generational issue.

"I think as a generation, we want to be cool, and for our kids to be cool, if we weren't. Our parents didn't give a shit about their kids being cool. We all want our kids to be cool. Our parents wanted us to be successful . . . and now we want our kids to be cool." (A friend, upon reading this, remarked "God, our parents were so cool to not care!")

The funny distinction there is that cool and (traditionally) successful don't always overlap, or that it's not as important to L.A. parents if they do. I can "name-therapize" this down to two reasons. Most people come to L.A. from elsewhere to make it in entertainment, and being in entertainment tends to mean you like attention. It stands to reason then that you'd like the same for your kids, so you set them up for attention as early as possible, starting with a dose the day they're named.

Alpert, a name aficionado and L.A. transplant whose sons are Myles and Clive, agrees with me: "We're not naming them to become senators, doctors, lawyers, insurance agents. We're naming them because we want them to be cool kids that as children we wanted to be friends with. That's my personal theory."

Alpert's "we" refers to the creative community—the writers and musicians and other "showbiz people" who populate L.A. In fact, she says the L.A. elementary school set is full of what she calls "cowboy" names: Wyatt or Colton or Austin. Their classmates are right on trend with emerging North American tastes too—Declan or Aiden, and lots of "rock and roll" names, like Crosby and Tex and Jagger. I'm inclined to roll my eyes at the idea that calling your kid Bowie will make him some sort of utterly chill, Teflon persona, but Kayla points out that there's a long game, and our clucking about "silly" names is not it. (Kayla recently had my same realization about stripper names once she realized that a stripper she met named Kayla was wearing it as a stage name. She was dismayed that her name, which she's always liked, now qualified as a stripper name.) "What we as adults think of as these ridiculous names that are attached to strippers or rock and roll artists . . . like, Mick Jagger's going to die [someday] and some kid named Jagger is going to become a doctor and it's going to become normalized."

While this is likely true, it doesn't make me like the idea of a kid named Leaf (not Leif) any better. But maybe I need to get over myself. Maybe massive exposure to the "hippie dippie" L.A. names like Mantra and Savasana, so often bestowed by people named Anne, onto their children, will make me a convert. I decide to seek out the most Hollywood of Hollywood families, in their natural habitat—which means I beeline straight for a Sunday at the very fancy Brentwood Country Mart.

I am bracing for brushes with celebrity— after all, this is where Apple and Moses themselves are spotted regularly. Instead, the name trend is . . . utter normalcy. I come across a Johnny and an Henri and a (very whiny) Colin and an Olivia and of course, an Ella. There's an Ekatiya and a Lenny. These are in line with current celebrity baby names—recent A-list mothers have given birth to a Rose, an Edie, a Briar, an Otis. Natalie Portman's Aleph is the last "wacky" baby name I remember hearing about recently. I don't hear of anyone called Rhythm or Edamame. Maybe the creative L.A. name is becoming a myth.

But I hope not, because normalizing "ridiculous" L.A. names might negate one of my all-time favourite twitter feeds, @losfelizdaycare.

The comedic feed is ostensibly written by teachers at a daycare in the family-oriented L.A. neighbourhood of Los Feliz, where the focus is on eschewing gender pronouns, patriarchy, vaccination and processed foods. But the real joke comes in the bordering-on-ridiculous yet still believable, names of its pupils. A few examples, in 140 characters or less:

*Congrats to Orson's dad, Nellie's moms, Cece's mom, Byron's spin instructor and Queso's shaman for their appearances in the *Entourage* film!

*In the spirit of inclusivity, we asked Apricot and Kai to not wear their Apple Watches until everyone has one. Just waiting on (other) Kai.

*Ruth-Bader (ten months) mysteriously showed up with no shoes today. Creative expression or political statement? Both resonate with us.

And, one of my favourites among all my other favourites (note the pronoun):

*So cute! Little Jennifer made his own sweat-lodge near the Lou Reed memorial zen garden. He's being very inclusive by welcoming all ages!

The author of the Twitter feed, twenty-seven-year-old comedy screenwriter Jason Shapiro, told me that he too got inspired while sitting around a table in an L.A. writers' room:

"In writers' rooms, you spend a lot of time just talking about your life and hearing about other people's. So the parents in these rooms would inevitably talk about their kids and the daycare situation. And so many of them ended up living around the Silver Lake and Los Feliz area that it always came back to the daycares and the ridiculous e-mails that they would get from the teachers."

Originally, Jason was trying to prank his fellow writers, hoping they'd believe the feed was actually written by the proprietor of a new daycare. They caught on eventually, but Jason says there's still an element of surprise, since even people who quickly realize that it's a parody account assume it's written by a mother with kids. But while Jason has over 64,000 twitter followers on the account, he doesn't have any children yet. "I don't even really live in Los Feliz," he laughs.

The names of the Los Feliz Daycare pupils are so expertly chosen it can be hard to believe Jason isn't meeting them all at after school pickup, especially since most obviously jokey names (Noodle, Ayahuasca, Castro) are mixed together with the most absolutely on-trend for toddlers (Beckett, Ruby, Jackson).

I ask Jason how he walks the name line, balancing every "Yolo" with a "Stella" so the Twitter feed is collectively just this side of believable. "I do spend a lot of time in Los Feliz," he confesses. "So if I'm getting coffee and I hear someone mention their kid or their friend's kid, I write it down." But part of the game is balancing authentic Los Feliz names with those that aren't . . . yet. "Some of the weirder ones— sometimes I'll just make up a name like Bixby, or something like that, where I'll put a couple of sounds together and make up a [first] name. Because I think there are parents out there who want to be original enough that they do that."

He also admits he sometimes hits close to home with parents who read the feed—often he gets an e-mail from a friend confessing that one of the "parody" names he's made up actually belongs to one of their children. He even takes suggestions: "My cousin pitched me one of the favourite names I've used, Sorkin [as in *The West Wing* showrunner Aaron Sorkin], and I was just like 'Of course, of course. Yes! Showrunner names!'" I didn't even think of this as an L.A. trend. I tell Jason there are probably babies being born right now named Shonda, after ABC's showrunner extraordinaire Shonda Rhimes. Jason agrees: "I have not used Shonda. I have to use Shonda, if you're okay with it."

I graciously grant Jason the use of a name that isn't actually mine to begin with—though he is also welcome to use "Duana." Mostly I'm just gratified that The Name Therapist can help discover not only the names you love and what they mean, but the names you haven't used yet that you wish you could.

But of course, not all the names in L.A. are crazy-original. People love to cite "crazy celebrity names," and usually what happens is that they mention, in order, Apple, Blue Ivy, and then . . . shrug, as if their case has been won. The truth is that for every wacky celebrity name, either worn or given to a child, there are dozens of Charlottes and Maxes and Finns. Not everyone or everything out of L.A. is going to set the world on fire, namewise. But it's also true that the city is not half so full of Ephreesia and Roeverhampton as movies like *L.A. Story* would have you believe. Extra points if you just wrote SaNDeE* surreptitiously on your hand.

"My Mom Heard It on TV"

One of the reasons TV and film writers can have an inflated sense of the importance of names is that so many people inherit their names from the screen. Many are attributed to an actor or actress—ask any woman named Lindsay and chances are she'll say one or both parents were taken with Lindsay Wagner, the actress who played the Bionic Woman—but just as many are from the characters themselves. There is a notable pocket of women named Fallon currently in their early thirties, because at the time they were born, this name on the sexy nighttime soap *Dynasty* seemed impossibly sophisticated.

Why do we need others to greenlight a name before we find it attractive? That is, why are there two distinct popularity spikes for Gwyneth on baby name sites, right around the time that Paltrow's fanbase reaches childbearing age? Partly it's parents hoping their children will be imbued with the qualities associated with a particular famous person—there are lots of baby Rihannas and Baracks, and countless Williams born in the wake of the Prince's birth in 1982. You can predict these trends, after the first wave of popularity or a birth or particularly seminal moment. But sometimes a certain kind of name will spring up seemingly out of nowhere and people flock to it, as if at a signal of some kind, and you have to wonder, why now, exactly? What was the gateway drug that provoked this trend?

I think the answer lies in Bronx Mowgli Wentz, born in 2008 to 2000s-era pop stars Ashlee Simpson and Pete Wentz. This name, the most inflammatory "crazy celebrity baby name" of its time, is very obviously created just out of places and things his parents liked. That is, Bronx is a place (maybe they liked the zoo) and Mowgli is a character from Disney's

The Jungle Book (and Rudyard Kipling's, too, of course, but for some reason I am sure the Disney reference was more resonant for Simpson and Wentz).

Why not choose those names for humans? It seemed to open floodgates. Not because cities hadn't been used as baby names before, but because there was no particular concession to an "actual" name. Why couldn't any place, character, weather, or food be a name? Simpson's daughter, born in 2015 with Evan Ross, is called Jagger Snow. By contrast, Beyoncé's "crazy" celebrity baby name, Blue Ivy, seems downright reasonable. People who write to me seem to think that having a weird name is invariably hard on a kid. But—while it might have been true for me and my name-hairbrush-deprived childhood—I can't see how it would be the case today, when names have become brands, under which you do just about everything. Sure, you may not be thinking about what "brand" Henry or Rebecca might impart, but North West's parents, Kanye West and Kim Kardashian, most definitely are.

Whether or not you call it branding, having a distinctive name means always being the only person associated with it, and there is a downside: never being able to hide. For celebrities and other one-name notables this is an asset, but it's always made me anxious. I've always been a little nervous about call-in shows or online comments on web articles, because people use their own names as they give their opinions on inflammatory issues. If you're Elizabeth or Adrian nobody's going to know if you were *that* Elizabeth or Adrian, but if you're a Duana and you want to make a cranky anonymous comment, it could come back to get you. Your Googleability is at 100 percent, but that means the good and the bad are both there for the finding. You often hear people in their mid-thirties say they're so glad they came of age—that is, made all kinds of dumb decisions—before the advent of social media, but what is it like for someone who didn't? Nobody can hide online, sure, but what if you can't even try?

A. V. Club writer Pilot (yeah, like airplane pilot) Viruet agrees that everything she writes can be traced back to her, since, unlike a Courtney or a Jake, there's really only one Pilot writing on entertainment blogs. Her unusual name has helped her make a decision about what she says and does online, but she doesn't hold back: "I overshare on the Internet to begin with, so I'm just used to everyone knowing everything about me and I don't really have anything *to* hide. If I do something shitty, or say something awful, then I'll have to own up to it" . . . which, she admits, makes the case for not saying awful things much simpler, especially since the only other Pilot it could be is the most famous owner of a "crazy-Hollywood-kid-name," Pilot Inspektor Lee. Similarly, if in 2015 you heard a popular movie actor named Chris got into trouble, you'd have to wonder, and then remember, whether it was Chris Pratt, Chris Pine, Chris Hemsworth, or Chris Evans. There was never any such protection for Lindsay Lohan.

So in Hollywood, as in life, there are benefits and some minor drawbacks to having an unusual name—most of which I've come to terms with by now. However, there are distinct pluses on the "common name" side of the equation that must be considered. Possibly the most romantic of all . . .

Jude Law and a Semester Abroad

"Jude Law and a Semester Abroad" seems like the title of a middle-grade novel—but it's actually a song by the band Brand New. I can't say for sure that Jude Law has ever heard it, but I know for sure that someone—maybe many some-ones—has sent it to him. How could they not?

Having a song named after you seems impossibly romantic and plaintive and touching and, as someone who will never have a song written about me, it seems kind of urgent, in the loveliest way possible.

I remember the first time I realized this. I was maybe ten or eleven years old when I first absently misheard the titular lyric to Kool & the Gang's "Joanna" as *Duana*. My breath caught in my throat, because the sort of generic love-song lyrics were so not-generic when I thought they were about me—even though I knew they couldn't be. Imagine someone putting their feelings out there for the real Joanna—singing her name over and over in the space of a three-minute song. It's so open and honest. It's the opposite of my every romantic instinct, which is to hide and obfuscate, but maybe if I'd had a song written about me I'd be able to be a lot more up front.

There's a wide breadth of names in song—so many alone written about Johnny, any number about Susie and Annie, and even less common names like Marcello or Patience or Orville are immortalized in song. There's a great guessing game, of course—*which* Daniel or Kate is that song about? There are musical cultural dilemmas people ask me about in my column—like can they use the name Elise if the Cure's song "A Letter to Elise" is about suicide, or why everyone sings

"Jessie's Girl" to girls and women named Jessie (answer: because that song is too fun not to) even though "Jessie" is a man in the song. Soon our associations are attached to the song. Donna—as in Richie Valens's "Donna"—brings to mind a girl who doesn't know tragedy's coming at her. Layla—as in "you got me on my knees"—seems imbued with drama and foreboding. She's got people begging! Stuff could go wrong! Billys and Jimmys are always having adventures in songs, but Johnny is always being bossed around. Be good, be angry, Johnny Angel—it's enough to give someone a complex. I've always been driven crazy by people using "little Johnny" as an expression for what would happen with every kid, but maybe, given that there are multitudes of Johns in North America and most are becoming senior citizens, we'll start writing songs and talking about "little Taylor." Unisex, popular but not ubiquitous, and familiar enough that everyone can sing along. If you thought of Taylor Swift in that previous sentence, maybe that's the best possible outcome.

If "crazy and wacky" celebrity names are a thing of the past, or, more likely, "regular people" have been influenced enough by Hollywood that they take greater risks in their naming, and if ethnic names aren't as difficult for people to articulate as they used to be, and making up names *is* a way to actually make new names, you might think the name therapist's job was done—that there are no more bruises for people to experience with their names, no other aspects of their personalities or lives they haven't yet investigated. But luckily for me, names are the gift that keep on giving.

11

HAPPILY EVER AGNIESKA

Throughout this book I've discussed reasons why being the Name Therapist is the best. But the most glorious thing about it is that everyone has an opinion and at least one good story. A lot of people don't think they do, initially. They tell me their name is Theodoric, or Buffy, and they sort of shrug—it is what it is. Sure, Jemima is used for little girls in the U.K., but in North America it's too profoundly associated with the smiling syrup lady, so what? Sure, my mother gave me her mother's name, and then got upset when I modified it to use it my own way—so what? Sometimes it's hard to see the significance of the thing you've had literally since birth—for some people, the Name Therapist might as well be trying to explain the significance of a particular freckle.

But people always open up when you start asking about names. It's almost as though they didn't know they were allowed to have feelings and thoughts about them, but there's always more to everyone's story, and they are often as surprised to find it as I am to discover what it is. Either they always thought their name was for the good kids, and they're not one, as in the case of an Emma I know, or they disliked the name until it was in a hit song, as a Linda I know told me, or their name means "king" and so they felt pressure (but kind of a good pressure) to be kind and fair and strong and powerful.

But ironically, one of the reasons people don't discuss these things is because who would you talk about it with? Sure, there might be plenty of people called Daniel or Francine who could find one another and commiserate, but the actual names are only part of the package. It's what makes the name your own—the nicknames you have, the relatives you think of, either happily or ruefully. Most people realize eventually that, yes, their names have had an impact on them that followed them from childhood into adulthood. Not everybody is as neurotic about it as I was as a child (oh, fine, as an adult too), but we all have a personal relationship with our names. Whether we wish it were less downmarket, like Kayla and Krystal, or find a whole new side to ourselves, like Hilding, everyone has their own name hurdles.

But, even allowing for everyone's stories, this journey has taught me three things—three name revelations, if you will—about name culture that apply to virtually everyone.

Revelation number 1? Everyone—everyone, I tell you!—is a slave to name keychains.

Name Commerce

My friend Lorella, who's living in Britain, has been intent on sending me anything she can find about her own name, because when it comes down to it, we all just want to believe we belong in the world, and that means you may get validation from an entry on UrbanDictionary.com, which says Lorella is "super fun to hang out with" but also "usually a little conceited." (I wish I could scoff at this, but the UrbanDictionary entry for Duana says "OMG that girl is such a Duana, I wish I was her," so it's obviously gospel!) Lorella also found a town in Oregon called Lorella and a Lorella website from Helsinki that sells plus-size clothing.

All of this could have been alleviated if she'd just been able to get her hands on a keychain with her name on it. Or, as Lorella corrects me when I tell her this, a mug. Lorella likes tea.

The mug-with-your-name-on-it thing was kind of astounding in how often it recurred as a gripe from those bereft of a common name. People who didn't ever get a thing with their name on it, whatever the *thing* was, have never forgotten. The fetish objects are particular to the person; some people wanted a licence plate or a keychain or a nameplate for their bedroom door—I seem to be hung up on the hairbrush. I can't remember who had a hairbrush with her name on it but I can remember exactly the colours and the feel of the brush. They were so relentlessly late 1980s in lavender and bright teal and I can see the font—a sort of trendy '80s cursive meant to look like it was rendered by a paintbrush—as clear as day. *Duana*—that's what it would have looked like.

What kills me about this is that I *had* a nameplate (and actually, also a tiny inscribed trophy from my dad that read "to my greatest Duana"—as though he had other ones?). And where things could be personalized, they were. I had an airbrushed T-shirt with my name on it from an amusement park and my name written in icing on my birthday cake. It's not as if I was "She Who Shall Not Be Named." But somehow it just wasn't the same when your parents had to resort to customized mugs or hairbrushes. There wasn't that same social endorsement of the world in general saying "You're in"; when you were on that rack, you had made it. Actress Alanis Peart tells me a great story of being in elementary school, and having received some personalized purple pencils at a time when that was more difficult to do than now. She couldn't

believe it when a classmate swiped one of them—and then vehemently maintained that it was hers! It had "Alanis" right on it!

My inquiries at a souvenir shop near Canal St. in New York about who made their licence plates initially caused some anxiety, as though I might complain to government agencies. But all I wanted to know was

New York souvenirs. Ask me if they have my name.

who made the decision to put "Juan" on the list of the fifty names they produce, because I thought it was fascinating. Like it makes sense, obviously there's a market for Juan licence plates in New York but—does this mean there are regional shipments? Would it have been worth it to make Duana brushes if I and the other three Duanas had happened to live on the same continent? Basically, I hoped to learn who was the architect of my misery back then.

Ironically, the situation is completely different now that CafePress exists (along with many other online custom retailers) and you can order anything you want. The carrels of name products still exist in the Toys 'R' Us store and souvenir shops, but it's obvious to any four-year-old with access to an iPad that you can put your name on anything just about anywhere. In fact, customized name products are a hugely popular gift— personalized books to include not only a child's name but their friends, their hobbies—anything and everything. It's a name utopia, and I'm furious.

But I can't stay mad when I talk to the general manager of The Name People USA, a company that produces every mug, iPhone cover, ribbon and holiday ornament with a name on it. Joe Pirrucello is so endearing and sympathetic, and tells me that although they still provide the store racks with licence plates and keychains to your average beach town or local tourist attraction, everything can now be customized. Good for Joe's business, bad for my resentment factor.

He acknowledges, though, how it might have been hard for me. "Yes, that's quite a name you have. I find names as being very interesting as well, and feel anything that sets us apart in this world only adds value to who we are." That is easy for *Joe* to say.

But business is business. Joe knows that lesser-known names—quantity-wise—don't make for good sales, especially when the entire business model is built on impulse purchasing and sentimentality (and, of course, ego—we can't forget ego!). As Joe says, "We sell product just about everywhere we can get in a display, and I would say discount, dollar and souvenir shops are our biggest customers." Yes, because, the biggest bang when you're travelling and don't have a lot of bucks is something that says "I was here, ME."

So, if you can order everything all the time, what makes a Boston Santa Claus fridge magnet such a big deal? Sometimes it's novelty—you have to get 'em while they're hot. "Most personalized products have a fairly short life span, so most names are only updated in new product development based on target customer." That is, in the '80s when these things were popular among school kids, I *was* the target customer, I just wasn't named properly to benefit.

Still, I wish Joe had a little more . . . I don't know, nuance and variety in the honoured name lists. . . . "The names we choose come from the U.S. Social Security website. We have to select our names based on the targeted customer for the specific product. Be it a thirty-something woman or a little girl, to grandmas and grandpas. We can see the most popular names by year for the last 100 years [on the Social Security website]. We then pick the most popular names in these years that meet the criteria of the product." Right, so Emily and Erica are getting shunted to the "Novelty Apron" pile now. Joe says business is still good, but admits that they sell more products targeted to adults than not—maybe because baby boomers are the last generation more inclined to buy a novelty cow mug bearing their name in a store, rather than order one online. The glory of the impulse purchase. Lord knows I've bought enough lipsticks whose colours are called "Carina" or "Merle" or "Jaz"—how many more would I buy if they actually made them with my name on them?

I can completely see that it's a solid business model. Ironclad, actually. But when I complain to Joe that, well, my name was never on there, he thinks I might have better luck now—but my "brother" Niall wouldn't: "The top male names do not change a whole lot, based on the fact that men are usually named after a relative. Girls' names seem to get more and more creative, the problem is that the number of total names has grown and that makes it harder to develop a good solid name list. Nothing surprises me any more."

I believe Joe believes this, but I don't believe it's actually true, because nobody thought there was anything new to be done with name products. That is, you can slap them on hairbrushes or keychains, but there's no real way to build on that.

Unless you find a totally new and innovative way. Revelation number 2? *Everyone* wants to Share a Coke.

Canned Love

The hairbrushes or keychains were just the beginning. After all, not everyone has hair, or keys for that matter, and you grow out of wanting a Thomas the Tank Engine doorplate around the age of twenty-five or so. But virtually everyone loves a refreshing beverage, which is why Coca-Cola scored such a massive marketing win when it debuted its "Share a Coke with . . ." campaign, markets cans with first names on them, so that you could share a Coke with anyone whose name you could find. The campaign originally started in Australia, and the idea is just so simple. People like things with their names on them. In fact, Lucie Austin, who was the director of marketing for Coca-Cola South Pacific said that when she first saw her name on a bottle of Coke, "My response was childlike." Of course it was, for two reasons:

1. It's unexpected to see your name in such an iconic place. We all probably know the Coca-Cola logo instinctively, so it's surprising every time you look at it and see your name.

2. It's not just a trick of Photoshop. Instead of plugging your name into a product online and, to mix my food metaphors, see how the sausage gets made, you get to physically take the Coke with you. It feels special. Oh, and:

3. Let's face it, as a child Lucie probably never saw her name on anything either. I'm sure she checked the racks over and over, just waiting to see if they were ever going to deviate from L-u-c-y. (I feel you, Lucie.)

The original Australian campaign featured just 150 names and, though of course everyone in marketing hoped the campaign would be successful, nobody realized *how* successful. But it makes perfect sense. People love hearing their names, they can afford to buy a Coke over and over again, or, as per the campaign, buy one for someone else.

And then it snowballed. The campaign rolled out in over eighty countries and in many of them it has gotten bigger every year. But there was scarcity at work—in the U.S., the campaign in 2013 originally used only 250 names, but by the summer of 2015 it was relaunched with "1,000 of America's most popular names." Assuming these are 500 male and 500 female, there are a lot of obscure names that wind up in the mix.

There are "Mom" and "Dad" and "Soulmate" cans, among other nicknames, which are all specific to the regions they're launched in. I thoroughly enjoyed the South African site where you can personalize and then order your can—though that might be because you could put "Duan" on your can there, which might be as close as I'll ever come to seeing my name on a Coke. There's something about it that seems special—of all the millions of Cokes in all the world, this one is specifically for you. I felt even surer of this when I saw actress Sarah Michelle Gellar ask on Twitter whether Coke—or, actually, Diet Coke—could find a can labelled "Sarah Michelle" for her. This is an actress who's been working since she was a kid, been enormously successful and has made not a little money. But the fact that she uses both names meant no plain Sarah or Michelle can would do; one that was specialized just for her was precious. No matter what experiences you've had, hearing—or seeing—your name just never gets old.

Sarah Michelle Gellar knows that. Coke knows it. And every interviewee who complained that the *Romper Room* lady never said their name definitely knows it. The complaints about the lady with the mirror who would "see" children in her TV viewing audience, but never managed to see Ronit or Divya or Hilding, rivalled the ones about the keychains. Maybe more, because there was a new possibility each day for Miss Molly to say your name, and she just never did. This was maybe one of the first tears in the fabric of fantasy for kids. How could she be looking at you and not saying your name, unless she *wasn't* looking right at you? But the other scandal I unearthed about Miss Molly is equally incendiary.

There was more than one *Romper Room* lady, there were *dozens*, and we never knew. Revelation number 3—There were many *Romper Rooms*, not just one.

Rompity-Stompity Romper Room

Everyone who talked about *Romper Room* to me said the host "never said my name." For the uninitiated, a host named Miss Betty, or Miss Fran, or Miss Molly would, at the end of the show, look through a hand mirror with no glass in it, and say that she saw Melissa and Leah and Jason and Nina and Michael (never, ever, Duana). The show aired every day, so there were five opportunities a week, but the names she said were always resolutely normal. The show began in 1953(!) and was supposed to resemble an actual kindergarten class. From the name therapy sessions I've conducted—in which just about everyone, no matter how commonly named, said she never said their name—kids took their omission very much to heart.

But I was shocked to discover *Romper Room* was franchised, not syndicated. The theme song and basic sets were the same but the show we were watching in suburban Toronto had a different host than the one in Cleveland or San Francisco or wherever. Each *Romper Room* was produced locally, and kids were apparently encouraged to write in so that their names would be said on the air. But I don't remember this invitation and I never did it—maybe because I imagined *Romper Room* was far away or Canadians weren't eligible, or maybe I felt like it was fraudulent enough that it wasn't worth it.

Regardless, the names Miss Molly *wasn't* saying were also specific to the places we were living. That is, sure, she still never said your name—but at least she was omitting it locally! Eventually the show was syndicated instead of franchised, but each market could choose to keep producing their local version, and in fact the various Canadian versions were produced and broadcast until 1992. Which explains why there's an entire generation who are still smarting from never having their name said on television.

No wonder the keychains are such a big business.

The old "A rose by any other name" thing that people like to bring up has always seemed beside the point to me. Yeah, a rose would still smell as sweet, but if we didn't associate that scent with the word "rose," it would be meaningless. Would we think it was a nice name? Would it be deemed "a classic"? Would we still think it was, more than anything else, a middle name that lots of people have?

Probably not. But there would be something else—some other name. And there will be. As I keep reminding myself, Jaydens will be grandmothers and grandfathers someday. Names are defined by those who give them—that is, by the person who hopes to have a son who embodies all the qualities that are "Nigel"—but they're shaped, redefined and remixed by the people who wear them. Basically, names represent parental expectations. Some names fit and some don't, but all are going to be refracted through the prism of the kid who's on the receiving end.

That's why name culture is fascinating—it's a constantly moving target as our society changes, and we have new and evolving ideas of who we want to be, and who we want our children to be. As our tastes and influences change, new names enter the lexicon all the time, racing up the charts from ridiculous to perfect. Nicknames people thought they'd finally escaped will come back to haunt them, or to be worn as a rueful badge of honour. They're no less a part of our person than our personality, our emotions, or our physical beings—in large part, we're stuck with them.

Similarly, the ideas and opinions and even name favouites expressed in this book will ebb and change in real life, because everyone you meet continues to have a positive or negative effect on their name, and because there will inevitably be heroes and tragedies and news stories and breakout secrets that make stars out of Nevilles and send Kimberly tumbling towards earth. Which is kind of the beauty of the name game. Not only is it entirely subjective, where the micro-experiences of each name far outweigh the macro—it's never over. There's always a new name left to learn, and often to love.

Most of the people who ask me for advice about names just want permission to use a name they already like. I grant that—giving a child a name you like, hopefully for a multitude of reasons, is a great gift, and I'm happy for you, if you've really looked and found the name you love, and not just settled on Payton because it's fine.

However, I would expand the therapist's recommendation further—learn to like your own name. Find things about it that make you happy—an association or a sound or a nickname, or, if none of those work, choose another name, one that does work for you, that makes you happy. It's difficult to face life if you're going to cringe every time you announce the label that will be you until the day you die.

People accept their names and automatically think they're great, or they find ways to manipulate them until they have an association or meaning that they want (like the Kelly who became Raquel) or they find other name friends in common who can feel their pain. Everyone has to figure it out for themselves, of course, just as everyone comes to terms with their physical body—but it's worth the time, because it's with you every day.

As I reach the end of writing the book I am struck by a horrifying idea. What if I've done everything I can with names? That is, I'm as much at peace with my weird moniker as I'm ever going to be, and twist-of-fate-ishly, I'm now the first person who comes up when you Google it. I maintain not only that everyone has a name story, but that they're underrated and fascinating. Not to get all Oprah about it (did you know she was supposed to be called Orpah, as in the Bible, but the name was wrong on her birth certificate?), but there's a story hiding in your name somewhere. Either because someone chose it with care and thoughtfulness, or because they didn't, and so you, in turn, chose a name—for your child, or your pet, or your car—with deliberate care and thoughtfulness. Sure, there are both brilliant and terrible choices made on the name front every day, but they reveal so much about the parents and the children who will wear them that I could go on happily, because my opinions and strong reactions make this a frankly delicious topic to be immersed in—and I am thrilled that I don't have to stop just because we are at the end of the book. There will be names as long as there are people, world without end, Amen.

I have a parting thought, though. When someone asked me about this book and I talked about it, they joked, "Oh, it's your legacy." And it made me stop and think for a moment.

I'm not terribly sentimental where family heritage is concerned. Maybe that's because, as I've discussed, my four-person nuclear family seemed like we started a new chapter from scratch, and all the history had less relevance and prominence than if I were someone who lived where my ancestors had. Theodore is my "legacy," I suppose, even though his name will send him on a far different path than mine, and I'm certain he's inheriting my lack of coordination instead.

But the people I've met on this journey are all people who have always been interested in names and the way they shape people, but who never thought they would be asked about them. Though their opinions in every case were interesting enough to rate an interview, they often had a tendency to be reticent about sharing their feelings, about names in general and specifically about their own name. I think this is because everyone knows they're coming at things from their own personal worldview, and no matter how much you may have in common with another person, your name is your very own, and therefore a little bit private.

My own name journey began because I had parents whose names were quite common. My friends are amused by my interest and have told me they feel an affection for names they might not have if I didn't mention them constantly. The people I advise online never just ask whether I prefer Grigor or Roman—they always have stories, reasons and qualifiers about the way names make them feel, and the way they hope others will feel when they hear the names.

All of these things, of course, have an effect on me and who I am—and the traits we associate with the name Duana. I know that's only "my" Duana experience, and I also know I have a greater opportunity than most to define what it means. Still, I can't imagine what would happen if I someday met a baby or child called Duana. I don't think it's likely, but I would want her to know that the odder the name, and wackier the nicknames and misspellings and comments, the greater the chance she'll be able to carve out her own world, and create her own identity within it.

AUTHOR'S NOTE

The names and people in these pages are real, even though you might not believe me when you read them.

In a couple of small instances, when referencing people in passing, I've changed a first name to a comparable, but less unusual, first name, for anonymity's sake.

Let's see if they noticed.

APPENDIX A
A Small Collection of Names I Love
(for Reasons That Are Not Immediately Apparent)

One of the most alarming things I've realized about this whole exploration of names I've undertaken is that I'm not as original as I thought. I mean that in a couple of ways, of course—sure, when push comes to shove I am more likely to prefer the name Leilani over Luzulu. But I was also surprised to realize, when I began writing this book, that I'd referenced names I loved years ago—and that they were the same names. When I look back on my name columns, favourites come up all the time, even when I try to restrain myself. Names I'd considered for my son, thinking I was so creative, had actually appeared in scripts I wrote years before he was ever a possibility. Names are habit-forming, I guess.

And, as I've discussed elsewhere in the book, I am most definitely not having a dozen children or more, so most of these favourite names will go unused by me, and possibly unloved by anyone, especially since some of them have elicited scorn from people who think I should know better than to like them.

So, here are my unadulterated favourite names—for personal reasons, or no reason, or for reasons that shouldn't make them favourite names but do anyway.

Girls and Women

Talia/Thalia: I am often supposed by casual acquaintances to be Greek, and while Mediterraneans share a lot culturally and genetically, I have no Greek heritage as far as I know. But I have a weakness for Thalia and the Hebrew Talia, and Talia Balsam didn't hit my radar until *Mad Men* so it's not in reverence of her. Also Tavi, which I 100-percent clocked when Tavi Gevinson came on the scene. Would we have cared as much, or as early, if her name was Abby?

Wilhelmina: I definitely remember coming across this one. It was in the book *Come a Stranger* by Cynthia Voigt. The character is called Mina for chapters upon chapters, and then, as she comes of age, takes on her full name (though the book uses the spelling 'Wilhemina.') I loved the book, and the name left an indelible impression on me.

Daphne: I've named about six characters Daphne, as well as a would-be daughter. I'm incurable. Why will nobody catch on about this name, though? Sure, there's a *Scooby-Doo* element, but that's all but lost to an entire generation now, right?

Greta: This is a relatively recent adoration, I think. I've always liked the *G-r-e-* beginning, and I've struggled with the fact that Gregory is wonderful but that the inevitable

"Greg" is just so . . . I don't know, Brady Bunch, and that Gregor is likely to have the extra "y" put on the end by accident more often than not. So maybe that's why Greta feels like a secret, like I'm getting away with something.

Saoirse: You know, in the back of the mind of everyone who loves Gaelic baby names, there's a "Try to spell *this* one, why don't you." Saoirse's absolutely preposterous spelling isn't why I love the name, but it doesn't hurt to have a little of the "only those who know, know" factor. (It's SEERsha, and it's great.) Actress Saoirse Roman is bringing it into sharp focus now.

Xiomara: This name seemed utterly untenable until *Jane the Virgin* came into my life last year. The show is full of great names, of course—I have long loved Jane, and there's an Adriana and a Rafael and a Rogélio (it's fun even to *say* Rogélio—Ro-HAYL-ee-oh) but hearing the way the characters throw around "Xiomara" (Zee-oh-MAR-a) and the nickname "Xo" has made me realize the name is a lot more wearable and a lot less "Oh, look at me, I have an 'x' in my name."

Veronica: After Mom, or after Sister Veronica, or in reference to their epic battle of wills, and the way that Mary Veronica ANTHONY was able to make the name mean "badass" in a way that would have horrified the sister. I love it. I can't help it.

Hermione: This is the closest I will come to jumping on a name bandwagon, I think. No, I didn't know how to pronounce it either. Yes, I love it. No, I don't care if there are comparisons to the Harry Potter character. You could do worse, couldn't you?

Lesia/Dasha: I know it seems strange to group these two together, but I can never decide. Dasha sounds, you know, dashing, and I suspect I like the D sound because I'm a narcissist. Lesia, spelling be damned, is pronounced "Lasha." [Although the author Mary Karr said her sister Lecia pronounces it "Lisa"] I've met two Lesias in my life, and though they were on the surface very different, they were both very talkative, very funny people who really appreciated a good joke. I can get down with that.

Aziza: it's Arabic. It's THE BEST. I defy you to say that it's not "zippy." Moreover, since a former favourite Arabic girl's name, Zara, is now a major retail behemoth with lovely wool coats, Aziza is an important player in my cultural name library.

Agnieska: I was in high school when I met an Agnes, and I felt pity for her, because who wanted to be fifteen with that name? Then, when I found out her Polish family called her Agnieska, I was envious all over. It seems like a secret identity name. However, if you're going for Agnes I would nudge you towards the somehow much more wearable Agatha.

Boys and Men

I didn't think I had a theme for this section, but it turns out I do. You want to know one of my pet peeves with men's names? Everyone's afraid of the letter B. I once met this incredibly charismatic and good-looking musician. Funny and dynamic and the kind of person who was only barely held to the ground by gravity. You know what his name was? Brainerd. If he can be all of those things with that name, why are you so hard on Clyde?

Barnaby: Man, I love this name. It is energetic and smart and unusual and peppy. It has everything going for it, but every time I say it, people look at me waiting for the punchline. Barnaby. It's great! Come on! I will also accept Barnabas if your leanings are Latin.

Lionel: I will admit that my love for Lionel is recent, not going as far back as Mr. "All Night Long" Ritchie. But while I don't know why it's in this temporary downswing, I look forward to its prompt return. I have a related love for **Zion**— while I'm not into political statements for names, this one bounced onto my radar via Lauryn Hill's son (and song) of the same name, and it's felt resonant and relevant ever since.

Demetrius: I know—it's heavy on syllables, it's overwrought. I can't help it, I love it anyway. It's so surprising and offbeat, relative to most of the names you hear these days, you know?

Clive: I think I like this name because it reminds me of "Clever." I think that's a good enough reason, too, plus you could make Clifford the long form, which is great. Having said that, get out of here with "Cleave." Not the same at all. Though Cliff is entirely workable.

Malik: This is an Arabic name that I love no matter how it's pronounced (I've also seen the variant "Malek"). Somehow doesn't seem to lend itself to "Mal," which is a good thing, in my opinion. Also one of those great "man" names that you somehow rarely hear on a little boy.

Damian: You would not believe the grief I get over loving this beautiful Irish name. For the uninitiated, someone decided to name the (ahem) Antichrist character, in *The Omen* franchise, Damian—though they used the spelling "Damien." And *some* people, who I'm MARRIED to, can't let it go. It's a great name, it does not indicate demonic possession, don't listen to those who say it does.

Hamish: I would have loved to use this name, and I was roundly mocked. Hamish! He's not all the way Haim, he's just Haim–*ish*. No? I'll show myself out. But I do like this name a lot. This guy is up for a drink, and not necessarily alcohol, don't stereotype—doesn't Hamish also seem like he'd be into artisanal cold-pressed coffee, but like you wouldn't be annoyed with him for it?

Leif: This name has everything going against it when it comes to being liked by me personally. I don't know who Leif Garrett was, beyond being a teen idol from yesteryear, I think the "Leaf" homonym is too nature-y, ungrounded and silly, and nobody is ever, ever, going to spell it right—and yet, I love this name. Points also go to **Liev**, which will also never be spelled right.

Hobart: This one is definitely because of the rogue uncle character from *Ramona Forever*, who was amusing and constantly making people look at him with an exasperated but delighted expression. Basically, that's what I aspire to every day.

APPENDIX B
Names I Cannot Abide

A s in an earlier appendix, there aren't always real reasons for my dislike. Usually it's visceral—either a "feeling" or a sound that I associate with something else. The good news is there aren't many—most names that are on my "nah" list are just names that are overused right now, that I'm tired of hearing. And, as I mentioned earlier, a name book is never "done," so many more names will cycle in and out of favour, and I look forward to it.

But there are a few that do make me crazy. Real names, that is—I'm not going to insult your intelligence by including "Nevaeh," which everyone knows should never be used (Wait, you don't know? The shortest story is "It's heaven spelled backwards," First of all, a word spelled backwards is not a name, and furthermore, if it's a wonderful word spelled backwards, does that imply that the name is the opposite of the wonderful word? Don't do this).

Herewith my no-goes. If your name is included, I'm so sorry. But . . .

Lee-Anne: There are much more attractive variants on this name. I have no bone to pick with Liana, for example. But the first time I saw Lee-Anne I just thought it was the most clumsy, terribly assembled, Luddite-y name I'd ever heard. At least remove the hyphen.

Travis: It's not Travis's fault that it's halfway to "travesty," but it's still the first thing I think of. Just doesn't feel warm to me, and, probably from my childhood in the 1980s, makes me think involuntarily of little boys with brush cuts.

Al: Alex is lovely. Allen is lovely. Alexandra and Alice—yeah, you know where I'm going with this. But the potential for "Al" taints them all so badly that I pre-emptively dismiss all of them. There was a girl in school who was nicknamed "Allie," for Alison, but as soon as it turned into Al, I avoided saying her name altogether. True story.

Madison: Partly it's the trying-too-hard, gender-bendiness of it. Partly it's the tendency to be not just a little misspelled, but woefully, terribly misspelled. Madicyn is a real thing that has happened. Partly I just don't think it's an improvement on Alison, which seems to be its ancestor. I feel similarly about "Dallas."

Gage: I didn't use to have opinions on this name, until a letter writer asked me for advice talking her sister out of using it, because it was such a horrible name. I replied that I didn't think it was so bad, and got one of my first deluges of mail response to a column. Many notes explaining that, in these writers' opinions, Gage has a terrible association in the

South. That Gage might be a fan of the Confederate flag, or, alternatively, someone who wears ear gauges to stretch his earlobes, or both.

I, on the other hand, was thinking of Gage the way I thought of Gabe, or maybe Paige. I don't necessarily think the people who wrote to me are correct, but now it's got that taintedness that means I don't consider it the same way anymore. Kind of the way you thought Kenneth, or Rebecca, or Philip was a beautiful name until the bastard cheated on you as soon as you both left your hometown for college, right?

APPENDIX C
The Ongoing Issue of Gaelic Spellings

The truth is that while many Gaelic names are gorgeous, the spellings of most of them are prohibitively difficult. To this day, the ones that have endured are those that are most easily adaptable to English, spelling-wise. It's not that Connor is the most favoured name of my people—it's just the one whose simplified spelling (from Conchobhar) most improves it. Similarly, Rory is so much better, even for die-hard Celts, than its original Ruadhri, that it seems like a no-brainer to go with the anglicized version. I narrowly missed out on being called Grainne, which looks like "Grain" but is actually pronounced "GRAWN-ya." Concerned friends of my parents told them they couldn't possibly saddle me with such an awful name that sounded like "groin" and was inexplicably spelled. I've since seen the name spelled "Grania," which seems beautiful and almost Italian in origin, but for Gaelic purists, simplifying the spelling means eradicating the Irish language.

Herewith the most beautiful Gaelic names that will never see the light of day outside an increasingly adamant subset of Irish-name fans determined to uphold the sanctity of Gaelic names, due to monstrously difficult spellings:

Sadhbh: Sive"
Saoirse: "Seersha"—which, yes, is one of my favourites no matter what.
Caoimhe: "Keeva"
Dearbhle: "Dervla"

The men's names are no easier—

Diarmuid: "Dermot"
Bearchan: "Barkan"
Caoimhin: "Keeven." Yes, it's basically Kevin, but with enough added complications to make life difficult forever.

The debate rages. Do we save some of these gorgeous names from obscurity by anglicizing the spelling? Or does turning Aoife into "Eefa" change everything that made the name beautiful in the first place? This debate made Neve Campbell enemy number one for Irish-name lovers, when they assumed her first name was an anglicized spelling of "Niamh." (The fact that she pronounces hers "Nehv," like the beginning part of "never," not "Neev," and gets it from her Dutch mother, didn't stop that same certain subset of North American Irish-name nerds from sniffing dismissively about the "Hollywood actress" who was ruining the name.) Where Gaelic names are concerned, tensions tend to run quite high—but it's hard not to feel sorry for the Irish-name lovers, since no amount of vigilance or insistence on the correct spelling will endear the original spelling of Orflaith to anyone. (It's pronounced "Orla." I know. I *know*.)

APPENDIX D
What to Do in a Name Emergency

Recently a woman wrote to me, annoyed that people were trying to "commiserate" with her over her eleven-year-old daughter's name—Isis. The woman was one of those awesome people we all hope to be who was able to shut it down with one comment, but it raised a question that came up in this book over and over again.

What do you do when your name is suddenly mud? You wake up and suddenly the senator who shares your relatively rare name is involved in an embezzlement scheme they're calling "GiselleGate," or Tropical Storm Courtenay devastates towns and dominates news coverage, or the only other Ichabod that everyone knows, other than Crane, is suddenly on the front page of the newspapers, due to a despicable act and a despicable pun that you know some copywriter is very proud of, using *your* name as the base.

Do Not Panic. Do not run to city hall with a name-change form. Do not claim that you have no association to the terrible person and how dare anyone imply that. Do not change your child's name, that he's had for two years, just because a character in a book was revealed to have racist opinions or any other unsavoury associations.

Here's what you do.

In the short term:

Use your middle name. That's not to say abandon your first name. But for the time being, introducing yourself as "Libby Arturo Lastname" will remind everyone that you're not that Libby Lastname.

Try to get down with the jokes. There will be some guy in your office who hears about this early, latches onto the joke as long as he can, and offers variants on it for as long as you both work together. Laugh once, nod in appreciation of his pun the second time, and ignore him after that. Don't pitch a fit screaming that you're *not* Hurricane Hazel—just recognize that this coincidence is the biggest deal in his work life, and ride it out accordingly.

Take a break. If all of the news is about the hurricane and destruction and it's wearing you out, turn off the news, pick up a book where the main characters are called Matthew and Lindsay, and tap out for a few days. This goes hand in hand with—

Don't follow the news story. If something really atrocious happens, there will be days and weeks of awful details. The less you know, the less you'll find to identify with involuntarily. You know how there's always someone who's the expert on a given tragedy? Be the opposite of that.

Get out in front. If you're a social media type, a

two-line status update that pokes fun at how your name is now ruined and you should probably go by Joe for the next six years will let people know that yes, you heard already.

If this happens to your kid:

Ninety-nine percent of the time I'm going to say, help them ride it out. Remind them of all the great people with their name, or ask what they think their name should be associated with.

Remember that the people who react to this kind of situation are mostly adults. If they're the ones remarking on your kid's name, a well-placed eyebrow raise and telling them to quit it should be half your battle.

I don't advocate a name change. It's a sliding scale, but you don't want to give your kids the impression that they should change themselves every time there's something about them that doesn't feel popular. They learn to deal when someone has an opinion of them that's less than flattering. I knew a young British boy named Dickon whose parents didn't realize the trouble their son's name was going to cause when he moved to Canada. They allowed him to go by his (much more common) middle name, but he was too old to really make the switch, and wound up remaining Dickon and being quite proud of it. For what it's worth, he employed the single eyebrow-raise too.

Terrible things happen all the time, but "Gilbert" is as likely to refer to Anne Shirley's lovely boyfriend (but kind of boring husband) as it is to the 1988 hurricane. Tragedies are all too common, sadly, and we don't outlaw the names attached to them—which is kind of a good thing, as putting names back into usage means the "bad" thing associated with them is diluted and forgotten over time. Don't sweat it.

(But if you absolutely, positively, can't hack it, take this opportunity to become a stealth first namer—or a stealth first initial. So they're calling it "The great dis-Grace"—so what? G. Elizabeth Lastname is always a great way to go.)

APPENDIX E
The Unlikeliest Names in Song

As I discussed in chapter 10, I always thought names in songs were unspeakably romantic. The fact that someone eats, sleeps and breathes *about* another person so intensely and completely that they actually write a song in that person's name has always been, to me, about 70 percent devastatingly dramatic (and earnest, I might add—there's no hiding in that scenario) and 30 percent hilarious. Part of the reason I've always been amused by it, especially as an outsider-who-will-never-hear-a-Duana-song, is that if there is a song with your name in it, people will sing it at you regardless of context. I had a childhood friend called Carrie-Anne, and everyone sang the Hollies' "Carrie Anne" at her, asking "Hey Carrie-Anne—what's your game?!," and not considering the implications of lyrics implying the title character has "lost her charm as she is aging" sung to a six-year-old.

The other hilarious part, to me, is that while everyone arguably deserves to hear their name in song, some names lend themselves better to titles than others. There are many many songs with "John" in them but some of the more obscure are more amusing. Here are some of my favourites:

Chez Keith et Anita: Why yes, I would like to be at a party at Keith Richards' house, thank you for asking.

Grizelda: There are a couple of songs with this name actually, I was thinking of the Yeasayer version. Compelling name, compelling song.

Henry's Made a Lady Out of Lizzie (not such crazy names, just a great title)

Hey There Delilah: You're welcome for having this song in your head now.

I Want a Girl Just Like Hillary: And yes, it's that Hillary.

Love Grows (Where My Rosemary Goes): I don't love this name but the song does a lot for it.

(This is) The Dream of Evan and Chan: Because, even after you hear the song, your ideas of who Evan is, who Chan is, and what their dreams could be together spiral endlessly.

Lucette Stranded on the Island: tells you everything you need to know.

Nadine (Is It You?): I've always liked this name. Why doesn't it get more play?

Unrepentant Geraldines: Another personal reference here. I have an aunt Geraldine, she's definitely unrepentant, and so the fact that this song crystallizes this very obvious-to-me Geraldine personality trait is a huge plus.

What Katie Did/What Katy Did Next: So, I was impressed with these titles because of the Katy books, obviously. But apparently each was written by Pete Doherty about different girlfriends—Katie Lewis and Kate Moss. The man could branch out, maybe.

You Can Call Me Al: Another one I'm happy to have put into your head.

Chris & His Connor (Whom I Already Love): And now, given that title, you do too.

David Duchovny: The kind of song I used to think was something I'd dreamed up that wasn't actually real, this is about a woman imploring the actor to love her. As far as I know, it did not work.

Jimmy Mack: I dare you to sing this, at all, but especially in the car, and not grin while you're doing it. It's the best.

APPENDIX F
How to Name a Baby in Five Simple Steps

If, after all this rumination, you're still left debating the merits of Emma versus Emily, caught in a never-ending loop running back and forth between names so similar you can't tell where one ends and the other begins, take heed. It's easy to choose a baby name you will love for years, but most people don't even make it past step one. Ready?

1. Eliminate outside influence

Do not float baby names for approval. Do not ask people what they think. Did they ask you? Probably not. If they did, did they actually take your advice? No? Then forget it. Even if they did, forget it. You do not need other people's opinions mixing you up. The gestation of a human infant is forty weeks because that's how long it takes to decide on a name. Anything else you've heard is just junk science, I promise.

2. Stop offering names

I get so many letters that say "Help! My husband hates every-thing." I've detailed it a little bit in my own life. I'm not pre-pared to say anything about gender here, but I am prepared to say that the people who are writing to me are universally trying too hard to "fix" the problem of not having a name. If he doesn't like the one you do, or you've offered a list of twenty and nothing works, stop offering. Let your partner come to you. Let him get worried that the kid might go home unnamed.

Why should you do this? Because there's no incentive for your partner to compromise or even search for an amaz-ing name if you're spinning your wheels coming up with dozens, trying to find the perfect name. If you're the one with the dog-eared baby book (yes, I mean metaphorically, I know you're on a baby name database), chill out. Let the name—and your naming partner—come to you. This may mean you have to employ step 3:

3. Let the baby remain unnamed (I *know*!)

Send the e-mail that says everyone's healthy. Go home and awkwardly eat a sandwich while the kid sleeps and you wonder what to do next. Then wait. You do not have to default to Hannah just because it's almost time to learn how to work the carseat for the first time. I've heard all those things that say they won't let you leave the hospital without a name. I'm telling you that they will, those maternity wards are way too busy for anyone to be fussed about your fluctuations between Duncan and Rossif. Take your time. You'll never regret wait-ing to look at the child in your actual home and environment.

Speaking of regrets:

4. You'll never regret an unusual name

This is true. Ask any parent of a child whose name is out of step with their peers, either a child or an adult. If they say "In retrospect, I wish we'd chosen to name her Sophia just like everyone else," I will buy you a copy of this book. Because I don't believe it. Even people whose actual choices may not have been perceived the way they wanted—as in names that "went stripper" or became too popular—will be very unlikely to say "If only we'd chosen Jacob." Your kid may not agree with me at age nine, but they'll come online.

5. Choose a name you love

I know it sounds like a cliché, but I'm talking about actual love. When you fall in love with a spouse or a career or Jason Priestley, you don't go "good enough." You're consumed by adoration for, and obsession with, the object of your affection. Even knowing what we know about love, and how it mellows over time, that's the kind of name you should be looking for—a name you love hearing, over and over again. That you can see on a two- and twelve- and twenty-five-year-old. Picture yourself mad at that person. Picture yourself coming across their name or photo in a newspaper (fine, online) and being proud. Choose a name that gives you little prickles at the back of your neck, because you so desperately want to hear it again. When you finally feel the prickles? That's the name you want. Now don't unpick everything by asking your Aunt Ellen what she thinks, okay?

ACKNOWLEDGEMENTS

Like all therapy, this book isn't about the bigger trends and statistics, but about individual people and their thoughts and feelings. So I cannot begin to thank everyone who participated in this book, who gave casual opinions or granted formal interviews, passed me on to a friend or filled out lengthy email questionnaires. Your stories shaped *The Name Therapist* and I hope you are as fascinated by your names as I am.

The utterly singular Deirdre Molina has championed from the outset, offered sage counsel, and rolled with the punches of my nonlinear mind. Thank you for your deft touch, genuine fascination, debates over self-definition, and the diner meals that made this book fully realized.

Amy Moore-Benson has been infectiously and firmly enthusiastic about this book since the first time we spoke. You're not just an agent, you are a good mood personified and the best hype-woman I've ever known. Thank you.

Thank you to Anne Collins and Marion Garner, who saw the spirit of this book so early. Thank you to Erin Kelly, my tenacious and creative publicist, Lindsey Reeder, Periscope Therapist, and to Charidy, Randy, and everyone else at Penguin Random House Canada who gave their stories either directly or indirectly, and who made me feel so warmly welcomed.

Elaine Lui, to point out the synergy of how everything has lined up for over a decade would invoke your superstition, which I've now inherited. But for a million late nights, "roommates," parents, and the most incredible gift—an open platform, whenever, which made this possible…I'll stop talking about it so you don't get squirmy.

Jacek Szenowicz is an unsung hero and loquacious charmer. You are an incredibly supportive friend, colleague, and godfather to Libby. Emily Huffman is smart as hell, delightfully upbeat, and always has my back. The entire Laineygossip.com readership, who sent questions and arguments and pleas, and who care about froth and feminism, names and *90210* in equal measure. Your e-mails and questions about all of pop culture remain a massive pleasure.

Glenn Cockburn, for your support and belief in all my endeavours, including this one, and Bryce Mitchell, Kerry Ball, Conrad Sun, and everyone at Meridian for keeping me so happily busy. Also for all the Starbursts.

Stephanie Cohen and Melinda Downie, for enthusiasm and scheduling help.

The connective tissue: All of my friends and colleagues whose names I didn't exploit in these pages—your support has been immeasurable. A particular thank you to those who told me great name stories or connected me to them:

Iain Christiansen, Esther Choi, Michelle Crespi, Stephanie Fontana, Andrea Gabourie, Nicholas Hirst and Kim Todd, Nanci Maclean, Ian Malone, Christopher Moloney, Sarah Underwood, Sasha Tong, Ziya Tong, and so many others I'm sure I've forgotten to mention. Rest assured, I already feel guilty. A particular shoutout to Lorella Berard, whose trans-Atlantic texts got me out of bed in the wee hours and whose last-minute assist will not be forgotten.

Lara Shaw, I trust your counsel for everything from word choices to life decisions. You are encouraging, challenging, and amazing, for 18 years and counting.

My Kerr/Stewart/Riffel family, for all the love, support, and unflagging enthusiasm. I am so lucky to have all of you.

My sister, Sheena Gereghty, corrected my memory of certain events and corroborated others. I love you and I'm not sorry about some of the pictures in this book. Matt Gereghty is stalwart, supportive, *and* cares about my spine.

Dad, thank you for always calling me a writer, and for making cheese soufflé, steak au poivre, bouillabaisse, and other weekday lunches (!) while I typed.

Mom, you inspired so many things, including my love of names. They say the Irish are storytellers—I've done my best to scratch the surface.

Mike, thank you for being so maddeningly sure that it would all go beautifully. Seeing the best in everyone is an excellent quality to frustrate me with. And to "Elizabeth," whose songs and stories and jokes are my favourite. The answer to "Read it, please?" will always be yes.

PERMISSIONS

INDEX OF GIVEN NAMES

DUANA TAHA wasn't allowed to watch much television as a child, which led directly to her career as a screenwriter for shows such as *Degrassi: The Next Generation*, *Lost Girl*, and *Lost & Found Studios*. She is also a regular contributor to *LaineyGossip.com*, where she writes about television and feminism, and where she launched her popular baby name column "Duana Names." Her opinions on name trends have appeared in *The New York Observer*, *The Globe and Mail*, and the *Daily Mail*. The author, who lives in Toronto, has never met another Duana.